BEFORE READING

BEFORE READING

*Narrative Conventions and
the Politics of Interpretation*

Peter J. Rabinowitz

CORNELL UNIVERSITY PRESS

Ithaca and London

First published 1987 by Cornell University Press.

International Standard Book Number (cloth) 0–8014–2010–5
International Standard Book Number (paper) 0–8014–9472–9
Library of Congress Catalog Card Number 87–47602
Printed in the United States of America
Librarians: Library of Congress cataloging information
appears on the last page of the book.

The paper in this book is acid-free and meets the guidelines for permanence and durability of the Committee on Production Guidelines for Book Longevity of the Council on Library Resources.

For Edward Ducharme

My dear fellow, you have got it wrong. The play *is* a success. The only question is whether the . . . audience will be one.

Oscar Wilde

Contents

Contents

Acknowledgments

Although I didn't know it at the time, this book began in twelfth-grade English, on the day that Mr. Ducharme was absent and the teacher from our junior year returned from retirement as a substitute. As soon as she found that we were studying *Hamlet*, her face lit up. "Let's recite!" she exclaimed, and launched into "O, what a rogue and peasant slave am I!" No one joined her. She gave a puzzled look and tried, "O that this too too sullied flesh would melt," only to find, once again, that she was reciting alone. "Do you know 'To be or not to be?'" she asked. We shook our heads. "Well, then, what speeches *have* you learned?" When we told her that we hadn't memorized any, she was utterly bewildered. "But, then, what have you been *doing* in class?"

That moment crystallized what had been so exciting about senior English: reading was no longer an act of memorization ("How many stab wounds had Caesar's body?" is the question that sums up my first encounter with Shakespeare in eighth grade), but as an activity in which we *did* things with texts. We did some pretty sophisticated things, too, and although I no longer remember all of them—and no longer practice many that I do remember—I have no doubt that it was the energy of that class that drew me away from nuclear physics to a career in literary studies. Because he showed me what it really meant to read, I respectfully dedicate this book to Edward Ducharme.

Edward Ducharme has not read any of the manuscript, but he was also my first teacher to take writing seriously, and I have so internalized his cynical red-pencil marks that even now, twenty-five years later, some of his imprint can be found in these pages. Other colleagues have had a more direct hand in the text that follows. Wayne Booth, who taught me to read criticism in much the same way that Ducharme taught me to read literature, went over an early draft of the book and, with his usual acuity, questioned some of the weaker links in the argument. Steven Mailloux also provided a painstaking reading of the text, offering a large number of suggestions that led me to clarify the precise nature of the claims I was making and to place them in a broader critical perspective. Sophie Sorkin helped streamline the style and pointed out embarrassing ambiguities in the writing. Janice Radway collaborated in an even more direct way. Not only did she, too, read an early draft, but she also contributed to the formulation of some of the theoretical arguments about misreading at the beginning of the section of Chapter 6 titled "Scapegoating Carmen," arguments that originated in a presentation we made jointly at the American Studies Association convention in 1983. She has generously allowed me to borrow from that paper here. Nancy Sorkin Rabinowitz read so many versions of the manuscript and criticized them so thoroughly that at times it is hard to tell whose voice is emerging from these pages.

I am also grateful to Rachel Arnedt, Teresa Noelle Roberts, Megan Wolf, and Jennifer Wynn for their assistance in finding articles and correcting footnotes, as well as to the librarians of Hamilton College, especially Lynn Mayo and Joan Wolek. In addition, I thank all those supportive friends who, over the years, have commented on the papers and articles that eventually found their way into this book. The book would certainly not have turned out as it did without the prodding of Don Bialostosky, Barbara Burns, Patricia Cholakian, Rouben Cholakian, Ann Coiro, Christopher Fynsk, Susan Hanson, Douglas Herrmann, Roberta Krueger, Sharon O'Brien, Jay Reise, Elizabeth Ring, Carla Stout, and many others. Rachel Rabinowitz did her part, too, ceaselessly encouraging me to return to the keyboard to "play more computer games."

Most of all, though, I thank Michael Samuel Rabinowitz. It was watching him learn how to read and listening to his patient explanations of the process that gave me my sharpest insights into how we make sense out of books.

Acknowledgments

Research for this book was facilitated by a Margaret Scott Bundy Fellowship from Hamilton College. I am also grateful for permission to reprint those sections that were previously published in different form. Portions of Chapter 1 and of the fourth section of Chapter 3 originally appeared in "Truth in Fiction: A Reexamination of Audiences," *Critical Inquiry* 4 (Autumn 1977); portions of the fourth section of Chapter 3 and a brief snippet in the fourth section of Chapter 5 originally appeared in "Assertion and Assumption: Fictional Patterns and the External World," *PMLA* 96 (May 1981); portions of Chapter 1 and of the first and third sections of Chapter 6 started out in "The Turn of the Glass Key: Popular Fiction as a Reading Strategy," *Critical Inquiry* 11 (March 1985); and portions of Chapter 1 and Chapter 7 appeared in "Shifting Stands, Shifting Standards: Reading, Interpretation, and Literary Judgment," *Arethusa* 19 (Fall 1986).

PETER J. RABINOWITZ

Clinton, New York

BEFORE READING

INTRODUCTION

Beyond Readings/Before Reading

For literature to happen, the reader is quite as vital as the
author.

Terry Eagleton, *Literary Theory*

Literature is political. It is painful to have to insist on this fact,
but the necessity of such insistence indicates the dimensions
of the problem.

Judith Fetterley, *The Resisting Reader*

Whatever critical affiliations we may proclaim, we are all New
Critics, in that it requires a strenuous effort to escape notions
of the autonomy of the literary work, the importance of dem-
onstrating its unity, and the requirement of "close reading."

Jonathan Culler, *The Pursuit of Signs*

    As its subtitle suggests, this book has a double focus. On the one
hand, it is intended as a contribution to the continuing project of
developing a coherent theory of how people read narrative—a project that has engaged critics as diverse as Wayne Booth and Roland
Barthes, Judith Fetterley and Wolfgang Iser. It starts from the assumption that one can study narrative structure not only in terms
of concrete textual features but also in terms of the shared interpretive strategies by which readers make sense of them. More
specifically, the book focuses on a particular *temporal* moment in
the act of interpretation. Very roughly, one can divide interpretation into three phases; while their boundaries are often fuzzy, and
while much valuable criticism tends to merge them unsystemati-
cally, it is possible to discriminate among them both in theory and
in practice. One can study interpretation in terms of what happens
after reading has finished, taking more or less completed in-

terpretations as a starting point (David Bleich, for instance, toward the end of *Readings and Feelings*, studies the ways in which communities negotiate among interpretations that individuals have already produced).[1] One can also look at what happens *while* the process of reading is taking place (as Kenneth Burke, in his pioneering essay "Psychology and Form," charts the changing moment-to-moment *experience* of a text).[2] In this book, I concentrate primarily on an earlier phase, moving one step further back to see what happens *before* the act of reading even starts. Readers need to stand somewhere before they pick up a book, and the nature of that "somewhere," I argue, significantly influences the ways in which they interpret (and consequently evaluate) texts.[3] Thus, while I will often need, in the course of my argument, to describe what readers do both while they read and after they finish reading, my fundamental concern will be with the ways in which those activities are already limited by decisions made before the book is even begun.

Needless to say, any complete discussion of this subject would have to account for the ways that, for instance, readers' medical presuppositions shape readings of such texts as *The Magic Mountain* and *The Death of Ivan Ilych*, the ways that historical knowledge shapes readings of Civil War novels (for example, *Gone with the Wind* or Margaret Walker's *Jubilee*), the ways that attitudes

---

1. Esp. 80–95. (*N.B.* In the notes that follow, full references are given only to literary texts and to those works of criticism that are not listed in the Selected Bibliography; other citations are given in shortened form.)

2. This approach was later taken up in different form by Stanley Fish in his "affective stylistics" ("Literature in the Reader: Affective Stylistics," in *Is There a Text?* 21–67), and by Roland Barthes in portions of *S/Z*.

3. As Jane Tompkins puts it, "Every reader is embedded in some network of circumstances or other when he or she picks up a literary work. Thus it is never the case that a work stands or falls 'on its own merits' since the merits—or demerits—that the reader perceives will always be a function of the situation in which he or she reads" (*Sensational Designs*, 8–9). At this point in her book, Tompkins takes a stronger position than I do with regard to how far the reader's context determines the apparent features of a text. As her argument progresses, however, she moves to a less radically contextual position, writing as if texts really had features in and of themselves which are simply rendered more or less visible according to the reader's perspective. See, for instance, her claim that "it is the *fact* of these dissimilarities and what they may or may not mean for the future of American society that form the true subject of *The Last of the Mohicans*" (104, emphasis in the original).

toward imperialism shape readings of Kipling and Mahasveta Devi, or the ways that attitudes toward women shape readings of practically everything. It would also have to account for the ways that readers' knowledge of Shakespeare influences their readings of *The Sound and the Fury*, the ways that fear of death by burial helps form experiences of "The Fall of the House of Usher," the ways that knowledge of comic tradition influences readings of *Catch-22*. It would also have to account for the differences (including psychological, gender, historical, cultural, racial, economic) among readers, both as individuals and as classes. As Janice Radway has pointed out in *Reading the Romance*, for instance, the initial assumptions (and as a consequence, the very *processes* of reading) are different for the women who read paperback romances and for academic critics. This is all, obviously, too much for a single work, and my aim here will be considerably narrower: to explore, through concrete analysis of particular texts, the ways in which Western readers' prior knowledge of conventions of reading shapes their experiences and evaluations of the narratives they confront.

In other words, this book is neither a complete theory of reading nor a complete taxonomy of narrative conventions, and it focuses less on the abstract possibilities of reading and writing than on what readers and writers have in fact done with narratives. Despite this strong emphasis on practical criticism, though, I do see *Before Reading* as part of ongoing theoretical conversations centered around reading and narrative, and I am therefore mindful of the criticism lodged against much reader-oriented theory a few years ago by Mary Louise Pratt in "Interpretive Strategies/Strategic Interpretations." Pratt was disturbed by what she saw as a tendency among reader critics to depoliticize the study of literature—and the second aim of this book is to help reverse that tendency by showing how study of reading and reading conventions can in fact help uncover the political presuppositions behind our literary practices. In particular, looking at readers' starting points can help us understand *how* interpretation comes about and what its implications are—not the implications of the particular texts at hand, but the implications of the very means we use as we go about making sense of them. In other words, in arguing that literature is political, I will be less concerned with the attitudes of particular authors

3

than with the ways in which the very act of interpretation is inevitably a political act.

This position—that interpretation is political—remains more controversial than it ought to be. To be sure, in the past few years, partly because of the pressure of feminist scholars, the study of literature has become more self-consciously political. Nonetheless, as Fetterley points out, those who argue for the political nature of literary study still meet considerable resistance in many quarters. For all the increased interest in the "politics of interpretation"—as evidenced, for instance, by a special issue of *Critical Inquiry* (September 1982) devoted exclusively to the subject—the recognition that no reading can be politically neutral is far from universal. Indeed, Edward W. Said goes so far as to claim that "an implicit consensus has been building for the past decade in which the study of literature is considered to be profoundly, even constitutively non-political"—and though one can debate whether this consensus has in fact been gaining ground, there is little doubt that it still has considerable sway in the academy.[4]

The persistence of the belief that it is possible (and even proper) to develop a nonpolitical interpretive practice stems in part from the continuing influence of New Critical assumptions. Recently, of course, it has become increasingly common to pledge dis-allegiance from New Criticism: feminists, Marxists, structuralists, Derrideans, Lacanians, and subjectivists all agree (if on nothing else) that it has outlived its usefulness and that we are living, in Frank Lentricchia's phrase, "After the New Criticism." Yet deeply ingrained ideologies are no more easily escaped when they are aesthetic than when they are political, and New Criticism remains a pedal point beneath our literary studies. It is not only, as Lentricchia points out, that one can find the "traces or scars" of New Criticism in the work of contemporary theorists.[5] Beyond that, New Criticism, in fairly unmodified form, still provides, among other things, the basis for secondary and undergraduate education in America, including the education that molded most American

4. Said, "Opponents, Audiences," 12.

5. Lentricchia, *After the New Criticism*, xiii. As he neatly puts it, New Criticism "is dead in the way that an imposing and repressive father-figure is dead."

"post–New Critics" and that continues to mold the students they now teach. And it continues as a lingua franca among literary scholars even today. No matter how forcefully contemporary critics insist on their distance from their forefathers (and I use the masculine advisedly), most of them maintain that distance only, as Jonathan Culler puts it, "with strenuous effort."

In order to understand how New Critical principles represented what Richard Ohmann calls "a flight from politics,"[6] let me begin by explaining more precisely what I mean by the politics of interpretation, since the phrase has come to mean different things to different people: note, for instance, the bewildering variety of definitions proposed in the special issue of *Critical Inquiry*. In this book, I will be using the term *politics* in a more limited way than, say, E. D. Hirsch, Jr., does in that collection, when he broadly equates politics and values; I will be using it in a less restricted sense than Walter Benn Michaels does, when he suggests that politics is at stake only when one is talking about free choice.[7] *Politics,* as used here, refers to the systems of power relations among groups (genders, races, nationalities, social classes, among others) in any social situation—systems that may be in part formalized (for instance, through law), but that are always in part invisible. (Indeed, one of the functions of ideology—and literature helps in this function—is to naturalize these power relationships. As Gayatri Spivak puts it, "Ideology in action is what a group takes to be natural and self-evident.")[8] And in my examination of the politics of interpretation, I will focus not so much, as Richard Ohmann and Steven Mailloux have so effectively done,[9] on the specific academic politics that have led certain interpretive practices to prevail, but more broadly on some of the ways in which any interpretive practice is always politically engaged. More specifically, I hope that my arguments will help us recognize that any interpretive practice is intertwined with politics as I have defined

6. Ohmann, *English in America,* 79.

7. Hirsch, "Politics of Theories of Interpretation"; Michaels, "Is There a Politics of Interpretation?"

8. Spivak, "Politics of Interpretations," 259.

9. See, for instance, Ohmann, *English in America,* and Mailloux, "Rhetorical Hermeneutics."

it in at least two ways: it is partially caused by (although not completely determined by) the political systems around it, and in turn it situates itself with respect to those systems (for instance, by reinforcing or by contesting them).

New Criticism obscured these relations between interpretation and politics in several ways. Most obviously, New Criticism tended to dehistoricize literary texts. David Daiches' claim that "ideally . . . every poem, as a self-contained work of art, should be regarded as though it were contemporary and anonymous"[10] may be an exaggerated version of a New Critical principle. But it is an exaggerated version of a principle still embedded in much academic practice, and it makes discussion of extratextual political relationships (including those that influenced the writer and his or her intended readers, as well as those that affect modern readers) by definition nonliterary.

But New Criticism depoliticized the study of literature in other, more subtle ways, too. Most important for my purposes was its treatment of reading, specifically its blurring of the distinction between the activity of the critic and that of the reader. True, New Critical theory suggested that the function of criticism was to describe the formal unity of a text; but in practice, especially when New Critics were studying fiction, description often gave way to interpretation. Literary critics, to a large extent, were considered expert readers who were expected to produce model interpretations, and academic publication turned more and more into the production of new readings.

This move from description to explication resulted, in part, from the New Critics' conception of theme, which they defined in such a way that it was quite close to what, in everyday speech, is called meaning. According to Cleanth Brooks and Robert Penn Warren in their extremely influential *Understanding Fiction*, for instance, theme is "what a piece of fiction stacks up to," "the pervasive and unifying view of life which is embodied in the total narrative."[11] Theme or idea was not simply one literary element among others; rather it was the dominant force in the New Critics' view of fic-

10. Daiches, *Critical Approaches*, 310.
11. 273.

6

tion, in much the same way that "end" was the shaping force in Aristotle's view of tragedy. Thus, despite claims to the contrary, there was a covert hierarchy in Brooks and Warren's first article of faith, "that the structure of a piece of fiction, in so far as that piece of fiction is successful, must involve a vital and functional relationship between the idea and the other elements in that structure." As a consequence, they insisted "that to be good, a piece of fiction must involve an idea of some real significance for mature and thoughtful human beings," and they therefore tended to equate aesthetic and philosophical value, broadly construed.[12] It may have often been labeled formalism, but New Critical analysis of fiction in fact steered more toward interpretation than toward formal description.

As Culler has argued, this emphasis on interpretation offered enormous pedagogical benefits, for it brought a refreshing democracy to the classroom.[13] The teacher was no longer a scholar whose task was to dispense information that students could never accumulate on their own; instead, he or she became the first among equals, engaged in the sharing of a learnable skill. This, especially when combined with New Criticism's ahistorical slant, tended to make the individual student count by promising that he or she too could, with practice, read well. But the scholarly impact was less salutary, for by equating the positions of the critic and the reader, New Criticism offered no perspective from which the act of reading itself could be critically examined.

Explication, of course, is not necessarily inimical to political analysis, and it would not be fair to say that New Criticism refused to touch at all on such concerns. But to the extent that they did treat politics, New Critics remained focused on the world view manifested by an individual author in the themes of a specific text or texts. Thus, while they were able and willing to discuss the value of the particular ideas expressed in a narrative, their analyses

12. Ibid., xvii.
13. Culler, *Pursuit of Signs,* esp. 3–5. Even among critics antagonistic to New Criticism, there is widespread appreciation of its democratic tendencies. See Ohmann's claim that New Criticism "at least aimed toward a democracy of critical ideas, available to all" (*English in America,* 85), and Said's claim that "New Criticism, for all its elitism, was strangely populist in intention" ("Opponents, Audiences," 4–5).

did not touch on the broader area of the politics of interpretation itself, did not touch on the ways that interpretive strategies, for instance, might be considered among the "practices" and "rituals" that Louis Althusser sees as part of the "material existence" of ideology.[14] For those shared interpretive practices were viewed as the basis, not the subject matter, for inquiry. New Criticism, in the end, was a style, not an analysis, of reading.

Of course, since Aristotle, there have always been critics whose work led, in Culler's phrase, "beyond interpretation" to an examination of the grounds of interpretation itself—to a study not of what a work means but of how it comes to mean. But when New Criticism dominated the American academy, such directions for study were the exception rather than the rule. It is only since perhaps the 1960s or 1970s that noninterpretive criticism has begun to reassert itself and that broader ideological questions, beyond the ideas of the author, have again become widely available as areas for extensive exploration. Not accidentally, this shift away from interpretation has gone hand in hand with a growing interest in reading—reading not as the end of criticism but as its very subject matter.

As Pratt's critiques make clear, however, the study of reading and interpretation as activities in their own right doesn't necessarily lead to a recognition of the politics of interpretation. Thus, for instance, although Wolfgang Iser does talk about the ways in which ideological commitment influences readers, he treats ideology much as the New Critics did, as something that simply interferes with proper reading.[15] And it might not at first seem that my central interest here—narrative conventions—would yield a particularly fruitful political harvest. Indeed, much of my description of reading conventions per se (Chapters 2–5) may not initially appear to bear directly on politics at all. But as Hayden White puts it, the politics of interpretation "arises in those interpretive prac-

14. Althusser, "Ideology and Ideological State Apparatuses," esp. 155–59.

15. Specifically, Iser claims that commitment reduces the reader's ability "to accept the basic theme-and-horizon structure of comprehension which regulates the text-reader interaction" (*The Act of Reading*, 202)—as if the kind of commitment to prior norms that he espouses were not an ideological commitment of its own.

tices which are ostensibly most remote from overtly political concerns, practices which are carried out under the aegis of a purely disinterested search for the truth."[16] Conventions, in other words, are one of the grounds on which the politics of art is mapped out; often invisible, they serve as enabling conditions for literature's ideological structures. Thus, study of literary conventions can help illuminate the connections between politics on the one hand and interpretation and evaluation, as the academy currently practices them, on the other.

The last two chapters reveal some of those connections. Let me say from the outset that I do not offer my analyses in a spirit of purely disinterested pursuit of knowledge. Rather, I hope to provide one more tool to help us change our world. As Spivak puts it, "One cannot . . . 'choose' to step out of ideology. The most responsible 'choice' seems to be to know it as best one can, recognize it as best one can, and through one's necessarily inadequate interpretation, to work to change it."[17] Study of conventions, that is, can help us escape some of the more confining effects of our culture by unmasking them, and can thus help us transform both reading and teaching into more liberating activities than they currently are. Not that I am proposing a specific program of social changes; nor, for that matter, am I attempting anything like an exhaustive account of the connections between literary conventions and political power. Rather, my analyses of specific texts and the ways readers approach them are intended as exemplifications of a *kind* of criticism that can be used more generally to make literature a source of social transformation. Thus, for instance, while I try to reveal some of the ways in which present practices of canon formation in the American academy influence our view of women's

---

16. White, "Politics of Historical Interpretation," 113. Although I agree with White about where politics is found, however, I do not follow his lead with regard to what it is. "This 'politics' has to do with the kind of *authority* the interpreter claims vis-à-vis the established political authorities . . . on the one side, and vis-à-vis other interpreters . . . on the other, as the basis of whatever *rights* he conceives himself to possess and whatever *duties* he feels obliged to discharge as a *professional* seeker of truth" (emphasis in original). This notion of politics seems quite restricted; it has little to do, say, with the activities of a nonprofessional reader as he or she happens to be "interpreting" a Harlequin Romance on the subway.

17. Spivak, "Politics of Interpretations," 263.

literature (and hence influence our gender relations), I would hope
that the analysis might not only change what and how we read, but
might also encourage a change in the way we live. I would hope, as
well, that the analysis would be expanded by others to deal with
the ways in which our academic practice marginalizes or excludes
other types of literature (and hence other groups): literature from
what is called the third world, for instance.

A word about my choice of texts. There is a complex relationship, not only between what you value and what you read, but
also between what you read and *how* you read. As Geoffrey
Hartman has argued, "We do not possess a careful study of theories
of criticism in the light of their *text-milieu:* how theory depends
on a canon, on a limited group of texts, often culture-specific or
national."[18] Still, even without that kind of study, it seems safe to
claim that the relationship between a theory and the texts called
upon to exemplify it works both ways. Once you know a reader's
critical principles, you can, within limits, predict what texts he or
she will gravitate toward. Given the theoretical perspective of *The
Rhetoric of Fiction,* it is not surprising that Wayne Booth refers to
Jane Austen and Henry James more often than he does to Gertrude
Stein. But you can also infer critical principles from a critic's basic
reading list. "To take the metaphysical poets as one's base or
touchstone," notes Hartman, "and to extend their 'poetics' toward
modern poetry and then all poetry, will produce a very different
result from working from Cervantes toward Pynchon, or from
Hölderlin toward Heidigger."[19] Or—he might have added—from
Ann Radcliffe toward Joyce Carol Oates.

I will speak in more detail in Chapter 7 about how the relationships among what you value, what you read, and how you read
(specifically, the interpretive strategies you use to make sense of
texts) help perpetuate canons. Meanwhile, let me point out that in
choosing my examples for this book, I have been wary of the ways
in which a presupposed set of exemplary texts can distort the theories built upon it. Thus, although I have drawn my examples

18. Hartman, *Criticism in the Wilderness*, 5. See also Eagleton's claim that
"most literary theories . . . unconsciously 'foreground' a particular literary genre,
and derive their general pronouncements from this" (*Literary Theory*, 51).
19. Hartman, *Criticism in the Wilderness*, 299.

largely from narrative fiction of the nineteenth and twentieth centuries, I have tried to make sure that they do not fall within the boundaries of any generally recognized text-milieu. My hope is that in making Chandler dance with Chekhov, Robbe-Grillet with Southworth, I have been able to sidestep at least one limitation of most contemporary practice.

I have been especially attentive to the noncanonical, including (but not limited to) popular fiction, for three reasons. First—and this is intended as a descriptive, not an evaluative, claim—the academy tends to favor complexity; as a result, the modern classics of our culture tend to be elaborate. Therefore, if one wants to examine literature that is more formulaic because its underlying principles are easier to spot, one is almost forced to study the noncanonical. Second, any study of reading will depend, implicitly or explicitly, in part on records of readings by others, including those public readings that take the form of articles and reviews. And it helps if those records are fundamentally accurate. Noncanonical literature has been less subject to willfully eccentric reading than the canon has, because it has (until recently) been less frequently studied in academic journals, which encourage novelty even at the expense of sincerity. Third, and most important, it is impossible to examine the mechanism of literary evaluation itself without studying both texts that are highly regarded by our literary judges *and* texts that are generally deemed inferior. Mary Louise Pratt has demonstrated how arguments about the distinction between "literary" and "nonliterary" language have been flawed by critics' tendency to scrutinize only the first half of the dichotomy.[20] The same charge could be leveled against much study of so-called literary quality: it tends to take, as its evidence, those works that are deemed good to begin with, assuming that the qualities discovered in them are the cause of that goodness. But there is no reason to believe that canonical texts are simply high-quality representatives of literature as whole, or that their goodness resides in discoverable features within them. Indeed, as I argue in Chapter 7, texts become canonized in part because they work with particular reading strategies. But if canonical texts are studied by themselves,

20. Pratt, *Toward a Speech Act Theory*, esp. chap. 1.

those strategies are never put to the test. Instead, they are implicitly universalized—treated as *the* way to read—a process that in the end serves to justify the initial canonical choice rather than to examine it.

As it is, my selection of texts—tied as it is to my own experiences—is narrower than it ought to be. Even beyond the focus on narrative (a narrow focus to begin with), even beyond the historical limits, there is little discussion of folklore, of oral literature, of literature from Asia, Africa, or Latin America, or even from parts of Europe with which I am unfamiliar. The conclusions I draw will therefore need to be refined or developed by others with different areas of expertise. Still, I hope that the book that follows will be one more step in the academy's slow retreat from the position that professional readings of *Moby Dick* and *Ulysses* are appropriate paradigms for *the* experience of reading narrative.

Let me point out, too, that the range of texts is more restricted in the last chapter and a half, where I engage in more sustained analyses of particular novels. Here, where I try to draw inferences about culture from the ways that people read texts, it seems appropriate to center on texts from the culture with which I have had the most experience—but also from a period from which I have some historical distance. I have therefore chosen my examples from American fiction of the 1920s and 1930s. However, although this is the most textually concentrated part of my argument, my concerns are methodological even here: I am less interested in the texts themselves than in providing concrete instances of a *type* of analysis through which we can become more self-conscious about what lies behind the ways we appropriate them. I therefore hope that my arguments will be of use even to readers with little interest in those novels or that period.

I have so far, rather disingenuously, used the words *reading*, *reader*, and *convention* as if they were unproblematic. Of course, they are not, as the various types of reader criticism now current make clear. Before getting to the conventions of reading in detail, it is therefore necessary to take a shorter detour to survey the process of reading more generally, to explain more fully what reading is, who readers are, and what kind of conventions they depend on as they read and interpret.

PART I

NARRATIVE
CONVENTIONS

I

Starting Points

> Any commentary on a particular poem *must* attend to more
> than is present in the verbal structure itself.
>
> Robert Scholes, *Structuralism in Literature*

What Is Reading?

Many of us had friends in high school who were, through their
religious training, capable of "reading" Hebrew or Latin in the
limited sense that they could pick up a text and make the appropriate sounds at the appropriate places. But they could not be said to
"know how to read" in a fuller (and more generally recognized)
sense—for the ability to read is usually construed (and is so used in
this book) to involve something more than the ability to parrot,
something more than phonetics and memory. It is, rather, somehow involved with "understanding."[1]

But what is understanding? How can we tell whether someone
does or does not understand? As long as understanding is viewed
strictly as a subjective phenomenon, there may be no answer. It is
probably impossible to determine precisely what the subjective
phenomenon of understanding involves—and because no one can
ever know what is happening in another's mind, it is impossible to
determine whether someone else is understanding. Most people,
however, have certain implicit but nonetheless *objective* stan-

---

1. See Louise M. Rosenblatt's discussion of this distinction, couched in somewhat different terms, in *Literature as Exploration*, especially chap. 3. See also
Gerald Prince's claim, "Identifying a series of symbols as specific graphemes (corre-
sponding to specific sounds) is not the same as extracting meaning from them and I
would not say, except as a joke, that I read German (or Rumanian or Russian) very
well but that I did not understand it" (*Narratology*, 104).

dards for determining understanding, for in our culture certain behaviors count as an indication that someone understands an utterance. Specifically, we rely on two commonsense means of verification: action and paraphrase. If a parent tells a child, "It's time for bed," the child can demonstrate understanding either by starting to put away his or her toys (action) or by asking, "Is it really eight o'clock?" (paraphrase).

As long as we are dealing with nonpoetic utterances, this may not seem a controversial claim. But when we deal with literature, we come up against the critical tradition of "the autonomous text." This traditional wisdom has many formulations,[2] but the most common in the American academy are variations of the New Critical axiom that a text says what it says in the only way it can say it. The text *means* what it *is*. Thus, a New Critic would view neither a paraphrase nor the act of sitting in at a lunch counter as a verification of the proper understanding of Chester Himes' *If He Hollers Let Him Go*. One is a different text altogether; the other is irrelevant to literature considered "as literature." Indeed, one of the most persistent residues of our New Critical heritage is our readiness to assume that when we speak of ethical effects, we are speaking of something extraliterary.

It would seem to follow logically that the only way for a reader to prove understanding of a text's meaning would be to repeat the text verbatim—in other words, that there would be no proper grounds for distinguishing mastery from memory. In fact, though, no practicing critics take such an extreme view; no matter what a critic's theoretical position may be, he or she always falls back on action or paraphrase as verifications of understanding. I will leave for some other book the vexed relationship between action and understanding (although I believe one can argue that there is a sense in which a racist whose actions were neither changed nor examined after reading *If He Hollers* had not "understood" the book) and limit myself here to the issue of paraphrase. *Paraphrase* is a difficult term, in part because it is entangled with the concept of synonymity. And if one uses the word *paraphrase* to mean an "absolutely synonymous" utterance, then no artistic text of any

2. For a good survey, see Frank Lentricchia, *After the New Criticism.*

merit or complexity can be paraphrased.[3] Indeed, since the meaning of any utterance depends on its context—at least if meaning is taken broadly to include tone, emphasis, and connotation—then no utterance is ever synonymous even with itself: you cannot step into the same meaning twice.[4]

But paraphrase need not imply identity of meaning; it can also be used in the wider sense of an imitation or transformation, with the recognition that imitations are by definition imperfect. Indeed, the prefix *para-*, in some of its meanings, suggests both imperfection (as in *paralexia*) and close resemblance without identity (as in *paratyphoid*). In this sense, a paraphrase is a translation into new terms that need not be judged in an on/off binary fashion in terms of equivalence (synonymous/nonsynonymous), but that can rather be evaluated along a continuum of greater or lesser adequacy or appropriateness. It is for this reason that "It's time for bed" could be paraphrased "It's eight o'clock"—not because "It's eight o'clock" is an exact synonym, but because in the given context, it comes closer to imitating the original sentence than most other sentences that could be uttered.

Whatever their theories, almost all critics act on the twin principles that paraphrases can be more or less adequate, and that, as Gerald Graff puts it, the act of paraphrasing or transforming is a "normal and unavoidable aspect of the reading process."[5] Roland Barthes claims that "to read is to struggle to name, to subject the sentences of the text to a semantic transformation"; E. D. Hirsch, Jr., defines interpretation as construing something else from the signs physically present in the text; Susan Sontag describes Beckett's plays as "delicate dramas of the withdrawn consciousness" in the middle of her argument against interpretation. All these critics admit, in their different ways, that to read—in the sense of to

3. See David Lodge: "I believe it can be convincingly argued that novels are non-paraphrasable" (*Language of Fiction*, 19). For a different position, see E. D. Hirsch, Jr., *Aims of Interpretation*, chap. 4. For a detailed account of the problems of paraphrase, see James Phelan, *Worlds from Words*. See also Barbara Foley's discussion in *Telling the Truth*, 45–46.

4. For an exploration of this phenomenon, see Jorge Luis Borges, "Pierre Menard, Author of Don Quixote," in *Ficciones*, trans. Anthony Kerrigan (New York: Grove, 1962), 45–55.

5. Graff, "Literature as Assertions," 99.

understand—a text is to imitate it in some way, to produce something "around" (*para*) it that is new but that bears some clear relationship to the original text.[6]

Indeed, the very institution of interpretive criticism betrays a belief that understanding is manifested in restating—and in making those restatements public. The question, then, is not whether works can be paraphrased, but rather how one determines what constitutes an adequate or acceptable transformation of the original. Paraphrases differ, after all, not only in their accuracy, but also in their emphasis and in their perspective. Different kinds of imitations are adequate under different circumstances, since the imitator's decisions about which features are essential and which are secondary will depend in part on his or her purposes. A doctor's standards for adequacy, when judging an anatomical chart that serves as his or her "imitation" of the human body, will differ substantially from a dressmaker's when judging a mannequin, and these are in turn different from those of a grandparent when judging a photo of a grandchild. Likewise, paraphrases will differ according to the context and the conventions surrounding them. In Swann's love affair with Odette, the phrase *faire cattleya* ("to do a cattleya") served as an equivalent for "the act of physical possession."[7] In a household where snacks are the custom before going to bed, the sentence "Let's get down the Cheerios" might be an appropriate paraphrase for "It's time for bed."[8]

6. Barthes, *S/Z*, 92; Hirsch, *Aims of Interpretation*, 75; Sontag, "Against Interpretation," in *Against Interpretation and Other Essays* (New York: Dell/Laurel, 1969), 18; see also her claim that "the task of interpretation is virtually one of translation" (15). This view is very widespread. Janice Radway remarks that an analyst's attempt to determine the significance that the act of reading has for a particular reader always involves the "activity of translation" (*Reading the Romance*, 9). Terence Hawkes uses the convenient notion of "recoding" (*Structuralism and Semiotics*, 104). Steven Mailloux discusses interpretation as "acceptable and approximating translation" (*Interpretive Conventions*, 146). See also Prince's discussion of the various ways one can "give an account of a particular text" ("*La Nausée* and Closure," 182–90, esp. 188–90).

7. Marcel Proust, *Swann's Way*, trans. C. K. Scott Moncrieff (New York: Modern Library, 1934), 336.

8. For a discussion of this point from a different perspective, see Stanley Fish, "Normal Circumstances, Literal Language, Direct Speech Acts, the Ordinary, the Everyday, the Obvious, What Goes without Saying, and Other Special Cases," in *Is There a Text?* 268–92.

For this reason, different kinds of reading involve different kinds of transformation and different standards of adequacy. Does the paraphrase more or less adequately imitate the latent psychosexual content of the original text? Does the paraphrase take into account the socioeconomic conditions under which the text was produced? Does the paraphrase maintain or at least represent the essential formal features of the original text? Whatever their origins, though, these standards for adequacy inevitably bring some extratextual context into the judgment of understanding. As Robert Scholes puts it, "The critic who 'recovers' the meaning of any given work always does so by establishing a relationship between the work and some system of ideas outside it."[9] Or, in Annette Kolodny's terms, "We appropriate meaning from a text according to what we need (or desire) or, in other words, according to the critical assumptions or predispositions (conscious or not) that we bring to it."[10]

Furthermore, this act of recovery is always both rule governed and reductive. Whether sitting on a beach or in a library, a reader can only make sense of a text in the same way he or she makes sense of anything else in the world: by applying a series of strategies to simplify it—by highlighting, by making symbolic, and by otherwise patterning it. It is perhaps worth stressing the reductive aspect of this process. Since all imitation is imperfect and incomplete, understanding—in the sense of being able to paraphrase—always involves the ability to *ignore*. Although many critics argue that in literature everything is significant, we know from experience that when we read literature (as opposed to the single sentences so many critics offer as examples), it is impossible to keep track of, much less account for, all the details of a text. As Michael Riffaterre's criticism of Jakobson makes abundantly clear, readers need to ignore or play down many textual features when they read lyric poetry;[11] they need to ignore even more in longer

9. Scholes, *Structuralism in Literature*, 9.

10. Kolodny, "Dancing through the Minefield," 11.

11. Riffaterre, "Describing Poetic Structures." See also Jonathan Culler's discussion of Jakobson in *Structuralist Poetics*, chap. 3; and Fish, "What Is Stylistics and Why Are They Saying Such Terrible Things about It?" in *Is There a Text?* 68–96. For a discussion of authorial memory and control with respect to revision—and the subsequent problems of producing correct texts in the first place—see Hershel Parker, *Flawed Texts and Verbal Icons*.

works like novels. As the Gestalt psychologists have shown us (and as Borges has reminded us in a more fanciful way),[12] perception involves simplification, which in turn involves some organizing principle, some hierarchy of attention and importance. The reader who pays no more attention to Hamlet's soliloquies than to Bernardo's opening sally has not yet grasped what most other readers have considered the play's basic figure/ground dichotomy.

Who Is Reading?

There can be no reading without a reader—but the term *reader* is slippery, not only because all individual readers read differently, but also because for almost all of them, there are several different ways of appropriating a text. This fact has been recognized, at least implicitly, by the large number of critics whose models of reading are multitiered. Usually, a two-leveled opposition is posited, although different critics use different terms. For Hirsch, it is "significance" and "meaning." For Wayne Booth, it is "understanding" and "overstanding." For Tzvetan Todorov, there are three terms: "interpretation," "description," and "reading."[13] Many other critics, despite the recent arguments of Fish, remain wedded, in one form or another, to the distinction between literal meaning and interpretation.

These distinctions all discriminate among activities that a reader can engage in under different circumstances or for different purposes. I would like to start with a different kind of distinction, one that discriminates among *simultaneous* roles that the audience of a text can play. There are three of these roles that will be central to my argument, but I will reserve the third for Chapter 3 and will only outline the first two here. First, there is the *actual audience*. This consists of the flesh-and-blood people who read the book. This is the audience that booksellers are most concerned with— but it happens to be the audience over which an author has no guaranteed control. Each member of the actual audience is differ-

12. Borges, "Funes the Memorious," in *Ficciones*, 107–15.
13. Hirsch, *Validity in Interpretation*, esp. 8; Booth, *Critical Understanding*, passim; Todorov, *Poetics of Prose*, 238–46.

ent, and each reads in his or her own way, with a distance from other readers depending upon such variables as class, gender, race, personality, training, culture, and historical situation.

This difference among readers has always posed a problem for writers, one that has grown with increased literacy and the correspondingly increased heterogeneity of the reading public. An author has, in most cases, no firm knowledge of the actual readers who will pick up his or her book. Yet he or she cannot begin to fill up a blank page without making assumptions about the readers' beliefs, knowledge, and familiarity with conventions. As a result, authors are forced to guess; they design their books rhetorically for some more or less specific *hypothetical* audience, which I call the *authorial audience*. Artistic choices are based upon these assumptions—conscious or unconscious—about readers, and to a certain extent, artistic success depends on their shrewdness, on the degree to which actual and authorial audience overlap. Some assumptions are quite specific. William Demby's *Catacombs,* for instance, takes place in the early 1960s, and it achieves its sense of impending doom only if the reader already knows that John F. Kennedy will be assassinated when the events of the novel reach November 22, 1963. One of the Encyclopedia Brown mysteries is soluble only by the reader who knows that skydivers always wear two parachutes. Other assumptions are more general: "Rip van Winkle" assumes readers who know that during the Revolution, the American colonies became independent of England. Some assumptions are historical: Flaubert assumes considerable knowledge of the revolution of 1848 in *Sentimental Education.* Some are sociological: at least one critic has argued convincingly that *The Turn of the Screw* makes proper sense only to a reader who knows something about the conduct deemed proper to governesses in the nineteenth century.[14] Some authors rely on our precise knowledge of cultural fads (Peter Cameron, in "Fear of Math," assumes that his audience will draw the proper conclusions about a character when he tells us that she eats a "tabbouleh-and-pita bread sandwich"),[15] others on our knowledge of more widespread cultural conventions (in

14. Elliott M. Schrero, "Exposure in *The Turn of the Screw,*" *Modern Philology* 78 (February 1981): 261–74.
15. *New Yorker,* March 11, 1985, 42.

Nabokov's *Lolita*, the refusal of the Enchanted Hunters to accept Humbert Humbert as a guest when he first shows up makes sense only if readers recognize both that they have garbled his name so that it sounds Jewish, and that the phrase in their advertising, "Near Churches," is a code phrase for "No Jews").[16] Some authors presume that we have a knowledge of specific previous texts (Stoppard assumes that his readers know *Hamlet* before reading *Rosencrantz and Guildenstern Are Dead*). Sometimes authors assume that our higher motives will triumph (Dostoyevsky assumes that we are capable of sympathy for the sufferings of Raskolnikov in *Crime and Punishment* even though he is a murderer). Sometimes authors—even the same authors—assume that we will be influenced by our baser prejudices (in *The Idiot* we are expected to be distrustful of Ganya because his teeth are "altogether too dazzling and even").[17] The potential range of assumptions an author can make, in other words, is infinite.

The notion of the authorial audience is clearly tied to authorial intention, but it gets around some of the problems that have traditionally hampered the discussion of intention by treating it as a matter of social convention rather than of individual psychology. In other words, my perspective allows us to treat the reader's attempt to read as the author intended, not as a search for the author's private psyche, but rather as the joining of a particular social/interpretive community; that is, the acceptance of the author's invitation to read in a particular socially constituted way that is shared by the author and his or her expected readers. Indeed, authorial reading is not only a way of reading but, perhaps equally important, a way of talking about how you read—that is, the result of a community agreement that allows discussion of a certain sort to take place by treating meanings in a particular way (as found rather than made). In this sense, what Susan R. Suleiman says

16. Although I have taught this novel several times, none of my students—coming as they do from a cultural context quite different from that of the authorial audience—has caught this, or any of the other references to anti-Semitism in the novel.

17. Fyodor Dostoyevsky, *The Idiot*, trans. David Magarshack (Baltimore: Penguin, 1955), 48 (pt. 1, chap. 2). In Dickens' *Dombey and Son*, we are expected to distrust Carker for the same reason.

about the notions of the implied author and the implied reader (which are themselves only variant formulations of the notion of authorial intention) applies to the authorial audience as well: they are, she says, "necessary fictions, guaranteeing the consistency of a specific reading without guaranteeing its validity in any absolute sense."[18] But it is crucial to note that this is not just an arbitrary convention invented by academics for their own convenience—it is a broader social usage, one that is shared by authors as well as their readers, including their nonprofessional readers. My position here is thus very close to that of Foley, who rightly sees fiction "as a contract designed by an intending author who invites his or her audience to adopt certain paradigms for understanding reality."[19] In other words, as Terry Eagleton argues, intention is best seen not in terms of "essentially private 'mental acts,'" but rather in terms of social practice.[20]

By thinking in terms of the authorial audience rather than private intention, furthermore, we are reminded of the constraints within which writers write. For despite the theoretically infinite number of potential authorial audiences, it does not follow that authors have total control over the act of writing, any more than that readers have total control over the act of interpretation. In a trivial sense, of course, they do: authors can put down whatever marks they wish on the page; readers can construe them however they wish. But once authors and readers accept the communal na-

18. Suleiman, "Introduction," 11.

19. Foley, *Telling the Truth*, 43.

20. Eagleton, *Literary Theory*, 114. See also Patrocinio P. Schweickart's claim that validity is not "a property inherent in an interpretation, but rather . . . a *claim* implicit in the *act* of propounding an interpretation"—that is, that validity is "contingent on the agreement of others" ("Reading Ourselves," 56). Fish argues similarly that authorial intention "is not private but a form of conventional behavior" ("Working on the Chain Gang," 213); Hirsch, with less enthusiasm, notes that "we can circumvent the whole question of author psychology by adopting a semiotic account of interpretation. Instead of referring an interpretation back to an original author, we could . . . refer it back to an original code or convention system" ("Politics of Theories of Interpretation," 239). Hirsch insists that this would not really be an adequate account, but I suspect it is as adequate as any that relies on actual psychology. It is worth remembering that this is not simply a matter of arbitrary definitions; as Mailloux's arguments in "Rhetorical Hermeneutics" make clear, the very act of treating readings in this way has serious effects on the ways in which people subsequently *do* read—on what counts as evidence, for instance.

23

ture of writing and reading, they give up some of that freedom. Specifically, once he or she has made certain initial decisions, any writer who wishes to communicate—even if he or she wishes to communicate ambiguity—has limited the range of subsequent choices.

Some of those limitations spring from what might be called brute facts. Writers of realistic historical novels, for instance, shackle themselves to events that are independent of their imaginations. As Suleiman has argued:

> The most obvious . . . difference between fictional and historical characters in a novel is that the latter impose greater constraints on the novelist who wants to be a "painter of his time." He cannot make Napoleon die—or win the battle—at Waterloo, just as he cannot make Hugo the court poet of Napoleon III. . . . And if the novelist chooses to place in the foreground events as well-known and public as the Boulanger affair or the Panama scandal, then he will have to bend to similar constraints even as far as the activities of the *fictional* characters are concerned.[21]

Thus, once Margaret Mitchell chose to write *Gone with the Wind* as a historical novel about the Civil War, she relinquished control over certain areas of her text. She could have saved Melanie had she wished, or killed off Rhett, but there was no way to give victory to the South or to preserve Atlanta from the flames.

More central to my argument, though, are *conventional* limitations on choice. There are no brute facts preventing an author from writing a religious parable in which a cross represented Judaism, but it would not communicate successfully. As Mary Pratt puts it, "Although the fictional discourse in a work of literature may in theory take any form at all, readers have certain expectations about what form it will take, and *they can be expected to decode the work according to those assumptions unless they are overtly invited or required to do otherwise*" (italics in original).[22] The writer

---

21. Suleiman, *Authoritarian Fictions*, 120.
22. Pratt, *Toward a Speech Act Theory*, 204. Pratt's own strong critique of speech-act theory (including her own work) can be found in "The Ideology of Speech-Act Theory." I think that my definition of fictionality (Chapter 3) solves

who wishes to be understood—even to be understood by a small group of readers—has to work within such conventional restraints.

Despite these limitations, however, there is still an incalculable number of possible authorial audiences; and since the structure of a work is designed with the authorial audience in mind, actual readers must come to share its characteristics as they read if they are to experience the text as the author wished.[23] Reading as authorial audience therefore involves a kind of distancing from the actual audience, from one's own immediate needs and interests. This distancing, however, must be distinguished sharply from the apparently similar kind of objectivity, represented in its baldest form by Dr. Blimber, in Dickens' *Dombey and Son*, who claimed "that all the fancies of the poets, and lessons of the sages, were a mere collection of words and grammar, and had no other meaning in the world."[24] Of course, few critics subscribe to Blimberism in its purest form, yet many critical windows are draped with remnants from Blimber's school. Northrop Frye insists that "the fundamental act of criticism is a disinterested response to a work of literature in which all one's beliefs, engagements, commitments, prejudices, stampedings of pity and terror, are ordered to be quiet."[25] Similarly, the reader postulated by Stanley Fish's once-popular "Affective Stylistics" is psychologically blank and politically unaware, an automaton who approaches each new sentence with the same anesthetized mind.[26] In a radically different critical

---

some of the questions that Pratt raises; while my book tends to focus on a type of reading that includes an attempt at author-reader cooperation, I have accepted many of the arguments on which her critique is based, and have tried not to "normalize" this particular kind of reading, nor to define others as "deviant" (see "The Value[s] of Authorial Reading" below). Even if one accepts her new position, though, much of Pratt's earlier work remains useful as a description of certain kinds of reading.

23. See Booth's discussion of this process in *Rhetoric of Fiction*, esp. 138–41.
24. Charles Dickens, *Dombey and Son* (New York: Dutton/Everyman's Library, 1907), 134–35 (chap. 11).
25. Frye, *Well-Tempered Critic*, 140. Frye backs off a bit from the implications of this statement by distinguishing later between the pure disinterested critical act and the act of ordinary reading.
26. Fish, "Literature in the Reader: Affective Stylistics," in *Is There a Text?* 21–67. Indeed, as Culler has pointed out, he or she does not even learn from reading; see *Pursuit of Signs*, 130.

tradition, Gerald Prince's degree-zero narratee—whom he assumes to be the addressee of the text except where "an indication to the contrary is supplied in the narration intended for him"—has no "personality or social characteristics," and although he (apparently, the degree-zero narratee is male) knows grammar and the denotations of words, he knows neither connotations nor conventions. He is, in other words, capable of reading a text without any distorting presuppositions; neither his "character" nor his "position in society . . . colors his perception of the events described to him."[27]

Authorial reading, however, is quite different. It does *not* escape "distorting presuppositions." Rather, it recognizes that distorting presuppositions lie at the heart of the reading process. To read as authorial audience is to read in an impersonal way, but only in a special and limited sense. The authorial audience has knowledge and beliefs that may well be *extra*personal—that is, not shared by the actual individual reader (I, for instance, do not personally share the racist perspective of the authorial audience of Ian Fleming's *Live and Let Die*). The authorial audience's knowledge and beliefs may even be extracommunal—that is, not shared by any community (and we all belong to several) of which the actual reader is a member at the historical moment of reading (what current community shares the belief in Zeus characteristic of the authorial audience of the *Odyssey*?). But these authorial audiences, whatever their distance from actual readers, certainly have their own engagements and prejudices. To join the authorial audience, then, you should not ask what a *pure* reading of a given text would be. Rather, you need to ask what sort of *corrupted* reader this particular author wrote for: what were that reader's beliefs, engagements, commitments, prejudices, and stampedings of pity and terror?

The reader, in other words, can read as the author intended only by being in the right place to begin with—and that can come about only through an intuitive mix of experience and faith, knowledge

27. Prince, "Introduction," 10–11. But see also his claim, "There may frequently be points in my reading where . . . I have to rely not only on my linguistic knowledge and the textual information supplied but also on my mastery of logical operations, my familiarity with interpretive conventions and my knowledge of the world" (*Narratology*, 128).

and hunch—plus a certain amount of luck. There is consequently no ideal point of departure that will work for any and all books. And since each point of departure involves its own corruptions, commitments, and prejudices, every authorial reading has significant ideological strands. As I suggested earlier, my primary concern here is with a particular aspect of the authorial audience's corruptions: the literary conventions that it applies to the text in order to transform it. As such critics as Culler are now making clearer, reading (especially the reading of literature) is not only not a natural activity—it is not even a logical consequence of knowledge of the linguistic system and its written signs. It is, rather, a separately learned, *conventional* activity.

In other words, literary conventions are not in the text waiting to be uncovered, but in fact *precede* the text and make discovery possible in the first place.[28] Note, however, that I speak here of discovery, not creation. The notion of reading as authorial audience is closer to what Steven Mailloux calls "textual realism" (the belief that "meaning-full texts exist independent of interpretation") than to what he calls "readerly idealism" (the belief that "meaning is made, not found," since "textual facts are never prior to or independent of the hermeneutic activity of readers and critics").[29] True, I share the idealists' belief that texts are incomplete when we get them and must be put together according to the

28. As Culler argues, "The implication that the ideal reader is a *tabula rasa* on which the text inscribes itself not only makes nonsense of the whole process of literary education and conceals the conventions and norms which make possible the production of meaning but also insures the bankruptcy of literary theory, whose speculations on the properties of literary texts become ancillary and *ex post facto* generalizations which are explicitly denied any role in the activity of reading" (*Pursuit of Signs*, 121). See also Mailloux's claim that "a reader's understanding of authorial intention always depends on shared communicative conventions, but the success of the intention to achieve certain perlocutionary effects is not guaranteed by those conventions, only made possible by them" (*Interpretive Conventions*, 106). This notion of reading is confirmed by research into cognitive psychology. See, for instance, Mary Crawford and Roger Chaffin's claim that "understanding is a product of both the text and the prior knowledge and viewpoint that the reader brings to it" ("Reader's Construction of Meaning," 3).

29. Mailloux, "Rhetorical Hermeneutics," 622. Mailloux attacks both schools and argues against doing "Theory" at all. Although I do not follow this path, I find his alternative—a study of the *institutional* politics of interpretation—a profitable one as well.

principles of the reader's interpretive community, but in the case of successful authorial reading, the author and readers are members of the same community, so while the reader does in fact engage in an act of production, he or she makes what the author intended to be found. Of course, as I will discuss in more detail in Chapters 6 and 7, not all attempts at authorial reading are successful. Even readers who try to find out what an author intends may thus in fact *make* something the author never expected; in such cases, though, the readers will still act as if they have in fact *found* the meaning of the text.

I am not arguing that we do not use logic to interpret literary texts. Given that Edna Losser is twenty in 1900 when Margaret Ayer Barnes' *Edna His Wife* opens, we can reasonably infer—as the author intended us to—that she is in her fifties when the novel ends, in the early 1930s. But such inferences are not sufficient for a complete authorial reading. Nor am I arguing that one cannot describe the features of literary artifacts or the rules that govern reading according to "logical" categories. Thus, for instance, Gerald Prince is quite correct when he claims, "Should an event A precede an event B in time, the two may be temporally adjacent, or proximate, or distant."[30] Similarly, we can claim, with some precision, that in any book, the rule that we should eliminate likely suspects either applies or does not apply. But providing a logical classification of all possibilities is quite different from providing a logical system that explains which of those possibilities will be actualized in a given novel. A reader who picks up Ellery Queen's *Tragedy of X* for the first time knows to eliminate obvious suspects, not because of some *systematic* understanding of possible literary types, but rather because it is the *conventional* thing to do in that kind of book. For this reason, discussions of the actual conventions of reading will always appear arbitrary and ad hoc compared to the classifications of structuralists.[31]

Knowledge of these conventions is a major part of what Culler

---

30. Prince, *Narratology*, 64.

31. For a different perspective, see Todorov's discussion of the difference between logical ("theoretical") and historical genres (*Fantastic*, chap. 1).

calls "literary competence."[32] It is not simply that we need to know conventions in order to read Joyce; even the simplest literary artifact (say, a comic strip) calls nonlinguistic conventions (such as the left-to-right spatial representation of the passage of time) into play.[33] As Janice Radway puts it, "Comprehension is . . . a process of sign production where the reader actively attributes significance to signifiers on the basis of previously learned cultural codes."[34]

As I will demonstrate, the reliance of reading on conventions that precede the text has enormous consequences for the processes of interpretation and evaluation, in many ways the central activities of the academic literary community.

The Value(s) of Authorial Reading

In this book, I will focus primarily on authorial reading. In so doing, I am not claiming that this is either the only or even the best way to read. I do not agree with Steven Knapp and Walter Benn Michaels that "the meaning of a text is simply identical to the author's intended meaning" or that "authorial intention is the necessary object of interpretation."[35] And I do not agree with Wayne Booth and E. D. Hirsch, Jr., who often suggest that there is a

32. Culler, *Structuralist Poetics*, esp. chap. 6. Conventions are also one aspect of Hans Robert Jauss' notion of "horizon of expectations." See, for instance, *Toward an Aesthetic of Reception*. For a strong critique of Culler's notion of competence, see Pratt, "Interpretive Strategies/Strategic Interpretations," esp. 215–21. Pratt points out that, as Culler uses the concept, literary competence can end up as a theoretical justification for the mainstream practices of academic criticism. Literary competence, however, need not be restricted to what the academy believes it to be; as I hope will be clear in Chapters 6 and 7, my own stress on actual authorial intention, rather than on received opinion about the "right" way to read "good" books, helps avoid this problem.

33. For a good unpacking of the conventions of the comic strip, see Seymour Chatman, *Story and Discourse*, 37–41.

34. Radway, *Reading the Romance*, 7. Radway sees this as a process of "making" meaning, but as I have argued, reading as authorial audience at least attempts to "find" a meaning that is in some sense already there.

35. Knapp and Michaels, "Against Theory," 724, and "A Reply to Our Critics," 796. For a series of incisive responses to Knapp and Michaels, see *Critical Inquiry* 9 (June 1983): 725–89.

moral imperative to read as the author intended.[36] At the same time, I would argue that authorial reading is more than just another among a large set of equally valid and equally important ways of approaching a text. Authorial reading has a special status for at least two reasons.

First, while Knapp and Michaels are wrong that "the object of *all* reading is *always* the historical author's intention" (italics added),[37] it is true that most people actually do read—or attempt to read—this way most of the time. Of course, different individuals may disagree about what the author's intention is, just as they may react differently to it once they think they have found it. Nonetheless, the initial question most commonly asked of a literary text in our culture is, What is the author saying? The critical revolutions of the 1970s and 1980s may have deluded us, but the millions of readers of Len Deighton's *SS-GB* or Judith Krantz's *Scruples* were interested neither in deconstructing texts nor in discovering their underlying semiotic codes. In fact, even among the most jaded readers—academics—the majority still attempts to read as authorial audience. Authorial reading continues to provide the basis for most academic articles and papers—and, even more, for classroom teaching.

Second, the perhaps more important for critical theory, reading as authorial audience provides the foundation for many other types of reading. True, some approaches to texts skip over the authorial audience entirely: certain kinds of structuralist or stylistic studies, for instance, or the kind of subjective reading proposed by David Bleich in *Readings and Feelings*.[38] But then again, many types of reading depend for their power on a prior understanding of the

36. See Booth: "It is simply self-maiming to pretend that any blissful improvisation on [Henry James'] words, sentences, or themes . . . can equal the value of his making" (*Critical Understanding*, 284). See also Hirsch, *Aims of Interpretation*. For positions that oppose Booth's, see, for instance, Barbara Herrnstein Smith, *On the Margins of Discourse*, esp. chap. 6; and "English 692" [Joanna Brent, Rita Conley, et al.], "Poem Opening: An Invitation to Transactive Criticism," *College English* 40 (September 1978): 2–16.

37. Knapp and Michaels, "A Reply to Our Critics," 798.

38. Esp. 80–95. For a further development of Bleich's ideas, see also his *Subjective Criticism*.

authorial meaning.[39] The manifest/latent distinction of certain Freudian studies, for instance, collapses if we don't have a manifest meaning to begin with. Georg Lukács' Marxist analysis of Balzac depends on the distinction between what Balzac wanted to see and what he really did see.[40] Most important—if importance has any connection to the power of a critical movement to make us recognize the world with new eyes—we see the same dependence on authorial intention in much feminist criticism. Judith Fetterley's "resisting reader" can come into being only if there is something to resist.[41]

Two examples may clarify how certain kinds of political criticism can be strengthened if they are built on a foundation of authorial reading. Imagine a critic who wanted to uncover Natasha's victimization in *War and Peace*—to show how Russian society restricts the development of her natural talents, how it curbs and punishes her spirit and individuality. Such a critic could well point out Natasha's unjust fate—even explain its social, psychological, and historical causes—without any reference to authorial intention. But if—and only if—the critic works through an authorial reading of the text, the scope of this political analysis can be enlarged to explore the *contradiction* between the authorial audience and the critic. For only by starting with an authorial reading could the critic analyze the social, historical, and biographical implications of the fact that from Tolstoy's point of view (and from the point of view of the authorial audience, as well as of

39. Booth has called such readings "parasitical" ("M. H. Abrams," 441). See J. Hillis Miller's response, "Critic as Host."

40. Lukács claims, for instance, that Balzac was faced with a contradiction between the torments of "the transition to the capitalist system of production" and his awareness that this "transformation was not only socially inevitable, but at the same time progressive. This contradiction in his experience Balzac *attempted* to force into a system based on a Catholic legitimism and tricked out with Utopian conceptions of English Toryism. But this system was contradicted all the time by the social realities of his day and the Balzacian vision which mirrored them" (*Studies in European Realism*, 12–13; emphasis added).

41. See also Mailloux's claim that "every feminist and nonfeminist approach must posit some kind of reading experience upon which to base its interpretation. Only after a reader-response description is completed or assumed can a feminist critique begin" (*Interpretive Conventions*, 89).

millions of actual readers), Natasha does not suffer in the end. Indeed, her victimization is worse than invisible—it is construed as a reward.[42] Without this grounding in an authorial reading, Tolstoy's misogynist text is indistinguishable from feminist irony.

Similarly, reading *Jane Eyre* in the context of Jean Rhys' *Wide Sargasso Sea*—and Mary Wollstonecraft's *Maria*—provides a useful perspective that underscores the inhumanity of Rochester's— and Jane's—treatment of Bertha and suggests that we look behind her function as a convenient Gothic plot device to consider her as a significant character who has been driven mad by her social and economic conditions. But again, with authorial reading one can go further to explore the extent to which Brontë was herself unable to see the oppression behind that convention.[43]

Thus, in arguing for the importance of reading as authorial audience, I am not suggesting that it is either the final reading or the most important. Were I teaching either Tolstoy or Brontë, I would be disappointed in a student who could produce an authorial reading but who could not, in Terry Eagleton's phrase, "show the text as it cannot know itself"[44]—that is, move beyond that reading to look at the work critically from some perspective other than the one called for by the author. But while authorial reading without further critique is often incomplete, so is a critical reading without an understanding of the authorial audience as its base.

So far, I have argued the importance of authorial reading on the grounds that many readers try to engage in it, and that it is a necessary precondition for many other kinds of reading. But it does not logically follow that it is actually possible. Indeed, I would argue that in a sense it is not. I am not referring here to the problems of interpretation that arise because authors simply fail at the act of writing, or because, when editors are allowed to muddle with

42. See, in this regard, Eve Kosofsky Sedgwick's discussion of the " 'happy ending' " of *Our Mutual Friend* and what it really means for Lizzie (*Between Men: English Literature and Male Homosocial Desire* [New York: Columbia University Press, 1985], 178).

43. For a different perspective on this problem, considered in the context of European imperialism, see Gayatri Chakravorty Spivak, "Three Women's Texts and a Critique of Imperialism," *Critical Inquiry* 12 (Autumn 1985): 243–61.

44. Eagleton, *Criticism and Ideology*, 43.

finished texts, authors, as Hershel Parker puts it, "very often lose authority, with the result that familiar literary texts at some points have no meaning, only partially authorial meaning, or quite adventitious meaning unintended by the author or anyone else."[45] Even beyond this, even among the most polished and accurately edited of texts, there are many (perhaps all) where neither scholarship nor imagination is sufficient to allow us to recover the text in the sense of experiencing the full response that the author intended us to have as we read. This impossibility stems directly from the actual/authorial split. These audiences differ in, among other things, the knowledge and belief they bring to a text. To the extent that the knowledge distinguishing the authorial from the actual audience is positive or additive (that is, to the extent that the authorial audience knows something that the actual audience does not), the gap can often be bridged through education. The reader of *The Catacombs* who does not know the date of Kennedy's assassination can be informed. But knowledge can also be negative. That is, sometimes actual readers can respond to a text as authorial audience only by *not* knowing something that they in fact know—not knowing, as they read John Steinbeck's *In Dubious Battle*, the actual (often unidealistic) course that the American labor movement would eventually follow; not knowing, as they read *U.S.A.*, that Dos Passos would later shift his political views. As for beliefs—they are usually neither additive nor negative, but substitutive: it was difficult for some college-age readers in the late 1960s to accept the passion with which Clarissa protected her virginity.

The problems of recovery caused by the actual/authorial split have a musical equivalent: what I call the authentic-performance paradox. Many performing groups assume that by recreating the physical sounds that a composer had available, they come closer to recreating the intended musical experiences. But do contemporary listeners really move closer to Beethoven's intended experiences when they listen to his sonatas on a Conrad Graf fortepiano? In at least one way, they take a significant step *away* from Beethoven. I am not convinced by those structuralists who argue that binary

45. Parker, *Flawed Texts and Verbal Icons*, 4.

oppositions underlie all of our perceptions of the world, but structuralists are surely right that we see things not in themselves but rather in terms of their relations, and specifically in terms of oppositions determined largely by culturally imposed categories that may change radically over time. Thus, when *I* hear Beethoven on an early-nineteenth-century fortepiano (and I think this experience is shared by many contemporary listeners), I hear it first and foremost *against* modern sounds. That is, the sound is defined by me (and hence experienced by me) partly in terms of its being not-that-of-a-modern-piano. That component of the listening experience was obviously not envisioned by Beethoven. Similarly, the range of choices that Mozart faced now seems restricted in ways that it did not in 1790, since we now know what Beethoven, Wagner, Schoenberg, and Jay Reise have added to available harmonic and formal vocabulary.[46]

In other words, we live in a world with a history and with traditions, and it is impossible to experience what an author wanted us to because it is impossible to forget all that has happened between the time when a text was written and the time when it is read. What reasonably educated member of our culture can read *Hamlet*—even for the first time—without being influenced by the traditions of interpretation encrusted on it? Of course, tradition is a factor in authorial reading as well; the tradition of literature out of which *Hamlet* grew is, to some extent, part of Shakespeare's assumed starting point. But the traditions coming *afterward* are assuredly not, and modern readers are more likely to be familiar with the latter (which cannot be erased) than with the former.

Thus, while books do sometimes have the power to take readers out of themselves, that power is limited. Nor is that limitation necessarily to be lamented. Despite romantic notions about the beneficial consequences of great art, books are in fact capable of moving readers in immoral as well as in moral directions. In the climactic chapter of Thomas Dixon, Jr.'s once-popular *The Leopard's Spots*, for instance, our hero, entering a chaotic Democratic convention, makes a stunning speech that unites the party, gains

---

46. For a fuller discussion of this problem, see my "Circumstantial Evidence: Music Analysis and Theories of Reading," *Mosaic* 18 (Fall 1985): 159–73.

him the nomination for the governorship, provides the first step toward the routing of the Republicans—and, happily, wins over the father of the woman he loves. Few of the readers who pick up this text have trouble recognizing that, for the authorial audience, this is an inspiring moment—especially since Dixon gives clear signals as to how we should react:

> Two thousand men went mad. With one common impulse they sprang to their feet, screaming, shouting, cheering, shaking each other's hands, crying and laughing. With the sullen roar of crashing thunder another whirlwind of cheers swept the crowd, shook the earth, and pierced the sky with its challenge. Wave after wave of applause swept the building and flung their rumbling echoes among the stars.[47]

But should the actual reader respond emotionally, as the author intended, to the *content* of the speech?

> "Shall we longer tolerate negro inspectors of white schools, and negroes in charge of white institutions? Shall we longer tolerate the arrest of white women by negro officers and their trial before negro magistrates?
>
> "Let the manhood of the Aryan race with its four thousand years of authentic history answer that question!" [436]

> "The African has held one fourth of this globe for 3000 years. He has never taken one step in progress or rescued one jungle from the ape and the adder, except as the slave of a superior race . . . and he has not produced one man who has added a feather's weight to the progress of humanity." [437]

The ability to "forget" the viciousness of this passage is not an ability to be nourished, even if it increases our aesthetic enjoyment of this text. And New Critical dogma to the contrary, it is not simply in works of lesser aesthetic quality that this problem

---

47. Thomas Dixon, Jr., *The Leopard's Spots: A Romance of the White Man's Burden, 1865–1900* (New York: Doubleday, Page, 1902), 443 (bk. 3, chap 13). Further references to this edition are made in the text.

emerges.[48] The ability to forget the ways that women have been abused is not a moral asset either, even if it increases our enjoyment of the way Don Giovanni makes a laughingstock of Donna Elvira, or our pleasure in Rochester's final release from the burden of a mad wife.

But while it is neither always possible nor always desirable to experience a text as an author intended, it does not follow that all interpretation need be subjective or idiosyncratic. We can, after all, describe what we cannot experience—and we can often determine what the authorial audience's response is without sharing it fully. A reader can, for instance, know what the authorial audience of *The Leopard's Spots* finds the speech gratifying, or that the authorial audience of *Jane Eyre* finds Bertha unsympathetic—even if, as actual audience, the gratification or the lack of sympathy are problematic. This is important because, as I have argued, authorial reading has a special status against which other readings can be measured (although not necessarily negatively); it is a kind of norm (although not necessarily a positive value), in that it serves as a point of orientation (although not necessarily as an ultimate destination). In short, authorial reading—in the sense of *understanding* the values of the authorial audience—has its own kind of validity, even if, in the end, actual readers share neither the experiences nor the values presumed by the author.

The Difficulties of Authorial Reading

Any discussion of reading must eventually come to grips with a fundamental fact: texts are often ambiguous. This claim of ambiguity, of course, is itself ambiguous, for it means several different

---

48. Thus, for instance, Brooks and Warren admit that there are some works that "offend us at too deep a level" for us to accept them. "But always we should be careful that we have made the imaginative effort to understand what values may be there, and what common ground might, with more effort, be found." It is significant, though, that they hasten to add, "Furthermore, in the end, we may find that we have rejected the story not because of its theme as such, but because we have found the story unconvincing" (*Understanding Fiction*, 276).

things. It means, for instance, that readers from different interpretive communities—readers who are using the text for different ends—may well find different things in it, and may well call on
different kinds of evidence to support their claims: Marxists and
Freudians may well see *The Trial* as different texts that are both
contained within the same marks on the page. It also means, as
many deconstructionist readings have made clear, that the nature
of our linguistic system is such that actual readers may find meanings in a text that subvert the meaning apparently intended by the
author. It means, in addition, that authors often attempt to communicate ambiguity itself—thus, even readers in the same interpretive community may well see different things in *The Trial*,
since Kafka was consciously trying to confuse.

The actual/authorial distinction, however, suggests yet another
type of ambiguity. Even among readers attempting to read as authorial audience (whatever they may call it)—that is, even among
readers who share ties to the same critical methodologies—there
are bound to be disagreements that literary theory can explain but
never erase. For even within a given interpretive community, interpretation depends radically on the reader's starting point, which
will influence (although not necessarily determine) his or her reading experience. And the proper starting point is always, as I have
suggested, presupposed by the text, not contained within it.

To be sure, it is often claimed that texts provide their own rules
for unlocking their meanings. "What attitude are we to take toward Walter Mitty?" ask Brooks and Warren. "The reader will
need no special help in deciding how to 'take' this story . . . The
action of the story serves to suggest the proper blend of sympathy
and amusement."[49] And it is true that we often apply rules of
interpretation with so little thought that the act of literary perception appears to be automatic; furthermore, texts do, to some extent, give directions for their own decoding. But the phrase "give
directions" is revealing. Every literary theoretician these days
needs a governing metaphor about texts: text as seduction, text as
fabric, text as abyss, text as system. I suppose that my metaphor

49. Ibid., 63.

would have to be text as unassembled swing set. It's a concrete thing that, when completed, offers opportunities (more or less restricted depending on the particular swing set involved) for free play, but you have to assemble it first. It comes with rudimentary directions, but you have to know what directions *are*, as well as how to perform basic tasks.[50] It comes with its own materials, but you must have certain tools of your own at hand. Most important, the instructions are virtually meaningless unless you know, beforehand, what sort of an object you are aiming at. If you have never seen a swing set before, your chances of riding on the trapeze without cracking open your head are slight.

The same is true of reading. You must be somewhere to begin with. Even when a text gives some fairly explicit guidance, you need to know how to recognize it and how to apply it. The moment I pick up Vanessa James' Harlequin romance, *The Fire and the Ice,* and find a story that begins with an erotically charged confrontation between a journalist heroine and her new boss (a wealthy playboy she had attacked in print two years earlier), I know a great deal about what to expect—but that is only because I have met the genre and its conventions before. One can well appreciate the kind of insensitive reading that led such critics as I. A. Richards to launch an attack on stock responses—but the fact remains that

---

50. See Gerald Graff's comment that "the reason most students are baffled by what we ask them to do is that they do not know what kind of thing it is that they are supposed to *say* about literary works, and they can't infer those kinds of things from the literary works themselves, because literary works themselves don't tell one what it is one is supposed to say about them" ("Joys of Not Reading"). See also Eagleton's remark, "The competent reader is the one who can apply to the text certain rules; but what are the rules for applying rules?" (*Literary Theory,* 125). Wolfgang Iser also relies heavily on the notion of giving directions; see, in particular, *The Act of Reading.* Iser, however, stresses what the text offers, rather than what the reader is presumed to bring; that is, he starts with a reader who already incorporates all the rules I am discussing here. And by suggesting that all worthwhile texts develop their own codes (see, for instance, 21), he smudges the line between the text's directions and the readerly presuppositions that allow those directions to work. He thus minimizes the different types of presuppositions required by different texts. Despite his theoretical insistence that "the reader's role can be fulfilled in different ways, according to historical or individual circumstances" (37), he rarely discusses different possible approaches to a text (for an exception, see his 201–2). As a consequence, his analyses, and especially his view of the canon, differ radically from mine.

without some stock responses to begin with, reading is impossible.[51]

Now suppose you are given something to assemble and a set of directions. If you make a mistake in construction, you may eventually find yourself in a self-contradictory position, one where you cannot go further—where following the directions is made impossible by the material reality ("attach the dowel to the holes in posts A and B"—where the posts are six inches further apart than the dowel is long). At this point, you have to reconsider your whole "interpretation," often starting over again from scratch. So it is with reading. The reader of *Crime and Punishment* who assumed that the rule of the least likely suspect applied and that, as in Agatha Christie's *A.B.C. Murders*, our protagonist had been framed—such a reader would eventually reach an interpretive dead end. And unless the reader were exceptionally dull witted or strong willed, he or she would eventually have to rethink what had been done so far.[52]

But sometimes erroneous assembly produces something internally consistent: the swing set holds up, but the swings are three inches closer to the ground than the manufacturer had in mind. And that can happen in reading as well. That is, there is a significant number of texts (perhaps all texts) where two or more starting points can result in conflicting, but equally coherent and consistent, *meanings*—using the word broadly to include the step-by-step experience of tension and relaxation, surprise, confusion, and euphoria. Jane Austen fans will remember the scene in *Emma* where Emma and Harriet have a conversation in which neither understands the other—although both *think* they are communicating—because they are beginning with different assumptions about the referent of the pronoun "he." This kind of misunderstanding comes up in our conversations with authors, too—more

51. See, for instance, Richards, *Practical Criticism: A Study of Literary Judgment* (New York: Harcourt, Brace, and World/Harvest, 1964), 223–40, esp. 232. See also Rosenblatt, *Literature as Exploration*, 113–23.

52. For an amusing exploration of this issue, see James Thurber's story about an attempt to read *Macbeth* as if it were a classical detective story: "The Macbeth Murder Mystery," in *The Thurber Carnival* (New York: Modern Library, 1957), 60–63.

often than we may believe.[53] An example may show more specifically what I mean.

On the surface, Agatha Christie's *Mystery of the Blue Train* is a commonplace member of the genre "classical British detective story." It has a murder; it has an adequate collection of readily identifiable cardboard characters, most with plausible motives and questionable alibis; it has trains and timetables, jewels and false jewels, accusations and false accusations, disguises and discrepancies; and, of course, it has an eccentric detective. A reader experienced in the genre will know fairly quickly what to fasten on to. Of particular importance will be such details as who has seen the victim after the train has left the Gare de Lyon. Such a reader, from his or her experience with other similar novels, will also know that in detective stories, "there must be no love interest."[54] He or she will therefore rightfully dismiss as window dressing the romantic story of the pure and simple Katherine Grey, who has just inherited a fortune from the crotchety old woman to whom she was a companion.

Read in this way, the book works well. As we expect, some of the apparent clues turn out to be important, others to be red herrings, and there is the expected unexpected twist so that the average reader will, at the end, experience that very special emotion that only a good classical English detective story can offer: the rush of "Oh! I should have caught that!" I have taught the novel several times as a model of the genre, and most students have enjoyed it and been both surprised and pleased by the ending.

I had two students, however, who used a different point of depar-

---

53. I thus disagree with Monroe C. Beardsley's claim that "the more complicated a text, the more difficult it becomes (in general) to devise two disparate and incompatible readings that are equally faithful to it" ("Textual Meaning and Authorial Meaning," 171). One problem with Beardsley's position is that he does not take sufficient account of the differing conceptions of what it means to be "faithful" to a given text. In this regard, see Thomas S. Kuhn's observation that when philosophers and historians read the same texts, they read them differently. "Undoubtedly the two had looked at the same signs, but they had been trained (programmed if you will) to process them differently" (*The Essential Tension: Selected Studies in Scientific Tradition and Change* [Chicago: University of Chicago Press, 1977], 6).

54. S. S. Van Dine, "Twenty Rules for Writing Detective Stories," in *The Art of the Mystery Story: A Collection of Critical Essays*, ed. Howard Haycraft (New York: Grossett and Dunlap/Universal Library, 1947), 189.

ture. The rule that love interest is secondary, after all, is not *in* the text. Nor, for that matter, is it an article of faith of any regularly constituted interpretive community. Rather, it is brought to bear *on* the text from the outside. And without a prior decision to apply that rule, there is no textually imposed reason not to pay more attention to Katherine Grey, especially since her actions are given considerable prominence, as is her perspective on the events. In fact, it is possible to treat the novel as a kind of romance. From this standpoint, the timing of the trains becomes a secondary consideration, and a different stock pattern emerges: a sympathetic and lovely young woman is wooed by two apparently suitable suitors. From our knowledge of such texts as *Sense and Sensibility* and *War and Peace*, we expect that one of them will be eliminated. But we wouldn't be satisfied if one were simply bumped off (like Tolstoy's Andrei) or one were simply rejected, for we like them both, and this is not the sort of novel in which the tragedy of life or even the sadness of having to make difficult decisions seems a major theme. The best solution, therefore, is to have one of them lose our respect, like Austen's Willoughby; he must turn out to be a scoundrel beneath the surface. Given the subject matter of the story, the most appropriate resolution would be to have one of the suitors turn out to be the killer. The author, in fact, fulfills the expectations raised by this pattern; indeed, so that we can maintain our love and respect for Katherine, Christie goes so far as to assure us that she has known the truth for some time. When Knighton turns out to be the villain, then, the reader starting off from this romance premise experiences something quite different from the surprise that the detective reader experiences: a satisfying, Austenesque confirmation of expectations.

These two readings of the book—and given the radically different effects they produce, they have to be considered two distinct readings—do not stem from differences in critical methodology. And for this reason, they are (in contrast, say, to Freudian and Marxist readings of *The Trial*) irreconcilable. The argument that Joseph K.'s experiences represent his inner psychodrama does not necessarily contradict the claim that they reflect the irrationality of modern-day society; one can well believe both simultaneously. But one cannot simultaneously be surprised and not surprised by the ending of *The Mystery of the Blue Train*. Each reading confers a different meaning on the text, and each is consistent and coherent in itself.

How can we explain this double-barreled detective story? We could, perhaps conclude that all texts are open, that they are all susceptible to multiple (even infinite) equally correct readings. Alternatively, we could claim that this novel plays on the conflict between knowledge and ignorance, and that it thus either speaks the truth through paradox or artfully deconstructs the genres to which it appears to belong. We might also conclude that it is a poor text. But there is another perfectly reasonable claim one could make: that it is a detective story that does not provide enough *internal* evidence for the actual reader to determine correctly the nature of the authorial audience. This does not make it any less of a mystery story—but to read it correctly (in the sense of successfully joining the authorial audience), you have to know what its genre is *before* you read it. In other words, it is a text that readily opens itself up to misreadings—a term that I use to refer not to readings that simply skirt the authorial audience, but rather to readings that *attempt* to incorporate the strategies of the authorial audience, but fail to do so. In this regard, as we shall see, it is far from an unusual case.

In Chapters 6 and 7, I have a great deal to say about the implications of such misreadings, especially about the ways in which they interact with ideology. But before doing so, I need to look more closely at the kinds of conventions on which competing authorial readings are apt to be based.

Rules of Reading

The term *convention* may appear, at first, somewhat restricted—for many people, when they think of literary conventions, think of formulas of plot and character. Conventions, however, inform our reading in far more complex ways. There are any number of ways of classifying them, and I would like to suggest now a four-part system. Let me make it clear from the outset that this framework is neither exhaustive nor privileged. That is, I intend neither to provide a complete taxonomy of interpretive conventions nor to oust other

systems that have been offered (my scheme, for instance, comple-
ments, rather than replaces, the typology suggested by Steven Mailloux).[55] Rather, I am offering what I hope will be a useful if rough
sorting out of an extremely thorny area—a system that is not only
convenient for organizing the ways that we can think abc t narrative conventions, but that also serves to illuminate some of the
relationships between them. Specifically, the system sets out four
types of rules. These rules govern operations or activities that, from
the author's perspective, it is appropriate for the reader to perform
when transforming texts—and indeed, that it is even necessary for
the reader to perform if he or she is to end up with the expected
meaning. And they are, from the other end, what readers implicitly
call upon when they argue for or against a particular paraphrase of a
text. The rules, in other words, serve as a kind of assumed contract
between author and reader—they specify the grounds on which the
intended reading should take place. They are, of course, socially
constructed—and they can vary with genre, culture, history, and
text. And readers do not always apply them as authors hope they
will—even if they are trying to do so, which they sometimes are
not.[56] Indeed, as I will argue in Chapter 7, canonization is, in large
part, a matter of misapplication. But even when readers do not apply
the *specific* rules the author had in mind, in our culture virtually *all*
readers apply *some* rules in each of the four categories whenever
they approach a text.

First, there are what I call rules of notice. Despite repeated
claims by critics that everything counts in literature (especially
poetry), we know from experience that there are always more details in a text—particularly a novel—than we can ever hope to

55. See, for instance, the distinction Mailloux proposes among traditional, reg-
ulative, and constitutive conventions, as well as among social, linguistic, literary,
and authorial conventions and conventions within individual works (*Interpretive
Conventions*, esp. chap. 5). See also the distinction among linguistic, pragmatic,
and literary conventions in Ellen Schauber and Ellen Spolsky, "Reader, Language,
and Character"; and the classification of codes in Barthes, *S/Z*.
56. See, for instance, Umberto Eco's claim that "we must keep in mind a principle, characteristic of any examination of mass communication media . . . : the
message which has been evolved by an educated elite (in a cultural group or a kind
of communications headquarters, which takes its lead from the political or economic group in power) is expressed at the outset in terms of a fixed code, but it is
caught by divers groups of receivers and deciphered on the basis of other codes"
(*Role of the Reader*, 141).

keep track of, much less account for. We have learned to tame this multiplicity with a number of implicit rules, shared by readers and writers alike, that give priority to certain kinds of details, and that thus help us sort out figures from ground by making a hierarchy of importance. Some rules of notice cover a wide spectrum of texts: for instance, there is the simple rule that titles are privileged. This may seem trivial, but it is a tremendous help for the first-time viewer of *Hamlet*. In the opening scenes, there are so many characters that he or she would not know where to focus attention without some cue. Similarly, the first and last sentences of most texts are privileged; that is, any interpretation of a text that cannot account for those sentences is generally deemed more defective than a reading that cannot account for some random sentence in the middle. Other rules of notice are specific to smaller groups of texts. For instance, when we are given some apparently obscure detail about a character's grandmother in a novel by Faulkner, we are supposed to pay more attention to it than we would in one by Dostoyevsky.

Second, there are rules of signification. These are the rules that tell us how to recast or symbolize or draw the significance from the elements that the first set of rules has brought to our attention. Included here are rules for determining symbolic meaning (the rules that tell us when to invoke the religious connotations of words, for instance); rules for distinguishing degrees of realism in fiction (the rules that allow us to discriminate, for instance, among the degrees and types of realism in the various representations of Napoleon in *War and Peace*, Anthony Burgess' *Napoleon Symphony*, and Woody Allen's *Love and Death*); the rule that allows us, in fiction, to assume that post hoc *is* propter hoc; rules that permit us to assume that characters have psychologies and to draw conclusions about those psychologies from their actions.

Third, there are rules of configuration. Certain clumps of literary features tend to occur together; because of our familiarity with such groupings, we know how to assemble disparate elements in order to make patterns emerge. We can thus both develop expectations and experience a sense of completion. Our ability to perceive form—in Kenneth Burke's sense of the creation and satisfaction of appetites ("Psychology and Form")—involves applying rules of configuration. As Barbara Herrnstein Smith's *Poetic Closure* demonstrates, so does our ability to experience closure. And so does our recognition of the plot patterns and formulas so often illuminated in traditional genre studies. One need not get much further than the opening scenes of Philip Barry's *Holiday* to know how it is going to end. But that is not because it signals its own unique form; rather, it is because we know how to put together a few elements—a charming man, a rigid fiancée, an attractively zany fiancée's sister—and see an emerging pattern.[57]

Finally, there are rules of coherence. The most general rule here, familiar in part through such critics as Wayne Booth and Mary Louise Pratt,[58] states that we should read a text in such a way that it becomes the best text possible. Of course, as Pratt notes, "this is not to say . . . that we do or should assume all literary works to be somehow perfect. It means only that in literary works . . . the range of deviations which will be construed as intentional is much larger" than in "many other speech contexts."[59] From this follow more specific rules that deal with textual disjunctures, permitting us to repair apparent inconsistencies by transforming them into metaphors, subtleties, and ironies. Even deconstructive readings, which widen rather than bridge textual gaps, often find some overarching theme or philosophical point in terms of which the discontinuities make sense.[60]

Now while there is a certain logical order to these rules, I am not

57. In the film version, there is an added signal, since we assume that the characters played by Cary Grant and Katharine Hepburn will be the ones who get romantically entangled.

58. See, for instance, Booth, *Critical Understanding*, esp. chap. 7; Pratt, *Toward a Speech Act Theory*, esp. chap. 5.

59. Pratt, *Toward a Speech Act Theory*, 170. See also Ronald Dworkin's rather more extravagant claim that "an interpretation of a piece of literature attempts to show which way of reading (or speaking or directing or acting) the text reveals it as the best work of art. Different theories or schools or traditions of interpretation disagree . . . because they assume significantly different normative theories about what literature is and what it is for and about what makes one work of literature better than another" ("Law as Interpretation," 183). In subsuming *all* interpretation under rules coherence, Dworkin is not the only critic to privilege this category of rules.

60. Thus, it is not surprising that Serge Doubrovsky, writing in 1966 of what was then "the new criticism" in France—and what now appears to have been the initial stage of what eventually grew into post-structuralism—argues as follows: "Unity, totality, coherence: I believe that to be a motto common to all the new critics or, if you prefer, their common postulate" (*New Criticism in France*, 119).

suggesting that we read a text by applying them one after another. Reading is a more complex holistic process in which various rules interact with one another in ways that we may never understand, even though we seem to have little difficulty putting them into practice intuitively. Thus, for instance, rules of notice would seem to precede rules of configuration, since we cannot perceive a pattern until we notice the elements out of which it is formed. But one of the ways elements become visible is that they form parts of a recongizable pattern. Thus, when Lisa is stabbed in the breast near the end of D. H. Thomas' *White Hotel*, the authorial audience notices that it is the left rather than the right breast in part because her left breast has been mentioned so many times in the novel (repetition is one of the basic means of attracting attention). But it is noticeable for another reason as well: the reference fills out a basic configurational pattern in the novel centering around the theme of clairvoyance.

In addition, a given convention may well be capable of reformulation so that it fits into more than one of the four categories. Take, for instance, the way we are expected to respond to the conventional use of literary parallels. It involves a rule of notice (it is appropriate to pay attention to textual elements that parallel one another), but it is also a rule of signification (parallel forms suggest parallel meanings), a rule of configuration (given an element A, there is a good chance that there will be an element A' parallel to it), and a rule of coherence (given elements A and B, their mutual presence can be explained to the extent that we are able to interpret them as parallel to one another). The division of conventions into these four types, therefore, is intended neither as a descriptive model of the way the human mind actually reads nor as an absolute and exhaustive classification. It is, rather, a practical analytic device, of value to the extent that it is useful for answering particular questions.

Let us now consider each of these types of convention in turn.

2

Trumpets, Please!:
Rules of Notice

I do not see how Mr. Stauffer can reject the proposition that
every word in a good poem counts and still continue to use the
term "poem" in a meaningful sense.

Cleanth Brooks, *Well Wrought Urn*

The Hierarchy of Detail

In his essay "How Readers Make Meaning," Robert Crosman
presents an interpretation of "A Rose for Emily" worked out by
one of his students.[1] The analysis is unusual: while it accounts for
many details in Faulkner's story that are usually passed over, it
does not come to terms with the ending, for the student fails to
mention, much less catch the implications of, the famous "long
strand of iron-gray hair" on the pillow.[2] Nonetheless, argues
Crosman, the interpretation is valid; it may fail to incorporate
certain textual features, but that is true of *any* interpretation.
While more traditional readings of the story all account for the last
sentence, they skim over elements that his student vividly illumi-
nates.

In one sense, I agree with Crosman: no interpretation can possibly account for all the details in a text. This position, however,
runs against the current of a strong critical tradition based on two

1. Crosman, "How Readers Make Meaning." See also his "Do Readers Make
Meaning?"—especially his claim for the validity of an interpretation of Pound's "In
a Station of the Metro" "as a statement that we should drink milk regularly" (153).
2. Faulkner, "A Rose for Emily," in *Selected Short Stories of William Faulkner*
(New York: Modern Library, n.d.), 61.

of what Susan Horton aptly calls "interpretive fictions": that "the 'best' interpretation can avoid leaving out as much as it takes in" and "that everything in the text means or ought to be forced into meaning."[3] These interpretive fictions have held a firm grip on contemporary criticism, especially from the New Critics onward. Wimsatt and Beardsley, for instance, claim that "poetry succeeds because all or most of what is said or implied is relevant; what is irrelevant has been excluded, like lumps from pudding and 'bugs' from machinery."[4] Similarly, Barthes' exhaustive analysis of Balzac's "Sarrasine" assumes that "everything signifies something."[5] Wayne Booth seems to agree in principle: in a discussion of apparently irrelevant features in *Tom Jones,* he notes that "if we really want to defend the book as art, we must somehow account for these 'extraneous' elements."[6] And Jakobson and Lévi-Strauss' famous analysis of Baudelaire's "Les Chats" is in harmony with this critical chorus, for it too hinges on an implicit assumption that all features of a text are fair game for the critic.[7]

There is, however, a countertradition as well, one that admits (sometimes grudgingly) that everything in a text is *not* really important. One variant of this countertradition assumes that texts are, in fact, abridgeable. To be sure, such condensations as those produced by the *Reader's Digest* have no academic standing. Still,

3. Horton, *Interpreting Interpreting,* 5.
4. W. K. Wimsatt, Jr., and Monroe C. Beardsley, "The Intentional Fallacy," 4.
5. Roland Barthes, *S/Z,* 51. See also his claim that "a narrative is made up solely of functions: everything, in one way or another, is significant. . . . There are no wasted units" ("Introduction to the Structure of Narrative," 244–45). He does admit later on, however, that not everything is *equally* important (247–48), a position also hinted at in *S/Z* (see, for instance, 112).
6. Booth, *Rhetoric of Fiction,* 216.
7. Roman Jakobson and Claude Lévi-Strauss, "Charles Baudelaire's 'Les Chats.' " In a very different tradition, see also Forster's claim that "the plot-maker expects us to remember, we expect him to leave no loose ends. Every action or word in a plot ought to count" (*Aspects of the Novel,* 61). And in a different tradition yet, see Ronald Dworkin's "Law as Interpretation." Even Jane Tompkins—while self-consciously aware that her "contextual reading" of *Wieland* is a "product of modern critical assumptions"—justifies her interpretation as "more satisfactory . . . because it is able to account for portions of the text that have hitherto been seen as irrelevant, inadvertant, or simply 'bad' " (*Sensational Designs,* 43). For attacks on Jakobson and Lévi-Strauss by Michael Riffaterre and Jonathan Culler, see above, Chapter 1, note 11.

the shortened *Clarissa* is more common in colleges and universities than is the complete novel; the Norton Anthologies, like the other collections that have served up the world of literature to college and high school students, tantalize with selections from longer works; many volumes in the widely used French series "Classiques Larousses" offer *extraits* rather than full texts. Such texts are not chopped up at random; behind their publication is the assumption that abridgement must be done according to certain rules, according to a systematic assessment of what is more important and what is less so.

This countertradition has its theoreticicans as well. Gary Saul Morson, for instance, argues that "to identify the structure of a work is to construct a *hierarchy* of relevance that makes some of its details central and others peripheral."[8] Tzvetan Todorov, similarly, argues against "a general refusal to privilege any part of the work whatever; we must not assume that there is only a monotonous reading which attributes an equal importance to every sentence of the text, to every part of the sentence."[9]

This countertradition, I believe, is the one that accords more fully with the way people actually read and write. Of course, anything in a text *can* be made to "mean" by an ingenious reader— even accidents of pagination. It would not be hard to give meaning, for instance, to the fact that in the original French edition, the murder in Robbe-Grillet's *Voyeur* appears to take place on a blank page that would be 88 if it were numbered, for the number 8 has been a motif throughout the novel.[10] But giving meaning is not the same as finding it or construing it; and to the degree that a novel is an attempt by a novelist to convey some more or less precise meaning, it is impossible for all of its features to bear weight. It is impossible because of limitations in both writers and readers.

8. Morson, *Boundaries of Genre*, 42. He goes on to claim that "the way readers go about this process of ordering . . . is not a constant. Different genres, for instance, imply different rules for ordering, and readers in different periods may estimate importance in different ways." In this regard, see Jane Tompkins' contention that Richard Adams was unable to notice a particular phrase in Hawthorne "because there is nothing in his interpretive assumptions that would make it noticeable" (*Sensational Designs*, 15).

9. Todorov, *Poetics of Prose*, 239.

10. Alain Robbe-Grillet, *Le Voyeur* (Paris: Minuit, 1955).

There are many reasons why writers cannot write so that everything carries an intended meaning. As producers in an economic system, they sometimes have to fill space for nonartistic reasons (one thinks, in particular, of large, popular blockbusters, in both the nineteenth and twentieth centuries), and their works are often altered by other hands.[11] Furthermore, as flawed humans like the rest of us, they sometimes lose their grip on the specifics of their texts. Dostoyevsky, especially when under the pressure of a deadline, was notoriously sloppy; in *The Idiot*, he was even able to change the name of a character between the third and fourth chapters of part 3, where Lieutenant Molovtsov becomes Kurmyshov. And even so painstaking a writer as Raymond Chandler, in wrapping up the plot of *The Big Sleep*, forgot to give his readers the real story behind the mysterious death of the chauffeur, Owen Taylor. Indeed, in his later years, he could not recall it himself. "I remember," he wrote to Hamish Hamilton, "several years ago when Howard Hawks was making *The Big Sleep*, the movie, he and Bogart got into an argument as to whether one of the characters was murdered or committed suicide. They sent me a wire asking me, and dammit I didn't know either."[12]

The limitations on an author's control over the details of a text, though, do not arise solely from economic pressures or from the human limits of memory. Such control is in fact *mathematically* impossible. As composer Ernst Křenek points out, if you try to organize a piece of music totally, you end up paradoxically with the equivalent of chance. For as soon as a composer asserts full control over one aspect of the score (say, melody), he or she relin-

11. For a fuller discussion of textual corruption, see Hershel Parker, *Flawed Texts and Verbal Icons*.

12. Chandler, letter to Hamish Hamilton, March 21, 1949, in *Raymond Chandler Speaking*, ed. Dorothy Gardiner and Kathrine Sorley Walker (Freeport, N.Y.: Books for Libraries, 1971), 221. Stephen Knight views the situation differently: "Chandler may well have forgotten and the others may not have read the novel carefully enough, but the explanation is there. He committed suicide; the lump on his head was given him previously by Joe Brody" (*Form and Ideology*, 150). He is right about the lump, at least to the extent that Brody *says* that he sapped Taylor. But Knight does not explain why he believes Brody or why he is sure it was suicide even if Brody is telling the truth. Indeed, given the limitations of the first-person point of view, it would be impossible for the novel to tell us definitively that it was suicide.

quishes control over another (for instance, harmony).[13] What is true for music, where each note has a fairly restricted range of features (e.g., pitch, timbre, duration), is even truer for literature, where each word has a far greater range of potential relationships to the words around it (e.g., phonetic, syntactic, connotative, denotative), as well as to other works of literature and to the outside world. A writer who aims at the most precise semantic distinctions cannot simultaneously maintain full control over the text's rhythms; once you have decided to write a play in palindromes, you severely limit your opportunities for subtle gradations of tone. All art is a matter of choice, and the most fundamental choice an author faces is the choice of where to direct his or her attention.

What is true of writers is true of readers as well. If one assumes that all features of a text are to receive close attention from an interpreter, then a text (even a lyric poem, certainly a novel) becomes an infinite and impenetrable web of relationships. In the end, such a view not only makes everything equally important, but also makes everything equally unimportant: only boredom can result. As Roland Barthes puts it, "Read slowly, read *all* of a novel by Zola, and the book will drop from your hands." But Zola would never have expected us to read that way. Thus, while Barthes is right that "we do not read everything with the same intensity of reading; a rhythm is established," he is wrong to see such reading as necessarily "casual, unconcerned with the *integrity* of the text."[14] That rhythm—if we catch the one the author intended—is very much a part of the integrity of the text.

In other words, since the attention of the author is not directed equally to all details in a text, then neither should the attention of the authorial audience be. The reader trying to recover authorial intention should, rather, try to duplicate the angle of the author's attention. Thus, while, as Crosman claims, no interpretation can account for all the details of a text, it does not follow that all partial interpretations are equally valid, since not all details equally deserve explication. This notion fits our commonsense experi-

13. Křenek, "Extent and Limits of Serial Techniques," in *Problems of Modern Music: The Princeton Seminar in Advanced Musical Studies*, ed. Paul Henry Lang (New York: Norton, 1962), 72–94.
14. Barthes, *Pleasure of the Text*, 12, 10–11 (emphasis in the original).

ence with texts: except perhaps when we are reading academically, we tend to read hierarchically, in the sense that we assume that, for any given text, certain features are more important than others. John D. MacDonald begins *Darker than Amber* as follows:

> We were about to give up and call it a night when somebody dropped the girl off the bridge.
> They came to a yelping stop overhead, out of sight, dumped her over the bridge rail and took off.
> It was a hot Monday night in June. With mood. It was past midnight and just past the tide changes. A billion bugs were vectoring in on us as the wind began to die.
> It seemed to be a very final way of busting up a romance.[15]

Then follow more than four pages of flashback to Travis McGee's fishing expedition and his attempt to help a friend recover from a failed marriage. Most readers who are likely to pick up this novel will recognize that these four pages are a detour from what is really important. Not that the detour has no function—it does serve to heighten our anticipation. But MacDonald's rhetorical device works only for the reader who views the events described as a deflection from what he or she really wants to know. No reader who pays as much attention to the fact that the fishermen had "lost seven"—rather than six or eight—"amid the pilings" (11) as to the description of McGee's attempt to free the victim from the cement block wired to her ankles will be able to experience the intended dramatic curve.

Basic Gestures of Noticeability

> "I begin now to understand you all, except Miss Price," said Miss Crawford. . . . "Pray, is she out, or is she not? . . ."
> Edmund, to whom this was chiefly addressed, replied, "I believe I know what you mean—but I will not undertake to answer the question. My cousin is grown up . . . but the outs and not outs are beyond me."

15. MacDonald, *Darker than Amber* (New York: Fawcett, 1966), 7.

"And yet in general, nothing can be more easily ascertained. The distinction is so broad. Manners as well as appearance are, generally speaking, so totally different. Till now, I could not have supposed it possible to be mistaken as to a girl's being out or not. A girl not out, has always the same sort of dress; a close bonnet, for instance, looks very demure, and never says a word."[16]

A text, then, has a hierarchical organization of details: we do not attend to everything equally. To be sure, there are many forms of attention. Some features of a text are rich or evocative, others are strange, others surprising, others climactic. But whatever their specific character, their weight in our reading experience is variable. This chapter centers on two interrelated aspects of noticeability: concentration and scaffolding. First, rules of notice tell us where to concentrate our attention. Some details are, quite simply, more skimmable than others. You can get through *War and Peace* without paying very much attention to the clothing that the characters wear, and you will still have a reasonable experience of the text. But if you nod off during the discussions of Napoleon's progress, your response—in particular, your failure to share the growing tension—will be far from the one Tolstoy intended.

Second, the stressed features in a text serve as a basic structure on which to build an interpretation. As authorial audience, we read with the prior understanding that we are more expected to account for a detail that is stressed by a rule of notice than for a detail that is not. And both while we read and after we have finished, we shape our interpretations to conform to this basic understanding. Interpretations start, at least, with the most noticeable details.

Communication can exist only if author and receiver agree beforehand about what is worthy of notice. And like Miss Crawford's distinction between "out" and "not out," this agreement requires precise cultural articulation. One need not subscribe to Miss Crawford's social code to feel that, in literature, it is—as she says—"very inconvenient indeed" when an author fails to give the proper signals and allows those details which should be "not noticeable" to "give themselves the same airs and take the same

16. Jane Austen, *Mansfield Park*, ed. R. W. Chapman, 3d ed. (London: Oxford University Press, 1934), 48–49 (vol. 1, chap. 5).

liberties as if they were"—or vice versa. For there are two ways in which communication can fail on the question of notice: the irrelevant can appear to be prominent, or the crucial can pass by unnoticed.

Sometimes, of course, authors are quite explicit, even forceful, in the ways they direct us. They may simply tell us in so many words that something is important. James Cain's chatty narrators are especially given to telling us where to direct our attention: "After the coop was built," Leonard Borland tells us in *Career in C Major*, "Craig dug in at his farm up-state, and that left me alone. I want you to remember that, because if I made a fool of myself, I was wide open for that, with nothing to do and nobody to do it with." Or, later on, when describing the fiasco during *Rigoletto:* "I want you to get it straight now, what happened."[17] But this is not simply a Cainian device. Almost all authors do the same thing to a greater or lesser extent. "Trumpets, please! Or still better, that tattoo which goes with a breathless acrobatic stunt. Incredible!"[18] So Hermann, in Nabokov's *Despair*, announces his "discovery" that Felix is his double. "The adventure that befell us on the way," we are told by Anton Lavrent'evich, the narrator of *The Possessed*, "was also a surprising one"—just to make sure we approach it in the right frame of mind.[19]

Only slightly more subtly, a detail can be emphasized through repetition. Thus, Naomi Schor's reading of Poe's "Mystery of Marie Rouget" starts out from the fact that the peculiar state of Marie's outer skirts is emphasized "by a combination of repetition and italicization. . . . For the reader, the hitch appears as a kind of marker, a signal, in a word: a detail jutting out above the plane surface of the text, providing the would-be interpreter or literary detective with a 'handle' on the text."[20] Similarly, the authorial

17. Cain, *Career in C Major*, in *Three of a Kind* (Philadelphia: Blakiston, 1944), 4, 109 (chaps. 1, 10).

18. Vladimir Nabokov, *Despair* (New York: Pocket, 1968), 5 (chap. 1).

19. Fyodor Dostoyevsky, *The Possessed*, trans. Constance Garnett (New York: Modern Library, 1936), 442 (pt. 2, chap. 10).

20. Schor, "Female Paranoia," 218.

audience of *The Great Gatsby* knows that Daisy's green light, like the ash heap and the billboard advertising Dr. Eckleburg, is important because it is mentioned so frequently.[21]

Certain semantic gestures serve as markers of stress as well—the use, for instance, of words like "immediately" or "realized." "He stood still as he suddenly remembered," notes the narrator in Francis Steegmuller's *Blue Harpsichord.* " 'Damn it—I've gone and left my thesis at Cynthia's' "[22]—and the authorial audience knows that this event is worth attention because of "suddenly" and (since it stands out in this particular text) "damn." Notice can also be directed through syntax. "It was after an August afternoon in a Times Square picture-house that Edna met Myrtle Throgmorton at the Schrafft's on West Forty-Second Street," writes Margaret Ayer Barnes in *Edna His Wife;* and because the sentence begins "It was" rather than simply "After an August afternoon," this particular August afternoon is singled out as especially important.[23] Similarly, an author may underscore importance by having a character perform the same actions he or she expects of the reader. After Inspector Roderick Alleyn reads through an entry in Arthur Rubrick's diary (*Died in the Wool*), Ngaio Marsh tells us that "Alleyn read this passage through again"—a clear sign to the reader that it contains something worth close consideration.[24] And in Charles W. Chesnutt's "Po' Sandy," if we use Annie's responses to Uncle Julius' tale-within-a-tale as a model for our own reading, we will know what *we* should invest with our primary attention.

Metaphors and similes, too, can underline in fairly straightfor-

21. Thus, James E. Miller, Jr., is able to say, "By now the signal is unmistakable" when the word "ashen" appears in Nick's attempt to imagine what Gatsby's death must have been like ("Fitzgerald's *Gatsby:* The World as Ash Heap," in *The Twenties: Fiction, Poetry, Drama,* ed. Warren B. French [Deland, Fla.: Everett/Edwards, 1975], 190). See also F. H. Longman, who emphasizes roses and the color white in *Gatsby* because of "verbal recurrence" ("Style in *The Great Gatsby,*" *Southern Review* [University of Adelaide] 6 [1973]: 58).

22. Steegmuller, *Blue Harpsichord* (New York: Carroll and Graf, 1984), 18 (pt. 1, chap. 2).

23. Barnes, *Edna His Wife: An American Idyll* (Boston: Houghton Mifflin, 1935), 533 (pt. 4, chap. 5.4).

24. Marsh, *Died in the Wool* (New York: Berkley Medallion, 1961), 215.

ward ways. In *The Ambassadors*, Henry James describes one of Strether's discoveries as coming like "the click of a spring."[25] John Barth announces the moment of Todd Andrews' revelation in *The Floating Opera* in a no less evident way: "For like that night in Baltimore when a dark alleyway turned me dazzled onto the bright flood of Monument Street, I now all at once found myself confronted with a new and unsuspected world."[26]

Typography can serve as a marker of stress as well. Todd's discovery itself, for instance, is printed partly in italics. Changes in typeface help guide the reader's attention in Horace McCoy's *They Shoot Horses, Don't They?* just as Manuel Puig's use of typography in *The Kiss of the Spider Woman* highlights shifts in the narrative that are crucial if we are to follow its drift. In Nabokov's *Lolita*, Humbert Humbert chides a detective story for presenting its clues in italics, but the criticism is ironic, since many of the clues in *Lolita* itself are in italics, too.

Still, such explicit markers of stress can go only so far in telling the authorial audience where to direct its attention. Authors need other—more implicit and often more economical—devices as well. Specifically, there are conventional rules for determining the primary objects of attention. True, different rules of notice apply to larger or smaller groups of texts. Some—for instance, the rule that tells the reader to attend to the first letter of each line of a poem, or to note what each line spells out when read in reverse—apply only to fairly limited types (acrostics and palindromes respectively). Others—such as the rules that stress beginnings and endings (see "Privileged Positions" below)—are more widespread. But while the specific rules may vary with genre, cultural context, and author, the authorial audience is expected to share them, whatever they are, with the author *before* picking up a text.

Let me stress, however, that while an author writes with the expectation that his or her readers have internalized certain rules, it does not follow that he or she is bound to follow those conventions rigidly. Quite often, rules will be twisted to special ends. One

---

25. James, *The Ambassadors*, ed. S. P. Rosenbaum (New York: Norton, 1964), 133 (bk. 5, chap. 2).
26. Barth, *The Floating Opera* (New York: Avon, n.d.), 271 (chap. 29).

of the most striking is the kind of dislocation that occurs when you read a passage (or even a whole book) assuming one set of rules to be in effect, only to find that you have been tricked. In "A Double-Barreled Detective Story," for instance, Twain—assuming that his readers will apply the rule permitting us to skim nature descriptions in a nineteenth-century detective story—begins his fourth chapter with the following evocation:

It was a crisp and spicy morning in early October. The lilacs and laburnums, lit with the glory-fires of autumn, hung burning and flashing in the upper air, a fairy bridge provided by kind Nature for the wingless wild things that have their homes in the tree-tops and would visit together; the larch and the pomegranate flung their purple and yellow flames in brilliant broad splashes along the slanting sweep of the woodland; the sensuous fragrance of innumerable deciduous flowers rose upon the swooning atmosphere; far in the empty sky a solitary oesophagus slept upon motionless wing; everywhere brooded stillness, serenity, and the peace of God.[27]

This almost surrealistic description was intended as a trap for the unwary reader, but even Twain himself was surprised by the success with which it worked, for it turned out that except for the presence of the oesophagus, nothing in the passage jarred *any* of his readers. Indeed, in order to make the joke effective, Twain had to resort to a footnote that ordered his readers to examine the paragraph again carefully.

The surprise ending of Nabokov's "Vane Sisters" also plays on confusion about the appropriate rules of notice. As I noted above, the rule that tells you to look at the first letter of every line (or every word) applies only to a small class of texts—and it is easy to miss the signals that the final paragraph of "The Vane Sisters" belongs to that group. The reader who fails to read acrostically, however, will misread the ending of the book, which has a buried message that inverts the story's apparent meaning.

No matter how much a writer wishes to play with conventions, however, he or she can do so only if the readers share those conven-

27. Twain, "A Double-Barreled Detective Story," in *The Man That Corrupted Hadleyburg and Other Essays and Stories* (New York: Harper, 1906), 312–13.

tions to begin with. Indeed, the more a writer wishes to undermine tradition, the more imperative it is that the tradition be understood to begin with. This may help explain why so-called serious avant-garde authors so frequently turn to formulaic popular fiction as a skeleton on which to hang their own works. In sum, whether a writer is twisting the rules or using them straightforwardly, he or she must work on the assumption that the reader has command over them to begin with, and regardless of the text, the reader reading without knowledge of the rules presupposed by the author is unlikely to uncover the intended meaning. The total number of rules of notice used in nineteenth- and twentieth-century novels is, of course, vast, and I cannot hope to discuss them exhaustively. I will, however, try to show something of their range by giving examples of three general types: rules of position, of intratextual disruption, and of extratextual deviation.

Privileged Positions

If you ask someone familiar with *Pride and Prejudice* to quote a line from the novel, the odds are that you will get the opening sentence. Similarly, most readers of *The Great Gatsby* have a stronger recollection of its final image than of most of the others in the text. This is not because those passages are inherently more brilliant or polished or interesting than their companions. Rather, out of all the aphorisms and images that these novels contain, these gain special attention because of their placement. For among the rules that apply quite broadly among nineteenth- and twentieth-century European and American prose narratives are rules that privilege certain positions: titles,[28] beginnings and endings (not only of whole texts, but of subsections as well—volumes, chapters, episodes), epigraphs, and descriptive subtitles. As Mar-

---

28. See also John Fisher's discussion of titles in "Entitling." In some ways, Fisher's arguments support mine: "The title tells us how to look at the work" (292), but he fails to deal with *why* this is so—that is, that we live in a community that has agreed to treat titles in certain ways, and that authors know this. See also Umberto Eco's enunciation of a rule that "(irony or other figure excepted), the title of a chapter usually announces the content of it" (*Role of the Reader*, 20).

ianna Torgovnick puts it, "It is difficult to recall *all* of a work after a completed reading, but climactic moments, dramatic scenes, and beginnings and endings remain in the memory and decisively shape our sense of a novel as a whole."[29] Placement in such a position does more than ensure that certain details will remain more firmly in our memory. Furthermore, such placement affects both concentration and scaffolding: our attention during the act of reading will, in part, be concentrated on what we have found in these positions, and our sense of the text's meaning will be influenced by our assumption that the author expected us to end up with an interpretation that could account more fully for these details than for details elsewhere.

The concentrating quality of a detail in a privileged position can be demonstrated by looking at *Anna Karenina*. The novel has a large cast of characters—so large that we might hardly notice Anna's arrival were the novel not named for her. But because of the title, we know from the beginning that we should look at the other characters in their relationship to her, rather than vice versa. Since they are the ground and she the figure, we pay more attention to her appearance and to the initial description of her character than we do to Dolly's. Of course, one could well argue that the novel is structured so that even without the title, we would eventually concentrate on Anna rather than on Dolly. That is undoubtedly true, but it does not contradict the importance of the title; it merely suggests that the title does more to orient our reading at the beginning of the book than in the middle and the end. And even so, our reading experience would be quite different if the title were *Levin*. Similarly, we know we are expected to pay special attention to the dog that Gerasim rescues halfway through Turgenev's

29. Torgovnick, *Closure in the Novel*, 3–4. See also Gerald Prince's claim that "the beginning or the end of various sequences" are "strategically important points" (*Narratology*, 72); and Barbara Gerber Sanders' justification of an analysis based primarily on the ends of chapters in *The Great Gatsby:* "Structurally, the beginnings and endings of chapters are strategic places for development of thematic images. . . . The reader's mind is, or should be, more alert at these transitions" ("Structural Imagery in *The Great Gatsby:* Metaphor and Matrix," *Linguistics in Literature* 1, no. 1 [1978]: 57–58). Films differ markedly from novels in this regard, perhaps because filmmakers must take late arrivals into account. People will start films in the middle, but they will rarely do the same with books.

"Mumu" because she is the title character. The effect is all the stronger because until this point, the title has been a source of puzzlement.

One way to highlight how titles concentrate the process of reading is to consider cases where novels have alternate titles, or where alternate titles were seriously considered. When a novel's cover proclaims *Pride and Prejudice,* we are immediately alert to certain contrasts. While the book incorporates a number of other oppositions as well (young/old, male/female, mother/daughter, rich/poor, light/dark, city/country), no reading could ever control them all—and Austen's choice of title makes it clear where she wanted us to put our attention first. The resulting experience is quite different from the one that would have been encouraged had the novel been published under the title that Austen used for her first version, *First Impressions.* With the early title, we would have been more alert to the elements *common* to Darcy and Elizabeth than to their differences (the fact that both exhibit pride *and* prejudice is beside the point; the published title encourages us to look initially for contrasts rather than for unity), and we would be more prepared on first reading to see Elizabeth's reaction to Wickham as part of the same package as her reaction to Darcy. In addition, the title *Pride and Prejudice* prompts us to concentrate on character, whereas *First Impressions* encourages us to concentrate on plot—more specifically, on change. Pride and prejudice are static qualities that may or may not be transformed, but first impressions imply the existence of second (and different) impressions.

Whatever one feels about the trial of *Madame Bovary,* therefore, the prosecutor Pinard had reasonable critical justification for starting with the title in order to get at the novel's central meaning.[30] First sentences operate in a similar way. "All happy families resemble one another, but each unhappy family is unhappy in its own way"[31]—so begins *Anna Karenina,* and from the beginning, the authorial audience is encouraged to pay more attention to family life than, say, to politics, which in this novel is subsidiary to

---

30. Ernest Pinard, "Réquisitoire de M. L'Avocat Impérial," in *Madame Bovary,* by Gustave Flaubert (Paris: Librairie de France, 1921), 382.

31. Leo Tolstoy, *Anna Karenina,* trans. Louise Maude and Aylmer Maude (New York: Norton, 1970).

individual action. The reader is further advised to see the novel in terms of a basic opposition between "happy" and "unhappy," and, more explicitly, to see happiness as a form of one's unity with others and unhappiness as a form of difference. No one could argue that the first sentence is essential to the book in the sense that if it were not there we would feel its lack. But without that sentence, the didactic message of the novel would be slightly muted, and it would thus engender a different reading experience for the authorial audience.

Titles not only guide our reading process by telling us where to concentrate; they also provide a core around which to organize an interpretation. As a general rule, we approach a book with the expectation that we should formulate an interpretation to which the title is in fact appropriate. This retrospective process of interpreting a completed book will be discussed in more detail in Chapter 5, but a few examples may be useful here. The title of James Cain's *Postman Always Rings Twice* does little to direct our attention as we are reading. There are no postmen in the novel, and while it is eventually obvious that the title is metaphoric, it is not immediately clear just what the import of the metaphor is. At the beginning of the novel, perhaps, after the first murder attempt fails, it might warn us to expect a second—as if the title were a twist on "Opportunity knocks but once." But by the end, we are encouraged to give a fatalistic reading of the text, because it is only in the context of such an interpretation that the title is appropriate. It is not only that Frank and Cora fail, but that they *had* to fail.

Ford Madox Ford's *Some Do Not . . .* provides a more elaborate example of how a title can serve as a skeleton on which to build an interpretation. As in all of the novels that make up *Parade's End*, the title has multiple meanings because the phrase is used in a number of different contexts. Its first appearance after the title comes in a privileged spot as well: a citation, at the end of a section, typographically set off:

> " 'The gods to each ascribe a differing lot:
> Some enter at the portal. Some do not.' "[32]

32. Ford, *Some Do Not . . .* , bound with *No More Parades* (New York: NAL/ Signet, 1964), 28 (pt. 1, chap. 1). Further page references are given in the text.

The phrase returns near the close of part 1 (chap. 7, also in a privileged position, half a page from the end), after General Campion has run into Tietjens and Valentine's horse. When Tietjens decides to stay with the animal, the fly driver says, " 'But I wouldn't leave my little wood 'ut nor miss my breakfast for no beast. . . . Some do and some . . . do not' " (149; ellipses in original). Later, when a "dark man" offers to help keep Tietjens out of the war, Tietjens tells him that he really wants to join the army; the dark man says, " 'Some do. Some do not' " (229; pt. 2, chap. 3). At the end of part 2, in chapter 5, after Valentine agrees to become Tietjens' mistress, the phrase becomes explicitly sexual: " 'That's women!' he said with the apparently imbecile enigmaticality of the old and the hardened. 'Some do!' He spat into the grass, said: 'Ah!' then added: 'Some do not!' " (284). But a few pages later, he realizes, " 'We're the sort that . . . *do not!*' " (287, pt. 2, chap. 6; ellipses in original).

The primary function of Ford's technique is not to create linguistic paradox by showing the multiple meanings latent in the title's language (although it does do that). Rather, the repetition of the title pressures the authorial audience to tie together the contexts in which the phrase appears and to interpret a number of apparently separate concerns (optimistic hope for the future, proper care for animals, willingness to fight in the war, and sexual honor) as in fact variations on a single theme. One might argue that the unity would be there without the title. Still, without the title to predispose the reader to notice its repetitions in the text, he or she would not be so likely to see them at all, much less to see them as contributing to a thematic unity. To put it another way: without the title, a reader who claimed to find this linguistic web uniting these disparate passages might reasonably be criticized for stretching things; with the title, a reader who refused to accept the connections could reasonably be accused of denseness. But this accusation carries weight only in a community where there is a prior agreement to privilege titles.

Last sentences, of course, cannot serve to focus a reading experience (at least, not an initial reading experience). But they do often serve to scaffold our retrospective interpretation of the book. The final image of Dashiell Hammett's *Glass Key* is Ned Beaumont staring at an empty doorway. Anywhere else in the novel, we might well slide over such a bland detail. By putting it at the end, though, Hammett is urging his reader to privilege that blankness and to tie it to all the other doors and entryways into mysterious psychological blanks that give the book much of its character.

Not *all* novels privilege opening and closing sentences; different genres stress different points to different degrees. Still, it is telling that novels that do not privilege the opening often make some linguistic gesture to signal their departure from the general rule. *The Postman Always Rings Twice* is a case in point. The opening paragraph tells us how our narrator, Frank, has been thrown off a hay truck. It gives us a general sense of his character, but we can tell that it is intended as introductory material (like the introduction of a sonata-form movement), rather than as the beginning of the exposition, because of the way that Cain begins the second paragraph: "That was when I hit this Twin Oaks Tavern."[33] The syntactic device "that was when" serves to inform us that this is the important point of departure.

At first, the claim that titles, openings, and closings are privileged may seem a trivial one—and in a sense it is, since it is one of the simplest rules of interpretation. Yet it is curious how often it can serve to answer interpretive disputes by supporting one reading over another. The privileged nature of closing sentences surely answers Robert Crosman's arguments, outlined at the beginning of this chapter; the privileged nature of beginnings supports a feminist-economic reading of *Pride and Prejudice*. Similarly, the opening sentence of *Little Women* ("'Christmas won't be Christmas without any presents,' grumbled Jo, lying on the rug") encourages the authorial audience to see the novel in terms of the interaction between love, friendship, and family on the one hand, and economics on the other. And the fact that Norman Mailer begins his *American Dream* with a reference to John Kennedy supports an interpretation that sees the whole novel as lit by the Kennedy mystique—although the evidence for that claim would be feebler

---

33. Cain, *The Postman Always Rings Twice*, in *Cain × 3* (New York: Knopf, 1969), 3 (chap. 1). For the rhetorical significance of the definite article in such contexts, see Walker Gibson, *Tough, Sweet, Stuffy*, esp. 37–40.

if the explicit mention of Kennedy came only in the middle of the novel.[34]

So far, I have considered position in the most literal sense, as a feature of the text as a physical, printed artifact. But textual features have positions within plot structures too, and a novelist can direct attention by careful placement in this regard as well. Threats, warnings, and promises, for instance, are almost always noticeable because of their role in predicting the shape of a text. This will be clearer after Chapter 4, where I discuss configuration in more detail. Still, it is possible to give a few examples by relying on our common-sense notions of novelistic structure.

Few authors are so skillful at emphasis through placement as Dostoyevsky. His novels are full of small, superficially empty moments that the authorial audience charges with psychic energy because of their placement. One thinks of Raskolnikov and Razumikhin staring at one another in the dark corridor (*Crime and Punishment*) or of Kirillov's bizarre empty stare when Pyotr Stepanovich goes to see if he is really going to shoot himself (*The Possessed*). Both moments exemplify a general rule: details at climactic moments (at peripeties, discoveries, revelations, recognitions) receive special stress. This rule can in turn be broken down into more specific variants that are known to most experienced readers of nineteenth- and twentieth-century literature, even if they are really formulated explicitly. A few examples: (1) When a character's moral choice serves as the linchpin for the development of the plot, then that character is to be read as an important character. On this basis, the reader of Ibsen's *Doll's House* can fairly assume that Krogstadt—whose decisions about whether to expose Nora's forgery determine much of the play's action—is intended to be a more important character than Mrs. Linde, who serves primarily as a sounding board for, and contrast to, Nora.

---

34. Of course, the Kennedy reference also conjures up an image of violent death. Since Mailer had written the first version of the opening before Kennedy's assassination, it was obviously not on his mind; still, one suspects that his decision to keep the reference (albeit with alterations) even in his postassassination revisions stemmed at least in part from the fact that the death imagery, too, fit in with the rest of the novel. For a detailed discussion of the editorial problems in this novel, see Parker, *Flawed Texts and Verbal Icons*, chap. 7.

(2) When an event changes a major character's relationship to other characters, that event is to be read as charged. Thus, in Marge Piercy's *High Cost of Living*, when the homosexual Bernard makes love to the protagonist, his lesbian friend Leslie, the act is a plot-stressed event since we know that, whatever happens, their relationship will be permanently altered. (3) When an event or a detail answers a question around which a narrative has been based, it is emphasized. Thus, the gray hair in "A Rose for Emily" is stressed not only by its physical position, but by its plot position as well, for it provides the final bit of information about what has happened to Homer Barron. (4) In addition, there are positions that are stressed only in certain genres: the meeting around the fireside at the end of a detective story, for instance, attracts our special attention.

Rules of Rupture

Politics in the midst of imaginative concerns is like a pistol shot in the middle of a concert.[35]

We tend to skim over the even and the unbroken; disruptions attract our notice. This explains why we notice the pyramid rising above the desert, and also why we notice certain details in literary works. Specifically, textual features stand out both when they disrupt the continuity of the works in which they occur and when they deviate from the extratextual norms against which they are read. Thus, for instance, silences interjected into a dialogue attract notice ("'My name is Gagin, and this is my'—he hesitated for a moment—'my sister'"),[36] just as violations of conventional expectations do (most detective story solutions are quickly forgotten, but almost everyone who has read Agatha Christie's *Murder of Roger Ackroyd* remembers its unconventional climax—a climax

---

35. Stendhal, *The Red and the Black: A Chronicle of the Nineteenth Century*, trans. Lloyd C. Parks (New York: NAL/Signet, 1970), 378 (bk. 2, chap. 22).

36. Ivan S. Turgenev, "Assya," in *First Love and Other Tales*, trans. David Magarshack (New York: Norton, 1968), 89 (chap. 2).

that I will not spoil for those who have not read the novel). Needless to say, however, the application of this general rule is problematic in particular cases.

Let me begin with intratextual disruptions—breaks in a given text's continuity—since they are somewhat more straightforward. Continuity, to be sure, itself depends on rules of configuration; as I have pointed out, notice and configuration are interdependent. Still, even at this point, a few examples can be given.

The blatantly irrelevant tends to be noticed. Any time a detail is mentioned when there seems to be no apparent reason for it, the surface of the text is ruptured; most of the time, such ruptures are appropriately treated as signals to pay attention. This is especially true when the irrelevance itself is explicitly mentioned: "Oh, yes—there had been one more episode, if one wanted to record every last detail: the visit to the milliner. But even Terence wasn't morbid about mere shopping encounters."[37] But such explicitness is hardly required. We pay attention when Gatsby and Tom Buchanan switch cars, because it seems such a pointless turn in the plot that we feel sure it will have consequences. Even nontraditional novels often make use of this rule. One of the most oft-quoted passages in Robbe-Grillet's *Erasers* is his description of a tomato—a description made memorable by the specificity of its detail (excessive even in this densely detailed novel), and especially by the apparent irrelevance of much of it: "Above, a scarcely perceptible accident has occurred: a corner of the skin, stripped back from the flesh for a fraction of an inch, is slightly raised."[38]

The inappropriate, too, tends to be noticed. There are numerous variations on this rule. For instance, inappropriate behavior by characters is always noticeable. Myshkin's verbal assault on Catholicism in Dostoyevsky's *Idiot*, for instance, stands out at least in part because a formal reception is an improper forum for such an impassioned outburst. A more specific variant applies to detective and spy novels: when a character displays a piece of knowledge

---

37. Steegmuller, *Blue Harpsichord*, 28 (pt. 1, chap. 3).
38. Alain Robbe-Grillet, *The Erasers*, trans. Richard Howard (New York: Grove, 1964), 153 (chap. 3, pt. 3).

that he or she has no apparent way of having obtained, the reader should watch that character. Indeed, mysteries are often solved because the criminal lets slip a piece of information that he or she could have only if he or she committed the crime. When Corky, in the Encyclopedia Brown story "The Case of the Knife in the Watermelon," lets slip that he knows how long a knife blade is—even though the knife is buried up to its handle in a watermelon—the careful reader can be sure that he is the guilty party.

More often than not, the authorial audience is also to pay attention when a plot changes direction. This can occur in fairly literal ways, as when, in *Robin Hood*, Little John physically stops moving:

> So he strode whistling along the leafy forest path that led to Fosse Way, turning neither to the right hand nor to the left, until at last he came to where the path branched, leading on the one hand onward to Fosse Way, and on the other, as well Little John knew, to the merry Blue Board Inn. Here Little John suddenly ceased whistling and stopped in the middle of the path.[39]

A less literal kind of change in direction is found in Aglaya's marriage at the end of *The Idiot*. This attracts our notice at least partly because it disrupts the neat closure of the circle provided by the final meeting of Myshkin and Rogozhin (whose first meeting opened the novel), and by Myshkin's return to the "idiocy" that had plagued him before the novel began. Indeed, shifts in plot direction also include changes in a novel's perspective—the move from a waking state to a dream, for instance (for this reason, the dreams in *Jane Eyre* are given special attention by the authorial audience)—as well as shifts in narrative distance. Thus, when Gogol, toward the beginning of "Nevsky Prospect," suddenly moves from the generalized, distant description of the crowd to a more detailed, close-up description of Pirogov and Piskarev, the shift in perspective makes us pay special attention to these two characters.

We similarly notice shifts in style. Dramatic effects in opera are often created in this way. For instance, when the Empress in the

39. Howard Pyle, *The Merry Adventures of Robin Hood* (New York: Grosset and Dunlap, 1952), 89.

Strauss-Hofmannstahl *Frau ohne Schatten* (*The Woman without a Shadow*) thinks that the curse has been fulfilled, she switches from singing to heightened speech in order to express her despair.[40] And any experienced operagoer, hearing that passage—even without knowing the plot or a word of German—would recognize it as a crucial juncture just because of the stylistic jolt. So it is in literature. The phrase "They ran" stands out in Faulkner's *Intruder in the Dust* because it is such a compact sentence following the long, stream-of-consciousness flow of the dreamlike fantasy of Miss Habersham caught in the traffic.[41] Rhymed couplets in Shakespeare's plays stand out for similar reasons.

Deviations from norms outside the text in question are just as noticeable as breaks in a text's continuity, but here we run into more severe interpretive problems, for a number of reasons.

What counts as a deviation will vary, for norms are radically context dependent. Indian musical tunings, which sound quite normal to someone raised in Delhi, seem strange and exotic when heard against the norms of American popular songs—at least, they did until they, too, became an American pop norm. The blandest American TV jingle would have the same shock value for an Indian unfamiliar with Western musical practice. In the same way, noticeability in fiction depends in part on what system of norms is invoked.

To make matters more complicated, there are two different kinds of norms involved in literary texts. On the one hand, there are what might loosely be called "real world" norms: norms that readers bring to works from their social experiences outside art, rather than from their experiences with literature per se. Thus, for instance, any violation of an actual cultural taboo will attract a reader's notice—although, of course, what constitutes a taboo will vary from culture to culture. The riveting power of Nora's departure in *A Doll's House* derives only partly from its privileged posi-

---

40. Richard Strauss and Hugo von Hofmannsthal, *Die Frau ohne Schatten* (London: Boosey and Hawkes, 1946), 571.

41. William Faulkner, *Intruder in the Dust* (New York: Random House/Vintage, 1972), 190 (chap. 9). See also Dennis Porter's analysis of the shift in sentence length as a way of "attention-grabbing" in the opening of Chandler's *Big Sleep* (*Pursuit of Crime*, 138–39).

tion. It is noticeable also because, in the social context in which Ibsen expected the play to be produced, the action itself was shocking, even though it may seem less so now. In contrast, a contemporary American reader of Chekhov's "Lady with the Dog," living in a social context where divorce is common, may be more surprised than Chekhov intended by Anna and Gurov's failure to consider this option. True, many texts teach their actual readers about the cultural perspective from which they are written. The social meaning of Lydia's elopement with Wickham is discussed exhaustively in *Pride and Prejudice*. But that discussion itself makes sense only to readers who have at least some prior knowledge of the importance of marriage and propriety in that culture.

In order to understand a text as the author intended, therefore, it is necessary to know in advance which social norms it was expected to be read against. But it is just as important to know the *literary* norms that serve as a text's background. Suppose, for example, we pick up a mystery story and find the characters comparing literature and life:

"You confess that you read detective stories, Miss Grey. You must know that any one who has a perfect alibi is always open to grave suspicion."

"Do you think that real life is like that?" asked Katherine, smiling.

"Why not? Fiction is founded on fact."

"But is rather superior to it," suggested Katherine.[42]

Are we to pay particular attention to that exchange and treat the novel as an inquiry into the ontology and epistemology of fictional discourse? The question cannot be answered in terms of how people confronting violent crime really operate, or even in terms of

42. Agatha Christie, *The Mystery of the Blue Train* (New York: Pocket, 1940), 130 (chap. 21). See also Michael Innes, *The Bloody Wood* (New York: Berkley Medallion, 1966): "'What if we're slipping sedately into one of those well-bred English detective novels of the classical sort? *Death at Charne House*'" (62); and P. D. James, *An Unsuitable Job for a Woman* (New York: Warner, 1982): "But it didn't surprise her . . . to hear that Sergeant Maskell . . . was tied up all morning. It was only in fiction that the people one wanted to interview were sitting ready at or in their office, with time, energy, and interest to spare. In real life, they were about their own business" (82, chap. 2).

how the authorial audience believes such people operate. Rather, the noticeability of this feature has to do with how such people behave in *books*. But *what* books? Different norms characterize different sets of narratives; what stands out as deviant, therefore, depends not only on social context but also on the intertextual grid against which the text is read. Generally speaking, formulaic elements—elements that regularly recur without significant variation in comparable texts—are not noticeable *unless* they are traditionally points of stress—that is, unless they are given specifically formulaic emphases. (Thus, as I have suggested, the fireside chat of the detective story is stressed because that is precisely its formulaic purpose—to point out an event worthy of special notice.) In a classical detective story, for instance, life-and-literature discussions are formulaic in this sense; like the formulaic descriptions of clothing in popular romances and of the storms that so often beset Southworth heroines, they are intended not to attract notice, but rather to fill space.

This is not to say that a sensitive cultural critic could not look at these formulas to unveil their implicit cultural values. Indeed, as I have suggested earlier, much of the most valuable political criticism comes from the decoding made possible by reading in a context that the author did not intend, a technique that often highlights precisely those elements of a text that the author and his or her intended readers took for granted—elements that can therefore reveal unexpected and unconscious aspects of the reigning ideology. Such reading against the grain, though, depends on authorial reading for its political force; it is valuable not because it points out certain features, but because it points out certain features that the author did not intend to be particularly noticeable.

What counts as a formula varies from genre to genre. The life-and-literature discussions in Pirandello's plays are intended to be read against a different intertextual grid than those in Christie, and in this context they are no longer mere filler. It would be just as wrong to ignore them in a reading of his work as it would be to stress them in a reading of *The Mystery of the Blue Train*. Readers frequently stumble on this point, missing what is important or stressing the irrelevant because they are reading in the wrong context. But the fault does not always lie with the readers. Authors can fail to assess properly the background their actual readers are likely to call into play.

For instance, writers (especially inexperienced writers) occasionally rely on what appears to be a deviation from a formula but what has in fact already been used so often that it has become a formula in its own right. The confusion of the border line between life and art that was an effective overturning of dramatic conventions in Pirandello becomes just another formulaic gesture in the work of student playwrights, just as the double and triple crossing that was so startling in the early novels of Le Carré and Deighton is by now no longer able to surprise us. We almost *expect* the true villain to be the head of a major spy operation on the good guys' side.[43]

The appropriate background group for a given text usually includes the previous works by the same author: the science fiction elements in Doris Lessing's later novels stand out more sharply against the stark realism of her earlier books, just as the return to realism in *The Diaries of Jane Somers* is especially noticeable in the context of that science fiction. The genre of the work in question, as we have seen, also alerts readers to the intended background, especially when the genre is announced by the title (Dinesen's *Seven Gothic Tales*, for instance); as a general rule, it is appropriate to give priority to deviations from works in the same genre over deviations from works in other genres. Still, every work has its own unique intended background (if only because every author has read a different selection of books). And although the variations in background may be so subtle as to be insignificant, interpretive questions often come down, in the end, to questions about choice of background group—a choice that the work itself cannot explicitly outline, and that will therefore depend to some extent on the reader's assumptions about the proper intertextual grid, assumptions made in part before even starting the book.

43. Thus, the impact of a book depends on when you read it with respect to other books. As Robert Champigny points out, "Suppose that a reader comes across *The Maltese Falcon* after reading several stories in which the murderer is a client who tries to seduce the detective. The fact that *The Maltese Falcon* exemplifies this pattern may disappoint him, not because he assumes that it is historically improbable (or probable) but because, in his eyes, the development of the story makes the denouement too likely. He may thus consider Hammett to be an imitator of authors who wrote after him" (*What Will Have Happened*, 32).

Thus, for instance, the reader who comes to Harriet Beecher Stowe's *Dred* with expectations drawn from experience with the works of Jane Austen is apt to be startled by the transformation of the heroine Nina. In the world of Austen, while characters change, the kind of flightiness exhibited by Nina in the opening chapters is unalterable; Nina's metamorphosis into a wise, independent-minded, and courageous woman appropriate for the virtuous Clayton to marry seems as unimaginable as Lydia's would be if she turned into an appropriate wife for Darcy. But such transformations were more common in the popular American women's novels of the day than in Austen. Indeed, Nina Baym argues that one of the two basic variants of the "single tale" told in "the many novels by American women authors about women, written between 1820 and 1870," starts with "a pampered heiress" who, after financial misfortune, "develops the capacity to survive and surmount her troubles."[44] Thus, what may seem surprising and unusual to us may in fact be merely formulaic. (Nina's death halfway through the novel, in contrast, is remarkable through either lens.)

In the case of *Dred*, modern readers can make a fairly reliable guess about authorial intention by looking at the historical context in which the novel was written and published. Sometimes, however, the available evidence is more ambiguous, with the result that recovery of the authorial meaning becomes more chancy. For instance, as I have noted, the comparison between the so-called real world and the stylized world of detective novelists is a common gesture in detective stories. Thus, if a reader of Eric Ambler's *Intercom Conspiracy* has experience with the genre, he or she might not pay particular attention when Valerie Carter tells novelist Charles Latimer:

> "I think [your novels are] highly ingenious and much better written than most. Above all nobody in them is made to behave stupidly. . . . One of the things I can't stand in that sort of book is the character who gets trapped in a dangerous situation and is forced to run appalling risks simply because he didn't, for some feebly contrived reason, go to the police when the trouble started. The author is assuming that the reader is a moron, and that's infuriating.

44. Baym, *Woman's Fiction*, 11, 35.

"So, when my father began explaining why he couldn't go to the police and tell them what was going on, I became angry."[45]

But since the theme is repeated as the novel progresses, the reader may begin to wonder about its intended importance. Is this simply an elaboration of a formulaic gesture? Or does *The Intercom Conspiracy* really aim to question which vision is truer: that of the individual participant (with his or her actual experience, but with the concomitant limitations) or that of the novelist (with his or her greater scope but also greater distance). One can, of course, apply the standard rules of notice for detective stories. Or one can apply a basic rule of coherence (discussed in more detail in Chapter 5), and assume that it should be read to make the best novel possible. In the case of *The Intercom Conspiracy*, we have a fairly weak spy novel, although as a novel about fiction and history it is somewhat more interesting. However we choose to interpret it, though, we are engaging in guesswork. In order to read it as the author intended, we have to know, before picking it up, what other texts Ambler wanted us to have in mind as we read.

Even after we have decided on the proper norms for a work, it is not always easy in practice to know what constitutes a real deviation. As I noted above, a textual element is formulaic if it regularly recurs without significant variation in comparable texts. But ascertaining what constitutes "regular" recurrence and "significant" variation is an act of judgment: one reader's significant variation is another's cliché. At the end of *Pride and Prejudice*, Lady Catherine is almost, but not quite, reconciled to Darcy's mismatch: "She condescended to wait on them at Pemberley, in spite of that pollution which its woods had received, not merely from the presence of such a mistress, but the visits of her uncle and aunt from the city."[46] Does the authorial audience view this as a formulaic reiteration of traditional comedy's love-conquers-all happy ending, with its reconciliation of warring factions through marriage of the younger generation? Or does the authorial audience pay special attention to the slight twist ("she condescended . . . in spite of that

45. Ambler, *The Intercom Conspiracy* (New York: Bantam, 1970), 140.
46. Jane Austen, *Pride and Prejudice*, ed. R. W. Chapman, 3d ed. (London: Oxford University Press, 1965), 388 (vol. 3, chap. 19).

pollution") and stress instead the novel's failure to resolve problems as neatly as the traditional formula dictates? Obviously, different actual readers will read it differently. But those differences do not stem necessarily from Austen's highly developed sense of paradox (there is no reason to assume that she did not intend one or the other of those readings unambiguously). Nor, more important, do they necessarily stem from a difference in the general rule being applied. Rather, they may well arise from a difference in the way that a generally agreed upon rule is being applied in one specific instance.[47]

To make matters more complex still, formulas are not as a rule given special attention, but specific references (parodies, quotations, allusions) are. Thus, the phrase "Look at Dick" is not noticeable in a children's reader, but it becomes so when it is used in Toni Morrison's *Bluest Eye*. It is not, however, always easy to tell a reference from a formula. Those who know Haydn's Symphony No. 13 may find citational significance in the fact that Mozart later used the opening theme of the finale to launch the last movement of his own *Jupiter Symphony*. In fact, though, the theme itself is a commonplace of counterpoint exercises, and there is no authorial significance to its appearance in both works.

In general, the border line between reference and formula—like the border lines between deviations and norms more generally—can be pinpointed only in the context of a particular intertextual grid. Take, for instance, Raymond Chandler's decision to name his series detective Marlowe. One can easily read this as a reference to Conrad's Marlow and draw symbolic conclusions from the parallels thus revealed between, say, *The Big Sleep* (the novel where Marlowe first appeared) and *Heart of Darkness*. But was Chandler really intending his readers to do that? The text itself does not provide an answer; the reader's interpretation, rather, will depend on his or her intertextual grid. If the reader groups *The Big Sleep* simply with traditional detective stories, then the connection between Philip Marlowe and Conrad's Marlow will appear to be purely coincidental (the name, after all, is not uncommon), not an

---

47. For good examples of the ways in which the same general rules can be applied differently by different critics, see Culler, *Pursuit of Signs*, chap. 3.

instance of copying and hence no more noticeable than the occurrence of the same name in Bentley's *Trent's Last Case,* Ambler's *Cause for Alarm,* or Allingham's *Mystery Mile.* If, on the other hand, the reader groups it with the so-called serious British literary tradition, the name immediately becomes charged. Sometimes an author will make the reader's task easier by being fairly explicit about references to other texts—as when Peachum explains the arrival of the Royal Messenger to the audience in *The Threepenny Opera* in terms of dramatic tradition: Even though in reality "mounted messengers from the Queen come far too seldom," Macheath will not be hanged because "this is an opera, and we mean to do you proud."[48] Sometimes, we can tell by context. Generally speaking, the importation of an apparently inappropriate formula (as the use of primer style in Morrison) signals a reference. Sometimes, we have to know the author. Only a reader familiar with Pushkin's style and wit will be comfortably sure that the completely formulaic last story in *Belkin Tales* is intended as a parody.[49] But there remain instances when even experienced actual readers will be baffled. It is not easy to be sure whether the apparently formulaic marriage between Annella Wilder and Valerius Brightwell in Southworth's *Allworth Abbey* is intended as a simple closure or as an attack on the genre. (For a fuller discussion of this text, see Chapter 5.)

Knowing where to direct our attention, however, is only the first step in literary interpretation. We also need to know how to construct textual meanings out of the details we have found. This leads to the next set of rules: rules of signification.

48. Bertolt Brecht, *The Threepenny Opera,* trans. Desmond Vesey and Eric Bentley (New York: Grove/Evergreen Black Cat, 1964), 96, 95 (act 3, sc. 3).
49. For a good discussion of this point, see Morson, *Boundaries of Genre,* 110–13.

3

The Biggest Black Eyes I Ever
Saw: Rules of Signification

Our public is still so young and naive that it fails to understand
a fable unless it finds a lesson at its end. It misses a humorous
point and does not feel irony. . . . [It] resembles a provicial
who, upon overhearing the conversation of two diplomats be-
longing to two warring Courts, is convinced that each envoy is
betraying his government in the interests of a most tender and
mutual friendship.

Mikhail Lermontov, *A Hero of Our Time*

Signification Defined

Once we know, through rules of notice, *what* to attend to, we
still have to face the problem of *how* to attend to it. Take the
opening sentence of the third section of Faulkner's *Sound and the
Fury:* "Once a bitch always a bitch, what I say."[1] It is clearly
noticeable. Not only does it begin a new section; in addition, coming after the elaborate grammatical and philosophical complexities
of Quentin's internal monologue, it hits us like a blast of cold air
with its immediacy. Yet what does it mean?

Out of context, Jason's remark may be somewhat obscure—but
difficult as the novel is, the reader who has gotten this far in it will
probably be able to make a variety of judgments about what the
sentence means. He or she will know, for instance, that its referent
is a woman, and not a dog; that the immediate source of the words

---

1. William Faulkner, *The Sound and the Fury*, bound with *As I Lay Dying* (New
York: Modern Library, n.d.), 198.

(that is, the dramatized speaker) is Jason (not Faulkner), who does not intend them to be ironic; that the act of making the statement reflects badly on Jason (at least, within the ideological norms according to which Faulkner expected his reader to judge); that the statement is false; and that, despite the authorial audience's disdain for the speaker, it sees certain factors in his life as causal contributions to his hatred of Quentin.

In a critical climate in which the very word *literal* has come under attack, where every act of shaping—be it in the form of a novel or a philosophical discourse or a newspaper editorial—is claimed to be a fiction, it is hard to know precisely what to call the process of making these determinations without appearing to be naive.[2] Nonetheless, the process does take place: in reading (decoding, unpacking, interpreting) Faulkner's sentence, the reader moves from what appears to be said to what is really said, or at least from one level (which, if not literal, is more immediate or more close at hand) to another (which is more distant, more mediated). I call this activity *signification*.

Authors can be quite explicit about the acts of signification that they intend readers to perform. It is not only in allegories and children's books (one thinks of Tom Swift) that characters' names serve as signposts of character: Dostoyevsky's Lev (from "lion") Nikolaevich Myshkin (from "mouse") trumpets his ambivalent character. (His name and patronymic may also refer, more subtly, to Tolstoy.) Alice Walker goes a step further and, in the opening of *Meridian*, gives us a detailed analysis of the implications of her heroine's name, providing a dictionary-style offering with twelve different meanings.[3] Nor is it only in fables and fairy tales that we find ourselves confronted with explicit statements about what it all means. In *Anna Karenina*, just as Levin's brother Nikolai dies,

2. For a strong attack on the notion of literal meaning, see Stanley Fish, "Normal Circumstances, Literal Language, Direct Speech Acts, the Ordinary, the Everyday, the Obvious, What Goes without Saying, and Other Special Cases," in *Is There a Text?* 268–92. For critical perspectives on the general expansion of the term *fiction*, see Barbara Foley, *Telling the Truth*, esp. chap. 1, and Gerald Graff, *Literature against Itself*, chap. 6.

3. Alice Walker, *Meridian* (New York: Simon and Schuster/Washington Square, 1977), [13].

the doctors discover that Kitty is pregnant. Lest we fail to recognize the cosmic implications of this coincidence, Tolstoy tells us directly—in a privileged position, at the end of a chapter: "Scarcely had the unexplained mystery of death been enacted before his eyes when another mystery just as inexplicable presented itself, calling to love and life."[4]

More often than not, though, authors rely on a set of unspoken agreements to get their readers to apply the correct rules of signification to texts. Rules of signification are vast in number, and teachers probably have more trouble teaching their students to understand them than teaching them other kinds of rules. It is perhaps for this reason that so much literary criticism is devoted to rules of signification. Most of it, however, has been focused on the fairly narrow area of figurative language, which critical schools as diverse as New Criticism and post-structuralism have seen as the essence of literary study. Cleanth Brooks, for instance, has argued that "the essence of poetry is metaphor," a statement that—except for its privileging of metaphor over other figures—accords quite comfortably with J. Hillis Miller's insistence that the "center of our discipline . . . is expertise in handling figurative language," and that the "teaching of reading" is therefore inevitably "the teaching of the interpretation of tropes."[5] Given this imbalance, there seems little point in trying to add yet more to what has already been said, for instance, about the ways in which readers know how and when to read textual features metaphorically. Instead, in this chapter I turn my attention to some other rules of signification that have not already been so well mined—specifically, to sketch out a few of them in four further categories suggested by my analysis of the Faulkner phrase above: rules of source, rules of morality, rules of truth and realism, and rules of causation.

4. Leo Tolstoi, *Anna Karenina*, trans. Louise Maude and Aylmer Maude (New York: Norton, 1970), 459 (pt. 5, chap. 20).

5. Cleanth Brooks, *Well Wrought Urn*, 248; J. Hillis Miller, "Function of Rhetorical Study," 13. Geoffrey Hartman would seem to agree: "Could we not say that there must be [in critical thinking] a willingness to receive figurative language?" (*Criticism in the Wilderness*, 27). Mary Louise Pratt has made a compelling case against the notion that the use of figurative language distinguishes literary from nonliterary discourse (*Toward a Speech Act Theory*, esp. chap. 1).

Rules of Source

Even the most rudimentary guides aimed at showing how to read literature include, fairly soon, the warning against confusion of author, narrator, and character. A study sheet devised by Hamilton College's English Department for students beginning their first literature survey, for instance, informs them that the question, Who is speaking? is one of the first that a reader must ask.[6] Because this distinction is stressed so often, it is only the most naive reader who makes gross errors on this score—who confuses Jason with Faulkner, for instance. Indeed, as Wayne Booth argued long ago in *The Rhetoric of Fiction* (the classic study of author/narrator relations), modern readers, if anything, tend to err in the opposite direction by ironizing everything, refusing to hear the implied author's voice even when he or she is speaking directly.[7] But in moments of stress—the furors surrounding the publications of *Madame Bovary* and *Lolita*, for instance—such niceties are often forgotten.[8] And the hazy area where fiction and autobiography melt into one another (as in *Remembrance of Things Past* or *Tropic of Cancer*) often finds even professional critics merging author and narrator.

To be sure, there is often good reason for this kind of uncertainty; some passages in *Madame Bovary*, for instance, are so clouded that it is impossible to be sure precisely whose words are represented in the text.[9] Still, what is surprising is not that we often find it hard to determine source (after all, difficulty is to be expected when we have one person taking on the voice of another). Rather, what is surprising is how easily experienced readers often figure out who is speaking even when the voice changes midstream. Indeed, even those authors, like Flaubert, who aim to muddle our thinking on this score can do so only because they assume we have certain procedures at hand that *can* be confused. Booth, in

6. Hamilton College Department of English, guidelines for English 200.

7. Wayne Booth, *Rhetoric of Fiction*, esp. 364–74.

8. For an interesting discussion of *Madame Bovary* in this context, see Hans Robert Jauss, *Toward an Aesthetic of Reception*, 42–44. See also Dominick LaCapra, Madame Bovary *on Trial*.

9. See LaCapra, Madame Bovary *on Trial*, esp. chap. 6.

A Rhetoric of Irony, has pointed to a number of devices that signal the presence of an ironic voice, including the proclamation of "known error," factual conflicts within a work, stylistic clashes, and conflicts "between the beliefs expressed and the beliefs we hold *and suspect the author of holding*" (italics in original).[10] While the procedures are somewhat subtler when irony is not present, similar signals operate in these cases as well. Take, for instance, the following passage from "Down by the Riverside," the second story in Richard Wright's *Uncle Tom's Children:*

> He walked to the window and the half rotten planks sagged under his feet. He had never realized they were that shaky. He pulled back a tattered curtain, wishing the dull ache would leave his head. Ah been feverish all day. Feels like Ah got the flu.[11]

Obviously, the speaker changes between the third and fourth sentences, from the narrator to the aptly named protagonist, Mann. The shift is extremely well marked in the text—overdetermined, in fact—because it is signaled in at least three ways.

Most obvious, there is a shift in person, from third to first. In traditional, realistic nineteenth-century novels, this is not an especially common device, except when the character's words—either thought or spoken—are placed in quotation marks. But it is found more frequently in contemporary novels, many of which use it in fairly complex ways. Nadine Gordimer's *Burger's Daughter* shifts between Rosa's first-person narration (addressed to different narratees as the book progresses) and various third-person viewpoints, in order to provide different perspectives on Rosa's life. Margaret Drabble's *Waterfall* also flickers between the first and third person—but here the different grammatical categories reflect not so much different people as different sides of the same speak-

10. Booth, *Rhetoric of Irony,* 57, 61, 67, 73. See also Pratt's discussion of violations of the Cooperative Principle, *Toward a Speech Act Theory,* esp. chap. 5. Wolfgang Iser gives a more extreme version of this notion in his discussion of pop art when he argues that "whenever art uses exaggerated effects of affirmation . . . their function is . . . to negate what they are apparently affirming" (*Act of Reading,* 11).

11. Wright, *Uncle Tom's Children* (New York: Harper and Row/Perennial Library, 1965), 54.

er.[12] Much the same technique (with the added complication of a second narrator) is used in John Fowles' *Daniel Martin*.

In addition to the shift in person, there is a shift in linguistic style to Black English. According to a basic rule of signification, such changes are usually to be interpreted as a sign that the narrator is no longer speaking in his or her own voice. As Booth argues, this is a standard technique in ironic works, but it is used in nonironic discourse as well. Shifts in linguistic style are especially important in distinguishing the source of particular phrases in texts that use free indirect discourse (what the French call *style indirect libre*), since they can work with extreme efficiency, even within a single sentence. Sometimes, the signification of stylistic shifts is reinforced by typography. As Dominick LaCapra points out, "The type of cliché from which Flaubert as narrator and as writer tried to take maximal distance was that of ordinary bourgeois stupidity. When this sort of cliché is employed in 'objective' narration in *Madame Bovary*, it is often (but not invariably) italicized."[13] Similarly, when the narrator, Vandyke Jennings, in Charlotte Perkins Gilman's *Herland* notes, "Terry, in his secret heart, had visions of a sort of sublimated summer resort—just Girls and Girls and Girls," the capitalization serves as a clue that the word "Girls" is Terry's, not Jennings'.[14] This rule, for all its apparent sophistication, is learned quite early. Sue Alexander's *Marc the Magnificent* may be aimed at first graders, but they are expected to know that the passages in parentheses and italics represent a different level of Marc's consciousness. The rule is harder to apply, but no different in principle, when employed without typographical support. In *Some Do Not . . .* , a reference to "Glorvina, who was the mother of two of Sylvia's absolutely most intimate friends" clues us in to a shift in source through the phrase "absolutely most intimate friends," with its inappropriate exaggeration.[15]

---

12. For a fuller discussion of this technique, see Nancy S. Rabinowitz, "Talc on the Scotch: Art and Morality in Margaret Drabble's *The Waterfall*," *International Journal of Women's Studies* 5 (May/June 1982): 236–45.

13. LaCapra, *Madame Bovary on Trial*, 111.

14. Charlotte Perkins Gilman, *Herland* (New York: Pantheon, 1979), 7 (chap. 1).

15. Ford Madox Ford, *Some Do Not . . .* , bound with *No More Parades* (New

Wright makes his shift even clearer by accompanying the shift in person and style with a shift in tense, from past to present. It is not, of course, the case that a shift to the present necessarily indicates a shift from narrator to character. Sometimes it indicates a swing the opposite way, sometimes no shift at all. Indeed, Seymour Chatman even argues that it always signals a move to the narrator: "If we read in a narrative otherwise in the preterite a sentence like 'War is hell,' the generalization is thought to hold for the narrator, as well as (or even rather than) for the characters. But 'War was hell' must mean that a character thinks so."[16] But as Chatman himself realizes, in his discussion of the opening of *Pride and Prejudice,* there are numerous other factors at hand—including the question of the possible irony of the sentence. The most we can say here is that tense shifts may be used in numerous ways, but that their presence alerts the reader to a possible change in source.

The Wright passage, of course, does not begin to exhaust the conventional techniques for dealing with source. Among the further factors that help us determine whose words we are hearing are perspective and knowledge. When a text suddenly changes its vantage point from a general perspective to the limited perspective of one of the characters—that is, when we are seeing what one of the characters sees—we can often assume that the words we are reading represent what the character is saying or thinking. Thus, Nabokov opens *Laughter in the Dark* with an overview of the story, ending with the narrator's claim, "and although there is plenty of space on a gravestone to contain, bound in moss, the

---

York: NAL/Signet, 1964), 170 (pt. 2, chap. 1). See David Lodge: "The novelist who uses [free indirect speech] is obliged to be particularly faithful to the linguistic quality of his character's consciousness" (*Language of Fiction,* 171). It is not always easy to distinguish the author's voice from the character's, however, when we are not sure of the standards being applied. Later on in Ford's series, Mark thinks—in *style indirect libre*—"Friend of Sylvia's friends in the government. To do her credit she would not stop with Jews. The only credit she had to her tail!" (*Last Post,* bound with *A Man Could Stand Up* [New York: NAL/Signet, 1964], 222 [pt. 1, chap. 4]). Since neither the narrator nor the implied author ever suggests that anti-Semitism is bad (indeed, all the Jewish and half-Jewish characters are devious), there is no way to know whether we should view this as an ironic criticism of Mark.

16. Chatman, *Story and Discourse,* 82. For a fuller discussion of the ways that linguistic devices can illuminate perspective, see his chap. 4.

abridged version of a man's life, detail is always welcome." When he abruptly changes gears ("It so happened that one night Albinus had a beautiful idea"), we have reason to suspect that the word "beautiful" is Albinus', not the narrator's—a suspicion confirmed by the ironic undercutting in the following sentence ("True, it was not quite his own").[17] Alternatively, when our vision of a scene is too large for a character to have, we can often assume that the accompanying words are those of the narrator or implied author. Note, for instance, the next-to-last paragraph of *Crime and Punishment:*

> She too had been greatly agitated that day, and at night she was taken ill again. But she was so happy—and so unexpectedly happy—that she was almost frightened of her happiness. Seven years, *only* seven years! At the beginning of their happiness at some moments they were both ready to look on those seven years as though they were seven days. He did not know that the new life would not be given him for nothing, that he would have to pay dearly for it, that it would cost him great striving, great suffering.[18]

In the phrase "Seven years, *only* seven years!"—which is implicitly in the present tense—we are clearly intended to hear Sonia's voice. The final words, however ("would cost him great striving, great suffering"), because they come from a vision of events that is beyond that available to the characters, must be assumed to represent the voice of the narrator.

Similarly, general statements that are too wise for the characters can generally be assumed to come from the narrator, at least when the narrator is a reliable representative of authorial norms. "His frock-coat seemed to have been made for someone else, and he had a beard like a tradesman's," we read of Dymov in Chekhov's story "The Grasshopper." "Of course, if he had been a writer or an artist everyone would have said that his beard made him look like Zola." None of the characters in the story has that kind of self-under-

17. Vladimir Nabokov, *Laughter in the Dark* (New York: New Directions, 1960), 9.

18. Fyodor Dostoyevsky, *Crime and Punishment*, trans. Constance Garnett (New York: Random House/Vintage, 1950), 492 (epilogue, chap. 2).

standing—so we can only assume that it is the narrator speaking. Alternatively, statements that obviously cut against what Booth calls the "known facts" can usually be assumed in reliable narration to represent the thoughts of the characters. A little later in the same Chekhov story, we read:

> They had a wonderful life after their marriage. Olga Ivanovna covered the walls of her drawing-room with sketches, framed and unframed, by herself and her friends, and surrounded the grand piano and the furniture with an artistic jumble of Chinese parasols, easels, many-colored drapes, daggers, small busts, photographs. . . . In the dining-room she hung cheap colored prints, bast shoes, and scythes on the wall, and grouped a scythe and a rake in the corner, thus achieving a dining-room *à la russe*. She draped the ceiling and walls of the bedroom with dark cloth, to make it look like a cave.[19]

Once we have read the description of Olga's paltry attempts at creating a chic environment, we can be fairly confident that the designation "wonderful" cannot be the narrator's.

Good Guys and Bad Guys: Rules of Snap Moral Judgment

"I didn't finish the book," said Maggie. "As soon as I came to the blond-haired young lady reading in the park, I shut it up, and determined to read no further. I foresaw that that light-complexioned girl would win away all the love from Corinne and make her miserable. I'm determined to read no more books where the blond-haired women carry away all the happiness. I should begin to have a prejudice against them. If you could give me some story, now, where the dark woman triumphs, it would restore the balance."[20]

---

19. Anton Chekhov, "The Grasshopper," trans. Ivy Litvinov, in *Anton Chekhov's Short Stories*, ed. Ralph Matlaw (New York: Norton, 1979), 70, 71 (chap. 1, 2).

20. George Eliot, *The Mill on the Floss*. ed. Gordon Haight (New York: Houghton Mifflin/Riverside, 1961), 290–91 (bk. 5, chap. 4). For an insightful discussion of this passage from a different perspective, see Nancy K. Miller, "Emphasis Added."

Whether Wayne Booth is correct when he claims that "the emotions and judgments of the implied author are . . . the very stuff out of which great fiction is made,"[21] there can be little doubt that the process of moral evaluation plays a central role in the reading of narrative fiction, and that for many readers, the greatest literature is that which forces them to probe the most difficult ethical questions with the greatest sensitivity (*A Hero of Our Time, The Ambassadors, Anna Karenina, Remembrance of Things Past*). Still, there are any number of reasons why an author might wish us to make quick judgments about his or her characters. Some narratives—for instance, adventure stories like the James Bond novels—depend for their effect on our experiencing the triumph over evil rather than on our understanding its nature. In such cases, efficient techniques are necessary so that the reader can know quickly who stands where. Furthermore, morality in fiction is closely tied to configuration; that is, ethical character—as we are reminded by the history of both the words *ethical* (from *ethos*) and *character* (meaning both moral quality and personage)—is often defined in terms of the kinds of actions we expect a character to perform in the future. Authors often need quick ways to set those expectations up. And even in novels where the primary end is ethical exploration, authors may need devices to allow readers to judge characters quickly—either because the characters are too minor for full development, or because the author needs an initial scaffolding that can then be developed (or undercut ironically) as the novel progresses. Dostoyevsky's subtle probing of light and dark imagery in *The Idiot* has the impact it does only because we start to evaluate fair-haired Myshkin and dark-haired Rogozhin as soon as we see them. Similarly, Gogol's play with the traditional patterns of light and dark in his treatment of the prostitute and the pure wife in "Nevsky Prospect," like Dashiell Hammett's reversal of the motif of the jolly fat man in *The Maltese Falcon*, can produce its intended effect only on readers who are prepared to make certain judgments to begin with.

Authors will often tell us quite directly what we should think of their characters. Mr. John Dashwood, we learn at the beginning of

21. Booth, *Rhetoric of Fiction*, 86.

Sense and Sensibility, "was not an ill-disposed young man, unless to be rather cold hearted, and rather selfish, is to be ill-disposed."[22] In addition, though, authors make use of a number of rules that they assume we have learned, and that allow us to make the appropriate judgments ourselves. Many of these rules are closely related to the New Critical doctrine of consistency of character. Although I would not agree with Brooks and Warren when they insist that the "thoughts and actions" of characters "must ultimately be coherent,"[23] it is certainly the case that when we read nineteenth- and twentieth-century narratives, we tend, on the whole, to *assume* a kind of consistency of character that hardly holds in life. This consistency, in fact, goes well beyond the meshing of thoughts and actions. There are many axes along which characters are generally assumed to be consistent, although most rules of snap moral judgment fall into one of two general classes: metaphorical rules of appearance and metonymic rules of enchainment.

The most basic rule of appearance is that we are to judge characters by their exterior, until the text gives us sufficient reason to judge them in some other way. Physical appearance, in other words, can be assumed to stand metaphorically for inner quality. The ability to make this metaphoric leap is a part of what Jonathan Culler calls "symbolic recuperation," which, in contrast to "empirical recuperation . . . operates where causal connections are absent. . . . We would presumably be unwilling to assume a causal connection between a perfect or a blemished complexion and a perfect or blemished moral character, but the symbolic code permits such associations and enables us to take the former as the sign of the latter."[24] But while it is not a direct analogue of the way

22. Jane Austen, *Sense and Sensibility*, ed. R. W. Chapman, 3d ed. (London: Oxford University Press, 1933), 5 (chap. 1).

23. Cleanth Brooks and Robert Penn Warren, *Understanding Fiction*, 173. See also Gary Saul Morson's claim that one of the rules of a novel is that "the statements, actions, and beliefs of any principal character (or the narrator) are to be understood as a reflection of his or her personality, and of the biographical events and social milieu that have shaped it." In this regard, he argues, novels differ from utopias (*Boundaries of Genre*, 77).

24. Culler, *Structuralist Poetics*, 225.

readers reason when dealing with their social realities, this symbolic code is neither constant nor purely literary. Specific applications will vary by text, and these variations are often echoes (and sometimes reinforcements) of the cultural norms within which the text is operating. Thus, for instance, the particular visual cues intended to inspire distrust in one text will not necessarily have the same meaning in another. The Late George Apley's father moved out of his old Boston neighborhood because seeing "a man in his shirt sleeves" on the steps was enough to tell him "that the days of the South End were numbered."[25] But the relevance of that physical feature is not the same in 1986 as it was either a century earlier, when the event took place, or a half-century earlier, when the novel was written. Similarly, nineteenth-century authors who expected their readers to make character judgments based on hair color did not expect their readers to decode the image of the blond woman in the same ways that writers of mid-twentieth-century hardboiled American fiction did. Still, the basic rule—that character is more or less revealed in appearance—holds steadily. Even a novelist like Southworth who argues philosophically and politically that character and appearance do not reflect each other ("At some former period in the history of the human race characters and countenances may have been in harmony, but not now")[26] is apt to find herself falling back on traditional literary markers of moral worth.

> Norham Montrose was, in form and features, the very counterpart of Malcolm, having the same tall, broad-shouldered, deep-chested, strong limbed athletic form, the same noble Roman features, and the same commanding presence. But in complexion and in temperament they were as opposite as day and night; for whereas Malcolm was fair as a Saxon, with clear, blue eyes, and light auburn hair, Norham was dark as a Spaniard, with jet-black eyes and raven-black hair and whiskers.[27]

25. John P. Marquand, *The Late George Apley: A Novel in the Form of a Memoir* (New York: Modern Library, 1940), 25–26 (chap. 3).

26. E[mma] D. E. N. Southworth, *The Bride of Llewellyn* (Chicago: Donohue, n.d.), 212 (chap. 30).

27. Emma D. E. N. Southworth, *Allworth Abbey; or, Eudora* (New York: Hurst, 1876), 139 (chap. 10).

Given the literary conventions according to which this text was expected to be read, in fact, both the phrase "in complexion and in temperament," and, even more, the next sentence of the text ("And where Malcolm was gracious, liberal and confiding, Norham was haughty, reserved and suspicious") are redundant.

Eyes are among the more reliable visual guides to character in fiction. As the narrator of Owen Wister's *Virginian* puts it, "Out of the eyes of every stranger looks either a friend or an enemy, waiting to be known."[28] It is no accident that Wells gives the hero of *The Time Machine* gray eyes, for he wants us to know, from the beginning, that he is keen, intelligent, controlled. When we are told that Olga, the protagonist of Chekhov's "Darling," has "gentle, soft eyes," or that Alyona Ivanovna, the pawnbroker in *Crime and Punishment*, has "sharp, malignant eyes," or that Cecil Carver, in *Career in C Major*, "had the biggest black eyes I ever saw" (in contrast to the Social Register types, who are "all so cultured that even their eyeballs were lavender")—we know a great deal more about the characters than simply what they look like.[29]

As a general rule, it is appropriate to treat the way characters sound much as we treat the way they look. Sometimes we are asked to judge by the quality of a voice per se (note Ippolit's squeaky voice in *The Idiot* or Daisy Buchanan's "low, thrilling voice," with its "fluctuating, feverish warmth," in *The Great Gatsby*).[30] Sometimes it is the way that language is used that serves as a guide to character. Ring Lardner assumes we will judge this narrator as soon as he begins to speak:

> Mother says that when I start talking I never know when to stop. But I tell her the only time I get a chance is when she ain't around, so I have to make the most of it. I guess the fact is neither one of us would be welcome in a Quaker meeting, but as I tell Mother, what did God give us tongues for if He didn't want we should use them? Only she

---

28. Wister, *The Virginian* (New York: Macmillan, 1902), 477 (chap. 35).

29. Anton Pavlovich Chekhov, "The Darling," in *Lady with Lapdog and Other Stories*, trans. David Magarshack (Baltimore: Penguin, 1964), 252; Dostoyevsky, *Crime and Punishment*, 4 (pt. 1, chap. 1); James M. Cain, *Career in C Major*, in *Three of a Kind* (Philadelphia: Blakiston, 1944), 17, 4 (chap. 3, 1).

30. F. Scott Fitzgerald, *The Great Gatsby* (New York: Scribner's, 1925), 9, 97.

says He didn't give them to us to say the same thing over and over again, like I do, and repeat myself.[31]

Once again, the specific conclusions to be drawn vary according to the context in which the book was intended to be read. Black English has different implications in Dixon's *Leopard's Spots* and in Wright's *Uncle Tom's Children;* in the Hardy Boys books, rough language is usually a sign of rough character, whereas in Chandler, refined English is intended to arouse suspicion.

We are also, as I suggested above, asked to judge characters by their names. This is not only the case with clearly allegorical names (Dostoyevsky's Golyadkin, from "naked"), or only in displays of linguistic virtuosity (the famous guest list in *The Great Gatsby*). Names also often imply, more subtly, a class or ethnic aura that, in a particular context, will carry a particular moral valence.[32] In Louise Meriwether's "Daddy Was a Number Runner," for instance, it is significant that the black narrator's mother gets a job as a cleaning woman in the Bronx with someone named Mrs. Schwartz, although the same name would have an entirely different resonance in a text about Jewish life.

In addition to metaphorical rules of appearance, which make it appropriate to assume that physical or verbal characteristics stand for moral qualities, we have metonymical rules of enchainment, which make it appropriate to assume that the presence of one moral quality is linked to the presence of another that lies more or less contiguous to it.

We are not only asked, for instance, to judge characters according to certain rules, but also to judge them according to how well *they* apply the rules. Thus, in mapping out the moral terrain of Southworth's *Allworth Abbey*, the reader is expected to judge peo-

---

31. Ring W. Lardner, "The Golden Honeymoon," in *How to Write Short Stories [With Samples]* (New York: Scribner's, 1925), 115.

32. See Ruth Prigozy's argument that Fitzgerald was "intrigued with the possibilities of names as social indicators, symbolic reflectors of class status and even moral outlook" ("Gatsby's Guest List and Fitzgerald's Technique of Naming," *Fitzgerald/Hemingway Annual 1972*, ed. Matthew J. Bruccoli and C. E. Frazer Clark, Jr. [Washington: Microcards, 1972], 99).

ple not only on their appearances but also on *their* ability to judge by appearance.

> The stranger listened with the deepest interest. At the conclusion of the narrative, he said:
> "The circumstances, indeed, seem to point out this young Eudora Leaton as the criminal; but from the glimpse I caught of her lovely face, she is just the last person in the world I should suspect of crime."[33]

Southworth's purpose in providing the stranger's assessment is not to guide our judgment of Eudora; we already *know* that she is beautiful and that she has been unjustly charged with murder. Rather, its function is to allow us to judge *the stranger*, who by his correct analysis shows himself worthy of our trust.

In another kind of chaining, many narratives also ask us, in the absence of evidence to the contrary, to assume a kind of innocence by association: we trust the friends of our friends and the enemies of our enemies. We can well appreciate Daniel Martin's method of appraisal.

> I took a little to judging friends, and not only the ones I shared my bed with, by Phoebe's reaction . . . how much she would chat with them, how discreet or voluble she would be, how much put on her old maidservant self or show her real one. It was all rather absurd, perhaps; but people got a bad mark if they didn't get on with Phoebe and learn to walk the delicate tightrope between giving her a hand in the kitchen and taking possession of it. [Ellipsis in original][34]

As with all narrative rules, authors frequently create their effects by tricking readers. The authorial audience of *The Maltese Falcon* at first trusts Brigid because she receives an unqualified endorsement from Effie Perrine's "woman's intuition":

> "What do you think of Wonderly?"
> "I'm all for her," the girl replied without hesitation.

33. Southworth, *Allworth Abbey*, 190 (chap. 14).
34. John Fowles, *Daniel Martin* (New York: NAL/Signet, 1978), 367 ("Westward").

"She's got too many names," Spade mused, "Wonderly, Leblanc, and she says the right one's O'Shaughnessy."

"I don't care if she's got all the names in the phone-book. That girl is all right and you know it."[35]

In the end, of course, the authorial audience discovers that it has been fooled, an effect that helps drive home the antifeminism of the text by showing that even "good" women like Effie are not to be trusted. But Hammett can use this rhetorical technique only because he can assume that his readers will apply the rule in the first place.

Similarly, we are often expected to assume that one moral failing naturally accompanies another. In Owen Wister's *Virginian*, for instance, we are expected to treat Balaam's failure to care properly for animals as a sign of a broader moral failing, just as in Charles W. Chesnutt's "Mars Jeems's Nightmare" (from *The Conjure Woman*), we are expected to think ill of McLean's overall character when we see him beating his horse "furiously with a buggy whip."[36] In *Gatsby*, we are surely not meant to be surprised when a man who has fixed the World Series—and who is Jewish and talks with an accent to boot—refuses to attend his friend's funeral. One could do a revealing cultural study by examining what flaws in particular are chosen—by what writers in what social contexts—as the material on which readers are asked to apply this rule. It is, I think, a sign of a particular kind of moral vision that Chekhov, for instance, so rarely invokes it.

One specific variant of the linking of moral feelings is the rule that Space Invaders are to be distrusted. Thus, in the beginning of *The Idiot*, the authorial audience is apprehensive of Lebedev in part because he imposes himself on Myshkin and Rogozhin. This rule applies not only to physical space, but to emotional and literary space as well. Andrew Garve, in *The Far Sands*, relies on this rule to create suspense. The novel concerns a man who comes to wonder whether his wife is planning to kill him for his money (as

35. Dashiell Hammett, *The Maltese Falcon*, in *The Novels of Dashiell Hammett* (New York: Knopf, 1965), 321 (chap. 4).
36. Chesnutt, *The Conjure Woman* (Ann Arbor: University of Michigan Press/ Ann Arbor Paperbacks, 1969), 69.

he thinks her identical twin did to *her* rich husband). It is therefore appropriate that Garve begins the novel, not after their marriage, but with him as a single man meeting her. The novel, in other words, is structured so that she enters the home space of *his* novel; she is thus especially subject to suspicion.

Novelists may also expect readers to use allusions as a basis for chaining their judgments. Of course, readers are often asked to transfer judgments when characters are explicitly or implicitly compared to characters in a previous, familiar text—we should, for instance, have already made a judgment about the heroine of Leskov's "Lady Macbeth of the Mzensk District" before we have even gotten through the title. More interesting for my purposes, though, readers are often expected to link ethical quality and aesthetic taste. In many texts, we are asked to assume—until there is evidence to the contrary—that people with the correct aesthetic views are also morally correct, while those with aesthetic failings have moral failings as well. We should not be surprised when Marianne, in *Sense and Sensibility*, turns out to have—at least by the standards of the authorial audience—moral flaws that mirror her foolish views on art; and Willoughby is suspect as soon as he echoes Marianne's aesthetic creed. Similarly, our judgments of the characters in *Remembrance of Things Past* depend to a large extent on their responses to music—especially, of course, on their responses to Vinteuil. And in James Cain's *Serenade*, we know that down-and-out Howard Sharp can trust the feisty Captain Conners to help him escape from Mexico, because Conners admires Beecham's conducting of the Beethoven Seventh and—even more—because Conners is susceptible to Sharp's demonstration that Mozart might be a greater composer than Beethoven.[37] But it is not only in the works of such novelists as Austen, Proust, and Cain—whose very themes, in part, are the interconnection of art and morality—that readers are expected to respond in this way. In *Farewell, My Lovely*, Marlowe keeps referring to Galbraith, a Bay City cop, as "Hemingway"—because he " 'keeps saying the same thing over and over until you begin to believe it must be good.' "[38]

37. Cain, *Serenade* (New York: Bantam, 1968), 56–58 (chap. 5).
38. Raymond Chandler, *Farewell, My Lovely* (New York: Pocket, 1943), 128 (chap. 24).

Galbraith's inability to understand the wisecrack is a point against him.

Needless to say, this convention depends not only on the reader's prior understanding of the rule itself and the prior knowledge of the works in question, but also on the reader's sharing of the author's judgments about those works. Without some knowledge of Chekhov's expectations about his readers' views on literature, it is hard to know, in "The Teacher of Literature," precisely how to take Shebaldin's criticism of Nikitin for his lack of familiarity with Lessing, or how to interpret Nikitin's consequent despair. Jane Gray's dismissal of Jane Austen in Drabble's *Waterfall* raises similar interpretive questions.

Truth and the Narrative Audience: The Rule of Realism

When I said above that Jason's statement (in *The Sound the Fury*) was "false," what exactly did I mean? Questions about the status of literary truth are as old as literary criticism, but they have become both more intricate and more compelling as literature has grown progressively more self-conscious and labyrinthine in its dealings with reality. One might perhaps read the *Iliad* or even Dickens' *Hard Times* without raising such issues. But such authors as Doris Lessing (especially in *The Golden Notebook*), Nabokov, and Borges seem continually to remind their readers of the complex nature of literary truth. How, for instance, are we to deal with a passage like the following from William Demby's novel *The Catacombs?*

> When I began this novel, I secretly decided that, though I would exercise a strict selection of the facts to write down, be they "fictional" facts or "true" facts taken from newspapers or directly observed events from my own life, once I had written something down I would neither edit nor censor it (myself).[39]

What does this sentence mean? When an apparently fictional narrator (who, to confuse matters, has the same name as his author

---

39. Demby, *The Catacombs* (New York: Harper and Row, 1970), 93 (chap. 6).

and is also writing a novel entitled *The Catacombs*) distinguishes between "fictional" and "true" facts, what is the status of the word "true"? It clearly does not mean the same as "fictional," for he opposes the two terms. Yet it cannot mean "true" in the sense that historians would use, for he calls what he is writing a novel, and even if he quotes accurately from newspapers, the events of a narrator's life are not historically true.

This is but a small version of other more famous literary questions. What precisely do we mean when we ask whether the governess in Henry James' *Turn of the Screw* is really a trustworthy witness? Or when we ask whether Dostoyevsky's Golyadkin (*The Double*) really has a double? Or what really happened last year at Marienbad?

To answer these questions, we must remember that all works of representational art—including novels—are imitations in the sense that they appear to be something that they are not. A piece of canvas, for example, appears to be the mayor or the Madonna; a tale about a nonexistent clerk and his overcoat appears to be a true account. As a result, the aesthetic experience of such works exists on two levels at once. We cannot treat the work either as what it is or as what it appears to be; we must be aware simultaneously of both aspects. A reader is hardly responding to the Sherlock Holmes stories as the author intended if he or she treats him as a historical being, makes pilgrimages to his home on Baker Street, and uses weather reports to determine when certain stories "actually" took place.[40] Neither, however, is the reader who refuses to fear for Holmes' safety as he battles Moriarty, on the grounds that he is simply a fiction.

In the proper reading of a novel, events that are portrayed must be treated as both true and untrue at the same time. One way of dealing with this duality is to add a third term to the distinction between actual and authorial audience. As I have noted, every author designs his or her work rhetorically for a specific hypothetical audience. But since a novel is generally an imitation of some nonfictional form (usually history, including biography and

40. For an encyclopedia, presumably tongue-in-cheek, of this sort of reaction, see William S. Baring-Gould, *The Annotated Sherlock Holmes*, 2 vols. (New York: Clarkson N. Potter, 1967).

autobiography), the narrator of the novel (implicit or explicit) is generally an imitation of an author.[41] He or she writes for an *imitation* audience (which I call the *narrative audience*) that also possesses particular knowledge. The narrator of *War and Peace* appears to be a historian. As such, he is writing for an audience that not only knows (as does the authorial audience) that Moscow was burned in 1812, but that also believes that Natasha, Pierre, and Andrei "really" existed, and that the events in their lives "really" took place. In order to read *War and Peace*, we must therefore do more than join Tolstoy's authorial audience; we must at the same time pretend to be a member of the imaginary narrative audience for which the narrator is writing. Whether they think about it or not, this is what all successful readers do when approaching the text.

The nature of the narrative audience can perhaps be clarified by distinguishing it from some other apparently similar concepts. For instance, the narrative audience is quite different from the narratee, the person to whom the narrator is addressing himself or herself.[42] The narratee is perceived by the reader as "out there," a separate person who often serves as a mediator between narrator and reader. The "narrative audience," in contrast, is a role which the text forces the reader to take on. The pretense involved in joining the narrative audience is also different from what Frank Kermode calls "experimental assent."[43] "Experimental assent" is an activity on the part of the actual audience through which it relates the novel to reality, accepting the novel if it turns out to be "operationally effective," rejecting it otherwise. The pretense I am describing is closer to Coleridge's "willing suspension of disbelief," except that I would argue not that disbelief is suspended but rather that it is both suspended and not suspended at the same time.[44]

41. For a development of the notion of literature as "fictive discourse"—that is, as an imitation of utterances rather than of actions—see Barbara Herrnstein Smith, *On the Margins of Discourse.*

42. See, for instance, Gerald Prince, "Introduction to the Study of the Narratee."

43. Kermode, *The Sense of an Ending,* 38–40.

44. I am not concerned here with the actual psychological processes by which a specific reader performs this act. This subject, however, is treated in Norman Holland's *Dynamics of Literary Response.* Holland starts out with the same observation that I do: we both believe and do not believe a literary text. But since he is

One way to determine the characteristics of the narrative audience is to ask, "What sort of reader would I have to pretend to be—what would I have to know and believe—if I wanted to take this work of fiction as real?" Normally, pretending to be a member of the narrative audience is a fairly simple task, especially when we are reading traditional realistic fiction: we temporarily take on certain minimal beliefs in addition to those we already hold. Thus, for a while we believe that a woman named Isabel Archer really existed, and thought and acted in a certain way; or, on a broader scale, that Yoknapatawpha County and its inhabitants really exist. Sometimes, however, we must go even further and pretend to abandon our real beliefs and accept in their stead "facts" and beliefs that even more fundamentally contradict our perceptions of reality. In *1984*, the narrative audience possesses "knowledge" of a series of "facts" about what was, at the time the book was written, "future" world history. In Mary Shelley's *Frankenstein*, the narrative audience accepts what the authorial audience knows to be false scientific doctrine.

If we do not pretend to be members of the narrative audience, or if we misapprehend the beliefs of that audience, we are apt to make invalid, even perverse, interpretations. For instance, the narrative audience of *Cinderella* accepts the existence of fairy godmothers (although the authorial audience does not share this belief). A reader who refuses to pretend to share that belief will see Cinderella as a psychotic young woman subject to hallucinations.

---

concerned with the psychological actions of readers (particularly with their unconscious fantasies) rather than with the conscious audience roles implied by a text, his resulting categories (intellecting reader/introjecting reader) differ markedly from mine. For another formulation of a similar dichotomy, see Pratt, *Toward a Speech Act Theory*, 174. See also Robin Feuer Miller's discussion of *The Idiot*, where she distinguishes between "the narrator's reader (who reads for pleasure, in a chronological and unreflective fashion)" and "the implied reader (who reads more carefully, attempting to discover the implied author's message)" (*Dostoevsky and* The Idiot, 127). These simultaneous roles are distinguished more by attitudes and values than by issues of truth; thus, her "narrator's reader" is closer to what I have elsewhere called the "ideal narrative audience" (the audience that the narrator wishes he or she were writing for) than to the narrative audience (see my "Truth in Fiction: Toward a Reexamination of Audiences," *Critical Inquiry* 4 [Autumn 1977]: 134–36), and is therefore of use primarily in analyzing ironic texts.

Although there are as many narrative audiences as there are novels, they tend to fall into groups, the members of which are quite similar. A reader does not really have to shift gears to move from *War and Peace* to *Gone with the Wind*, different as those novels are. Sometimes, however, a novelist is able to create a startling tone or mood by demanding a narrative audience that is unexpected or unfamiliar. Kafka's *Metamorphosis* is a good example. What is striking about this novella is not simply its fantastic premise, which is no more fantastic than the basic premises of *Alice in Wonderland*. Nor can the peculiar quality of Kafka's tale be explained purely in terms of the characters' odd reactions to Gregor's transformation. What strikes me as most curious about the book is the unusual nature of the narrative audience. In *Alice* we are asked to pretend that White Rabbits wear watches, that Cheshire Cats fade away, and that Caterpillars smoke hookahs. This is readily done by joining a narrative audience of a sort that is familiar from our experience with fairy tales. In *Metamorphosis*, however, we are only asked to accept the single fantastic fact that Gregor has been transformed into a gigantic beetle; in all other respects the narrative audience is a normal, level-headed bourgeois audience. Furthermore, we are asked to accept this without surprise; contrast the matter-of-fact opening of *Metamorphosis* with the equivalent passages in *Alice* or in Gogol's "Nose," where the narrative audiences are openly warned that the events portrayed will be strange and unusual. This curiously contradictory role—half mundane, half fantastic—contributes greatly to the novella's disquieting tone.

Although many critics have dealt with the implied audiences of texts, they have tended, on the whole, to ignore the distinction between authorial and narrative audiences—as Walker Gibson and Walter Ong do when they write, respectively, of "mock readers" and "fictionalized" audiences.[45] Granted, both the authorial and

45. Walker Gibson, "Authors, Speakers, Readers, and Mock Readers"; Walter J. Ong, "The Writer's Audience Is Always a Fiction." In fact, almost all critics who discuss the reader are discussing a hybrid form that crosses the lines I have set up. For example, Wolfgang Iser's discussions of the reader's discoveries (*Implied Reader*) are really studies of the narrative and authorial audiences combined. Only toward the end of his book does he suggest a duality in the reader. In Stanley Fish's

the narrative audiences are fictions (neither exists in the flesh), but they are fictions in radically different senses. When speaking of the authorial audience, we might more accurately use the term *hypothetical* rather than the term *fictional*. As I have suggested, most authors, in determining their authorial audience, try—within the limitations imposed by their aesthetic aims—to approximate the actual audience as closely as possible. For to the extent that an authorial audience is invented, footnotes or other explanations will be required before the text can work. Thus, while some authors (such as Joyce) are forced, because of the esoteric nature of their intentions, to idealize and write for an audience they know does not exist (or does not exist in significant numbers), few authors intentionally strive for such a situation. As T. S. Eliot puts it, "When a poet deliberately restricts his public by his choice of style of writing or of subject-matter, this is a special situation demanding explanation and extenuation, but I doubt whether this ever happens. . . . From one point of view, the poet aspires to the condition of the music-hall comedian. Being incapable of altering his wares to suit a prevailing taste, if there be any, he naturally desires a state of society in which they may become popular."[46]

The distance between authorial and actual audiences, in sum, may be inevitable—but it is generally undesirable, and authors usually try to keep the gap narrow. The narrative audience, on the other hand, is truly a fiction; the author not only knows that the narrative audience is different from the actual and authorial audiences, but rejoices in this fact and expects his or her actual audience to rejoice as well. For it is this difference that makes fiction

---

Self-Consuming Artifacts, the reader seems to be a complex combination: at least two actual audiences (the current, informed audience, with Fish as representative; the historical audience at the time the work was written), the authorial audience, and—when he is writing about fiction—the narrative audience. A primary difference between Fish's model (in that early book) and mine is that his is horizontal (he is concerned with the progress of a unified reader through time) while mine is vertical (I am concerned with distinguishing the different levels on which a reader operates simultaneously). Prince's distinction between real readers, virtual readers, ideal readers, and narratees (even though it does not, as I have pointed out, deal precisely with differing roles played by the reader) leads to more subtle analyses ("Introduction," 9).

46. Eliot, *Use of Poetry*, 22.

fiction and makes the double-leveled aesthetic experience possible.

From the authorial/narrative distinction emerges at least one fundamental reading convention: the rule of realism. Realism, of course, is a slippery concept. Although there are many ways to define it, recurring difficulties crop up whenever it is seen in terms of the relationship between the novel and some external, empirically verifiable world. For that empirical reality is, to a large extent, a changing social construct; thus, with any such definition, the corpus of so-called realistic works varies according to changes in readers' perceptions—it changes with each shift in scientific paradigms, with each shift in cultural norms. There is, to my mind, little value in a definition of realism that at best encourages us to dismiss older works as foolish and quaint—and at worst encourages us to twist them until they confirm our current prejudices, so that *Hamlet* is reduced to a verification of Freud, Poe to a confirmation of Lacan. Nor am I enthusiastic about a definition whereby Jules Verne, for instance, becomes more and more realistic as time goes on.

There is, however, another approach to the problem. If we look instead at the relationship between the narrative and authorial audiences, we find that there is something constant in most of the fiction that has commonly been considered realistic. In *The Portrait of a Lady*, for instance, the narrative and authorial audiences are quite close; the narrative audience is asked to accept very little beyond the beliefs of the authorial audience and virtually nothing that seriously contradicts those beliefs. Thus, while the narrative audience believes that Isabel exists, this hardly conflicts with the authorial audience's prior experiences; it is not improbable that such a person should exist and act as she does. Contrast this situation with that in novels generally thought to be antirealistic or fantastic. In Nathanael West's *Dream Life of Balso Snell*, for instance, the narrative audience takes on a good deal more—beliefs that, like the belief that one could stumble on the Trojan Horse, do contradict the experiences of the authorial audience.[47]

---

47. John W. Loofbourow's attempt to solve this problem is similar to mine, but is not entirely successful because he fails to distinguish between implied audi-

Of course, defining realism in terms of the distance between the two audiences does not provide a quantitative measure; literary distances may exist along several axes at once (scientific, historical, ethical, and so on), and they do not submit easily to the tape measure. This approach, however, does have the advantage of treating the realism of a given text as something that remains constant despite historical change. Furthermore, this definition reaffirms that realism is not a box into which some works fall and others do not, but rather a tendency, and it suggests that all novels are more or less, but at least somewhat, realistic in the sense of reflecting the beliefs of their authorial audience. Indeed, there is a general rule of realism to which virtually all nineteenth- and twentieth-century novels, at least those in the Western tradition, subscribe: the authorial audience knows it is reading a work of art, while the narrative audience believes what it is reading is real; but we can assume that in other respects the narrative audience shares the beliefs, prejudices, desires, fears, and expectations of the authorial audience, except where there is some evidence to the contrary, either in the text or in literary conventions. This principle can be broken down into two parts. First, there are areas of overlap between the two audiences, beliefs about reality that are common to both the authorial and the narrative levels; second, there is a more or less systematic way in which the areas of disagreement are mapped out. Let us look at these two claims in turn.

(1) No matter how fantastic a novel's premises, no matter how unrealistic the setting, the authorial audience and the narrative audience must share some beliefs about reality in order for the situations and actions to have the consequences they do and for the plot to get from point A to point B. That's because every fic-

---

ences. He locates realism in "any work in which the artist's assumptions about 'reality' are the same as those of his audience" ("Literary Realism Redefined," 434). But since he lumps together the authorial and narrative audiences, his definition falls apart. Surely the author and the *authorial* audience of *Alice in Wonderland* have the same preconceptions about reality; only the narrative audience has a different view of the world. And since, as Loofbourow notes, Dickens does undermine many of the preconceptions of his readers, we end up with the curious anomaly of realism that includes Carroll but excludes Dickens. For further development, see his "Realism in the Anglo-American Novel."

tional world, like every real world, requires a history, sociology, biology, mathematics, aesthetics, and ethics. The action of Goncharov's *Oblomov*, for instance, requires the institution of serfdom; the scenes of mental torture in *1984* can work their terror only because even in that world, two plus two really does equal four. And while in theory the writer of fiction can remake the world as he or she pleases, in practice no writer can create an entire world from scratch. Such a novel would be infinite, incomprehensible, or both.[48] Thus, novelists always require their readers to make inferences about characters and actions; those inferences are possible only if there are at least some points at which the novel's inner world—the world of the narrative audience—is congruent with the world of the authorial audience. Take, for instance, Robbe-Grillet's *Erasers*. It is an extremely unrealistic novel. It takes place in an imaginary city, where imaginary terrorists are threatening an imaginary government; more significant, the normal laws of cause and effect have been suspended: doubles appear unexpectedly, time stops. Yet when some women make suggestive comments about what goes on in the clinic of the gynecologist, Juard, readers catch the meaning. They can make the proper inferences, though, only because, fantastic as this world is, it is also assumed to coincide partially with that of the authorial audience— specifically, in the way in which abortions are handled.

(2) The characteristics of the narrative audience—that is, the respects in which it differs from the authorial audience—must be

---

48. Robert Scholes, working from a different critical perspective, comes to much the same conclusion; see "Towards a Semiotics of Literature." See also Chatman, *Story and Discourse*, esp. 27–31, 138; and Champigny's claim that in fiction, "the introduction of fantastic elements has to be restricted; otherwise, narrative coherence would crumble, and the story would turn into a poem" (*What Will Have Happened*, 23). For a discussion of the same point from the perspective of the "schema" theory of cognitive psychology, see Mary Crawford and Roger Chaffin, "Cognitive Research," esp. 4–11. As they argue, inferences are crucial because "no text can explicitly state all the information required by the reader" (10)—and inferences are possible because the reader comes to texts with "schema" which provide "default values" where the text has a gap (5). For a demonstration of the infinite regress that results when there are no unspoken assumptions and when, consequently, everything has to be stated explicitly, see Lewis Carroll, "What the Tortoise Said to Achilles," in *The Complete Works of Lewis Carroll* (New York: Random House/Vintage, 1976), 1225–30.

marked in some systematic way that is understood by author and reader alike. In other words, it is appropriate to assume that any novel is realistic (as defined above) unless there is evidence to the contrary. To use a comparison from music, realism is like the basic tempo from which nonrealism departs as a rubato; all fiction is at heart realistic *except insofar as it signals us to respond in some other fashion.* The opening of Marcel Aymé's "Le Passe-muraille," for instance, clearly tells us that, in this story, the narrative audience believes that it is possible to walk through walls. But since there is no signal that the narrative audience of S. S. Van Dine's *Canary Murder Case* believes in such a possibility, the narrative audience of *that* novel will not entertain this idea as a feasible explanation of how the famous Broadway beauty Margaret Odell was strangled in a locked room.

The specific signals used to chart out the overlap of authorial and narrative audience range quite broadly. As a general rule, the more potentially verifiable (by the authorial audience) the narrative audience's facts seem to be, the greater the overlap we should assume. Thus, in stories that take place in nonspecific or nonexistent times and places ("long, long ago in a distant kingdom"), we are justified, other things being equal, in assuming a high degree of nonrealism. For example, the counterfactual footnotes filling in the background of the "Second Revolt" at the beginning of Jack London's *Iron Heel* (in contrast, say, to Dickens' discussion of the legal system in *Bleak House*) provide no real links between the worlds of the authorial and narrative audiences; they must therefore be interpreted as a more sophisticated formulation of "Once upon a time." As such, they are a signal that what follows will contain counterfactual descriptions that the narrative audience should accept as true. In contrast, the more realistic details in the opening of John Marquand's *Wickford Point* set the reader up for a different kind of relationship between the authorial and the narrative audiences, a relationship typical of 1930s American naturalism. The author's disclaimer that his characters and incidents are fictitious does not in itself prove that what follows will be a narrative that could easily be confused with fact. But when the disclaimer is followed by the quotes from reviews of Allen Southby's book, by the details of his scholarly background, by the careful description of his letterhead, the characteristics of the narrative audience become increasingly clear. Given the first chapter, we are not expected to believe that Southby could turn into a dung beetle in the second.

In even more extreme cases, authors introduce into their texts not only realistic details, but even historically true details. Take the description of the storm in James Cain's *Mildred Pierce*. Here, the author not only describes an event, but gives us the specific location (Los Angeles) and the specific date (New Year's Eve, 1933). As a general rule, when a newsworthy event is described with enough specificity that the reader could, in fact, look it up in a newspaper, the reader is—in the absence of signals to the contrary—justified in assuming that the event more or less coincides with historical fact and that the rest of the text—again, in the absence of counterindications—is highly realistic.[49]

Some signals are genre bound. In John MacDonald's Travis McGee novels, for instance, the narrative audience is expected to take as true any generalizations made by the first-person narrator. Because, in this series, McGee stands as the author's representative, this can be seen as a specific variant of a general rule of detective stories, enunciated by Robert Champigny: "Since it cannot be attributed to a mistaken or lying character, a free comment [an authorial or unattributed comment that does not come from the point of view of one of the characters] should provide the reader with a valid axiom."[50]

Still, as the critical history of *The Turn of the Screw* has amply demonstrated, the signals of the degree of realism in a text are among the more difficult to interpret. Even in fairly straightforward detective stories, it is not always clear just what constitutes a "mistaken" character. In Josephine Tey's *Man in the Queue*, for instance, we are told by a police surgeon that because of the crush of a crowd, the mysterious victim could have been held erect for ten minutes after being stabbed, and in fact would probably not "even be aware that he had been struck."[51] Outside this novel

49. For a more detailed discussion of the use of verifiable facts in fictional texts, see Barbara Foley, *Telling the Truth*.
50. Champigny, *What Will Have Happened*, 69.
51. Tey, *The Man in the Queue* (New York: Pocket, 1977), 12 (chap. 1).

such a claim would seem preposterous, but in this context the narrative audience is apparently expected to accept it, for otherwise the mystery is insoluble. Fair enough; but at the end of the novel, we find the narrative audience was *not* to believe the same police surgeon when he assured us that the murder could not have been done by a woman—although there is no apparent way of distinguishing the validity of the two claims.

The problems get more complex still when we consider art that has, as its subject, the problem of perception—for instance, borderline fantastic novels with possibly mad narrators—where the signals can be so confused that actual readers simply cannot agree on how to take them. Thus, for instance, interpretations of Dostoyevsky's *Double* differ depending on how readers respond to the signals and what beliefs they consequently assume the narrative audience to hold. Depending on the strategies chosen, *The Double* can be read either as a realistic novel about madness or as a fantastic piece about doubles.

Post Hoc and Propter Hoc: Rules of Cause

The history of the novel—especially the realistic novel—has been tied closely to notions of causality and motivation. As Seymour Chatman puts it, "It has been argued, since Aristotle, that events in narratives are radically correlative, enchaining, entailing. Their sequence, runs the traditional argument, is not simply linear but causative."[52] The general expectation that narratives are causative informs reading processes in two separate and opposite ways. First, as we will discuss in more detail in Chapter 4, readers use their understanding of causation to move from cause to effect, in order to determine the future course of a novel they are reading. Knowledge, for instance, of the possible effects on health of severe drenching (at least in the early nineteenth century) helps the reader predict what will happen when Jane Bennet gets caught in a heavy rain on her way to visit the Bingleys in *Pride and Prejudice*.

Second, readers move in the reverse way, from effect to cause, in order to determine why things are the way they are, or why charac-

52. Chatman, *Story and Discourse*, 45.

ters act as they do. When we are introduced to the protagonist Pozdnyshev at the beginning of Tolstoy's *Kreutzer Sonata,* we are told that his hair is prematurely gray—and we are thus prepared to assume that he has suffered some severe anguish. (This example reminds us of the ways reading conventions—in this case, signification and configuration—interact. Once we realize that Pozdnyshev *has* suffered, we expect the novel to proceed to tell us about it.) The ease with which readers are able to make such determinations is one factor influencing the degree to which they find the book readable or comprehensible. Readers make these judgments in a variety of ways, but three very general techniques are important here.

(1) The authorial audience uses the realism rule to make a bridge between its visions of the external world and the novel at hand— that is, it generally assumes that the kinds of causal connections assumed to hold in the world around it will apply to the novel it is reading. In "A Rose for Emily," for instance, Faulkner assumes his readers' knowledge of how human aging affects hair color; it is on this basis that he expects his readers to infer from the presence of the "iron-gray" hair on the pillow not only that Emily killed Homer Barron years ago, but also that she has continued to sleep with his corpse into her old age.

(2) Sometimes an author cannot rely on the reader's conception of reality as a firm basis for cause-and-effect inferences. This may be, perhaps, because the author wishes to assert, in his or her fiction, a kind of causal relationship that does not, in fact, occur in reality. Or it may be because the author's notion of reality differs from that which he or she expects to find in the reader—this is especially common in historical periods when shared conceptions of reality are breaking down, or in books where writers are dealing with historical periods (past or present) the details of which they expect may be unfamiliar to their readers (present or future). In such cases, authors may wish to guide their readers through the use of maxims and other kinds of general statements. Chatman puts it well:

Both factual and rhetorical generalizations serve the same basic functions, for instance, the ornamental, and particularly the verisimilar. . . . Generalizations and other comments often arise because of the need for plausibility, since in troubled historical periods the codes are not strong enough to establish a seeming reality. Hence the greater prevalence of nonce-created, author-specific verisimilitude. . . . If a parish priest's desires are not satisfied by a large inheritance but require a canonship, it is because "Everyone, even a priest, must have his hobbyhorse" (*Le Curé de Tours*). But if he *is* satisfied, another generalization can accommodate that: "A sot does not have enough spunk in him to be ambitious."[53]

Thus, when Stendhal wants us to understand Julien Sorel's sudden suspicions about Madame de Renal's sincerity, he notes, "Such is, alas! the unhappy consequence of too much civilization! At twenty a young man's heart, if he has any breeding, is a thousand leagues removed from that casualness without which love is often no more than the most tedious of duties."[54] When H. G. Wells wants to ensure our understanding of why the Time Traveller's friends do not believe his initial claims, he notes, "But the Time Traveller had more than a touch of whim among his elements, and we distrusted him. Things that would have made the fame of a less clever man seemed tricks in his hands. It is a mistake to do things too easily."[55] When Chester Himes wants to be sure that his white audience understands why a black junkman might side with a person he had never seen before against the police, he uses the maxim, "It was the code of Harlem for one brother to help another lie to white cops."[56] The mainspring of the plot of Southworth's *Allworth Abbey* is maxim-ally justified by the claim, in a privileged position, "Flight! In that one short syllable lies the only safety from a forbidden passion, and where flight is impossible, passion becomes destiny."[57]

53. Ibid., 244–45. See also Gerald Graff's claim that "contrary to a popular view, modern literature tends to be more rather than less didactic than earlier literature, in part because the beliefs which earlier writers could assume they could presuppose as cultural givens in their readers now have to be made explicit" ("Literature as Assertions," 96). For an important discussion of maxims, see also Nancy K. Miller, "Emphasis Added."

54. Stendhal, *The Red and the Black: A Chronicle of the Nineteenth Century*, trans. Lloyd C. Parks (New York: NAL/Signet, 1970), 89 (bk. 1, chap. 13).

55. Wells, *The Time Machine*, in *Seven Science Fiction Novels of H. G. Wells* (New York: Dover, n.d.), 11 (chap. 3).

56. Himes, *A Rage in Harlem* (London: Allison and Busby, 1985), 82 (chap. 14).

57. Southworth, *Allworth Abbey*, 46 (chap. 3).

Such generalizations are not always in the form of maxims about human psychology. Sometimes they may provide reminders—or authorial claims—about the differences between historical periods. Chandler's Philip Marlowe notes, "Underneath a sheet of blue tissue paper in one corner I found something I didn't like. A seemingly brand new peach-colored silk slip trimmed with lace." And lest readers in the future be unable to follow the inferential chain because, having forgotten what life was like during the war years, they do not know *why* Marlowe does not like what he finds, Chandler adds an explanation: "Silk slips were not being left behind that year, not by any woman in her senses."[58]

Generalizations and maxims intended to clarify causal relations, however, need to be differentiated from several other types of maxims. Some are merely descriptive or—to use Chatman's word—"ornamental." "She was dressed in a leopard-skin coat with a matching hat. Real skin, of course. She was not the sort of lady who worried too much about leopards."[59] Some, given to us by a character or unreliable narrator rather than by a reliable narrator or implied author, serve not to create verisimilitude by describing the world, but rather to underscore the speaker's character by his or her *distance* from reality. When, in *Herland,* Terry insists that " 'women like to be run after,' " we are supposed to take it as a sign of his limitations, not of Gilman's world view.[60] Others serve as a way of expressing the author's or character's correct view of the world—they are, really, ends in themselves rather than means. "But sometimes Rennie liked to write pieces about trends that didn't really exist, to see if she could make them exist by writing about them. . . . Successes of this kind gave her an odd pleasure, half gleeful, half sour: people would do anything not to be thought outmoded."[61] Still others serve as predictors and help us determine the narrative's configuration. These will be discussed in more detail in Chapter 4.

(3) Beyond the realism rule and the use of maxims and generalizations, authors also depend on their readers' assimilation of what I call the rule of temporal causation. Like the realism rule,

58. Chandler, *The Lady in the Lake* (New York: Pocket, 1943), 65 (chap. 12).
59. Len Deighton, *Berlin Game* (New York: Knopf, 1985), 160–61 (chap. 12).
60. Gilman, *Herland,* 17 (chap. 2).
61. Margaret Atwood, *Bodily Harm* (New York: Bantam, 1983), 25 (pt. 1).

this is a rule of *literature,* one that need not have its analogues in real experience. In its most basic form, the rule of temporal causation assures us that in nineteenth- and twentieth-century narrative, it is appropriate to assume that temporally connected events are causally connected unless there is a signal to the contrary, and that the information necessary to determine the causal chain is available either in the authorial audience's prior knowledge or in the text itself. As Gerald Prince puts it, "Given two events A and B, and unless the text explicitly indicates otherwise, a causal connection will be taken to exist between them if B temporally follows A and is perceived as possibly resulting from it."[62] From this perspective, E. M. Forster's famous distinction between story ("a narrative of events arranged in their time sequence") and plot ("a narrative of events, the emphasis falling on causality") needs to be reformulated. As he puts it, stressing the objective qualities of the text, " 'The king died, and then the queen died' is a story. 'The king died and then the queen died of grief' is a plot."[63] From the reader's perspective, though, one can put it differently: if a work is known beforehand to be a novel, then we are invited to interpret "The king died and then the queen died" *as* "The king died and then the queen died of grief." Thus, Dostoyevsky writes, "The prince, however, heard them call him an idiot and he gave a start, but not because he had been called an idiot. He forgot 'the idiot' at once. He caught sight in the crowd, not far from where he was sitting, of a face."[64] According to this rule, the reader is entitled to assume that he gave a start *because* he saw the face.

This does not mean, of course, that a novelist cannot write a novel that resists traditional notions of causality, but special precautions must be taken to ensure that readers, generally used to

---

62. Prince, *Narratology,* 39. A more specific version of this rule, later quoted by Prince, is proposed by Roland Barthes: "There is a strong presumption that the mainspring of the narrative activity is to be traced to that very confusion between consecutiveness and consequence, what-comes-*after* being read in a narrative as what-is-*caused-by*. Narrative would then be a systematic application of the logical fallacy denounced by scholasticism under the formula *post hoc, ergo propter hoc*" ("Introduction," 248).

63. Forster, *Aspects of the Novel,* 60.

64. Fyodor Dostoyevsky, *The Idiot,* trans. David Magarshack (Baltimore: Penguin, 1955), 384 (pt. 3, chap. 2).

texts that operate according to the rule of temporal causation, will not fill in causal links where none are intended. Robbe-Grillet may very well be consciously trying to resist the nineteenth-century realist notions of causality in his novels, but as the analyses of Bruce Morrissette make clear, it is possible to make sense of them through the application of traditional rules for determining causal connections.[65]

Of course, even in the minimal narrative suggested by Forster, application of this rule is nowhere near so simple as I suggested. "The king died and then the queen died"—of grief? of remorse? of contagion? of relief? And the problems get more complex still when we deal with more extensive narratives. It is one thing to say that we can assume that the motives for Raskolnikov's murder of the pawnbroker lie *somewhere* in what we are told about the events leading up to it; it is quite another—as the conflicting readings of *Crime and Punishment* make abundantly clear—to pick out *the* appropriate details for assigning the cause. Learning to read—realistic texts in particular—is to a large extent learning to apply this rule as sensitively as authors require.

---

65. See Morrissette, *The Novels of Robbe-Grillet,* rev. ed. (Ithaca: Cornell University Press, 1975). For an opposing position, see Roland Barthes' foreword to Morrissette's study. For further discussion of their disagreement, see Stephen Heath, *The Nouveau Roman: A Study in the Practice of Writing* (Philadelphia: Temple University Press, 1972), esp. 119–21, 137–43.

4

The Black Cloud on the Horizon: Rules of Configuration

> Antigone is young. She would much rather live than die. But there is no help for it. When your name is Antigone, there is only one part you can play.
>
> Jean Anouilh, *Antigone*

Configuration vs. Coherence

Literary form—with its shadow twin, structure—has long been a vexed topic in critical discourse. At least part of the difficulty has stemmed from the frequent failure to distinguish carefully enough between the process of reading as it is taking place and the retrospective interpretation of that process once it has been completed. Thus, on the one hand, form refers sometimes to the reader's experience of an unfolding text during the act of reading. In Kenneth Burke's succinct phrase, "Form is the creation of an appetite in the mind of the auditor, and the adequate satisfying of that appetite."[1] On the other hand, the term can refer to the total shape of the work, as perceived by a reader who has completed it and reworked its elements into a total pattern. Form in this second sense is not a process, but something already achieved. As Cleanth Brooks puts it, "The structure meant is a structure of meanings, evaluations, and interpretations; and the principle of unity which informs it seems to be one of balancing and harmonizing connotations, attitudes, and meanings. . . . It is a positive unity, not a negative; it

---

1. Burke, "Psychology and Form," 31. A similar notion of form as process is found in Stanley Fish, "Literature in the Reader," in *Is There a Text?* 21–67.

represents not a residue but an *achieved* harmony" (emphasis added).[2] I call these two kinds of form *configuration* and *coherence* respectively, and different sets of rules govern each.

A reader applies previously learned rules of configuration while moving through the text. These rules are basically predictive—at least, on the level of discourse, although not necessarily on the level of story (that is, they permit us to make guesses about what will happen in the later parts of the *text*, whether the events described are chronologically before or after those we have already read about).[3] They are therefore always probabilistic. To put it another way, in a given literary context, when certain elements appear, rules of configuration activate certain expectations. Once activated, however, these expectations can be exploited in a number of different ways. Authors can make use of them not only to create a sense of resolution (that is, by completing the patterns that the rules lead readers to expect, either with or without detours) but also to create surprise (by reversing them, for instance, by deflecting them, or by fulfilling them in some unanticipated way) or to irritate (by purposefully failing to fulfill them). It is important to stress this point: a rule of configuration can be just as important to the reading experience when the outcomes it predicts turn out not to take place as when they do. Eugene Narmour's remark about music applies just as well to literature: "The structure of a work is a result of its implications, its realizations, *and* its non-realizations."[4] Thus, Raymond Chandler's *Big Sleep* was, at the time it was written, unusual among detective stories because the hero

---

2. Brooks, *Well Wrought Urn*, 195. See also Mark Schorer's claim "that to speak of content as such is not to speak of art at all, but of experience; and that it is only when we speak of the *achieved* content, the form, the work of art as a work of art, that we speak as critics" ("Technique as Discovery," in *Essays in Modern Literary Criticism*, ed. Ray B. West, Jr. [New York: Rinehart, 1952], 190).

3. Thus, the configuration/coherence distinction cuts across the story/plot distinction of E. M. Forster (*Aspects of the Novel*). Story and plot, of course, are textual categories, rather than classes of reader activities. More important, story is a matter of chronology, whereas configuration is a matter of order of presentation. Furthermore, application of rules of configuration involves an understanding not only of story but of plot as well, since readers often use their knowledge of causation to predict what will happen next.

4. Narmour, *Beyond Schenkerism: The Need for Alternatives in Music Analysis* (Chicago: University of Chicago Press, 1977), 184.

fails to restore order. But it does not follow that the rule of configuration basic to the classical detective novel—the rule that leads us to expect justice to triumph in the end—is irrelevant to this text. Rather, as I shall argue in more detail in Chapter 6, the final pages have the shock value they do only because Chandler encourages us to invoke the rule and then intentionally undermines our expectations.

Readers apply rules of coherence, in contrast, to the work as a completed totality (even though, of course, the rules have to be *learned* before the reading begins). Although a reader may posit certain coherences while moving through the work, he or she always does so by positing from some assumption about how the book will end. To put it otherwise: as we are reading, rules of configuration allow us to answer the question, "How will this, in all probability, work out?" while rules of coherence allow us to answer the question, "If it works out in that way, how will I account for this particular element?" Once we have finished the text, rules of configuration allow us to answer the question, "How did this particular element make me think, at the time I encountered it, that the text would work out?" whereas rules of coherence allow us to answer the question, "Given how it worked out, how can I account for these particular elements?" Rules of coherence allow us to make sense of, among other things, a text's failures to follow through on the configurations it seemed to promise— failures we cannot know about until the book is over. Thus while rules of configuration lead us to expect justice at the end of *The Big Sleep*, rules of coherence—which demand that the work fit together as a whole—allow us to interpret our frustration at the novel's irresolution in terms of Chandler's political message.

Let me stress that, according to my model, rules of configuration govern the activities by which readers determine probability. My perspective thus differs significantly from that of theorists who use apparently similar rules to describe *texts*. When Vladimir Propp claims, in discussing "Function VII" of the folktale, that "*interdictions* are always *broken* and, conversely, *deceitful proposals* are always *accepted* and fulfilled," he is not really enunciating a rule of configuration in my sense.[5] At best, rules like Propp's reveal

5. Propp, *Morphology of the Folktale,* 30.

consistent patterns in texts that have already been read; at worst, they lead to the kind of prescriptions for writers that Wayne Booth so rightly attacked in *The Rhetoric of Fiction*. Rules of configuration, in contrast, do not tell writers what to do—at most, they tell writers the framework within which their readers are likely to respond. Writers may use this framework any way they wish, either by accepting it, stretching it, or even ignoring it. Rules of configuration are prescriptive only in the following way: they map out the expectations that are likely to be activated by a text, and they suggest that if too many of these activated expectations are ignored, readers may find the results dull or chaotic.

Basic Rules of Configuration

In our current critical climate, academic writing tends to privilege novels that are surprising, experimental, avant-garde (or at least formerly avant-garde). For a variety of reasons, books that do not to a large extent forge their own paths are rarely accorded much attention in a college or university setting. But given that the Southworths and Dixons, the Ferbers and Robbinses outnumber the Melvilles and Coovers—and given that they're more widely read, as well—it is reasonable to claim that on the whole, novels are more or less predictable. Yes, it is hard, after one or two pages, to say very much about how the plot of Robbe-Grillet's *In the Labyrinth* is going to work itself out. But more often than not, readers have a good sense of the general course of future events before they have gotten very far into a narrative.

How are we able to predict with reasonable assurance the trajectory of a novel that we have not yet completed? It is surprising how much we depend on explicit guidance from the author or narrator. We may associate the "But the black cloud was already seen on the horizon"[6] technique of writing with literature of the second rank; but in fact, all authors—good and bad, popular and serious—lean on it heavily, in one form or another. It is not only modern "category" texts (Silhouette Romances, for instance) that announce the

---

6. Thomas Dixon, Jr., *The Leopard's Spots: A Romance of the White Man's Burden, 1865–1900* (New York: Doubleday, Page, 1902), 63 (chap. 9).

basic shape of their plots on their covers. Calling a play *The Tragedy of Hamlet* is not that much more subtle a way of warning us about how it is going to end. Nor, for that matter, is calling a novel *The Death of Ivan Ilych*.

Tolstoy, in fact, guides us even more firmly and prepares us for his ending not only through his title but also through his order of presentation: he begins with Ivan Ilych's funeral, and then narrates his life as a flashback. Similarly, Alice Walker begins *Meridian* with a chapter flagrantly called "The Last Return," which serves as a focal point toward which the other events of the novel—chronologically prior to it—are seen to be leading.

Epigraphs are useful devices for guiding readers' expectations, too. "Elle était fille; elle était amoureuse [She was a girl; she was in love]," the citation from Malfilâtre that opens chapter 3 of Pushkin's *Eugene Onegin*, clearly raises expectations about the events to come.[7] Alternatively, an author may preview the course of a story by comparing it to another familiar plot. In calling his story "Lady Macbeth of the Mzensk District," Leskov not only influences our evaluation of the main character, as I noted above; he also raises expectations about what will happen. Like Austen (who has her characters act out "Lovers' Vows" in *Mansfield Park*), Leskov may be more heavy-handed than Robbe-Grillet, with his concealed references to *Oedipus* in *The Erasers*. The underlying literary techniques, however, are similar in essence.

Whether authors use prophetic titles, inverted chronologies, mythic patterns, or simply straightforward descriptions of what is to come ("I called Flossie first," says Marcus Gorman at the beginning of William Kennedy's *Legs*, "for we'd had a thing of sorts between us, and I'll get to that"),[8] their warnings can vary in particularity. Sometimes, an author will merely give us a foreboding, a generalized hint about the sort of future that awaits the characters in a narrative, leaving the reader in suspense as to the precise form it will take. Southworth, for instance, writes in *The Hidden Hand:*

7. Alexander Pushkin, *Eugene Onegin*, trans. Walter Arndt (New York: Dutton, 1963), 59.
8. Kennedy, *Legs* (New York: Penguin, 1983), 14.

Let them enjoy it! It was their last of comfort—that bright evening! Over that household was already gathering a cloud heavy and dark with calamity—calamity that must have overwhelmed the stability of any faith which was not as theirs was—stayed upon God.[9]

"My last words," notes Pechorin in Lermontov's *Hero of Our Time*, "had been entirely out of place: at the time, I did not realize all their importance, but later had a chance to regret them."[10] Similarly, the Time Traveller of *The Time Machine* remarks, " 'I was to discover the atrocious folly of this proceeding, but it came to my mind as an ingenious move.' "[11]

But an author can be more concrete in prefiguring the course of a narrative, as well. Dostoyevsky begins *The Brothers Karamazov* as follows:

Alexey Fyodorovich Karamazov was the third son of Fyodor Pavlovich Karamazov, a landowner well known in our district in his own day (and still remembered among us) owing to his tragic and obscure death, which happened exactly thirteen years ago, and which I shall describe in its proper place.[12]

It is only a few paragraphs into the first chapter of *So Big* that Ferber sketches out the conclusion of the novel we have barely begun to read:

In fact, he never became as big as the wide-stretched arms of her love and imagination would have had him. You would have thought she would have been satisfied when, in later years, he was the Dirk De-Jong whose name you saw (engraved) at the top of heavy cream linen paper, so rich and thick and stiff as to have the effect of being starched and ironed by some costly American business process; whose clothes were made by Peter Peel, the English tailor; whose roadster ran on a

9. Emma D. E. N. Southworth, *The Hidden Hand* (New York: Burt, n.d.), 206 (chap. 27).

10. Mihail Lermontov, *A Hero of Our Time*, trans. Vladimir Nabokov and Dmitri Nabokov (Garden City, N.Y.: Doubleday/Anchor, 1958), 75 ("Taman").

11. H. G. Wells, *The Time Machine*, in *Seven Science Fiction Novels of H. G. Wells* (New York: Dover, n.d.), 59.

12. Fyodor Dostoevsky, *The Brothers Karamazov*, trans. Constance Garnett; rev. Ralph E. Matlaw (New York: Norton, 1976), 2 (bk. 1, chap. 1).

French chassis; whose cabinet held mellow Italian vermouth and Spanish sherry; whose wants were served by a Japanese houseman; whose life, in short, was that of the successful citizen of the Republic. But she wasn't. Not only was she dissatisfied: she was at once remorseful and indignant, as though she, Selina DeJong, the vegetable pedler, had been partly to blame for this success of his, and partly cheated by it.[13]

But widespread as such explicit prefiguring is, it is but one strand in a large network of techniques by which the authorial audience is prepared, while reading, for the shape of things to come. Most of these techniques provide foreknowledge implicitly, requiring readers to decode information given to them by applying rules of configuration. There are many such rules, often highly genre specific; as a result, we may tend to think of configuration—especially as it regards the course of action in a novel—in terms of total plot packages: the classical detective story, the Harlequin romance, the Russian fairy tale. But in fact, we perceive form as we read because we recognize far smaller building blocks. For this reason, a novel that may seem quite fresh in its total structure (for instance, its overall pattern of stress and resolution) can still seem orderly, familiar, even inevitable.

Many rules of configuration are so much a part of our intuitive understanding of literature that they seem almost trivial when made explicit. Nonetheless, it is worth looking at a few of them to see the kind of blocks from which even sophisticated, large-scale literary structures are built. The task will be somewhat easier if we start at a high level of abstraction. Generally speaking, the events in nineteenth- and twentieth-century fictional narratives appear, at least the first time through, to be neither completely determined nor completely free. The text's "horizon of expectations" (to borrow a term made popular by Hans Robert Jauss) is neither infinite nor zero.[14] As Umberto Eco puts it, "Every text, however 'open' it is, is constituted, not as the place of all possibilities, but rather as the field of oriented possibilities."[15] From this middle ground

13. Edna Ferber, *So Big,* in *Five Complete Novels* (New York: Avenel, 1981), 4 (chap. 1).

14. See, for instance, Jauss, *Toward an Aesthetic of Reception.*

15. Eco, *Role of the Reader,* 76.

come two metarules of configuration of which many of the more specific rules turn out to be special cases. First, it is appropriate to expect that *something* will happen. Second, it is appropriate to expect that not *anything* can happen. Literary communication depends heavily on these rules and their interaction.

Recast as a statement about texts rather than readers, the first of these metarules—that something happens, that things change in a way that is not *entirely* the result of inertia—is, for some theorists, the fundamental characteristic of narrative. Gerald Prince, for instance, defines narrative as "the representation of *at least two* real or fictive events or situations in a time sequence, neither of which presupposes or entails the other."[16] Mary Louise Pratt introduces the useful notion of tellability: "Assertions whose relevance is tellability must represent states of affairs that are held to be unusual, contrary to expectations, or otherwise problematic."[17] Narratives, the first metarule tells us, can reasonably be expected to be tellable.

Thus, when we pick up a narrative text, we can assume that the final situation will not be identical to the initial situation—or, if it is (as happens not only in texts that start at the end, such as *The Death of Ivan Ilych*, but also, less literally, in circular narratives, such as "The Fisherman and His Wife," *The Idiot*, and *Career in C Major*), that it will reattain that initial situation through some movement of departure and return. If, for instance, a book begins, as Jane Austen's *Emma* does,

> Emma Woodhouse, handsome, clever, and rich, with a comfortable home and happy disposition, seemed to unite some of the best blessings of existence; and had lived nearly twenty-one years in the world with very little to distress or vex her

—the first metarule allows us to predict that we will, in fact, read about events that distress or vex her.

The first metarule (something will happen) opens up the possibilities of the text; the second (that something will happen ac-

---

16. Prince, *Narratology*, 4. See also Cleanth Brooks and Robert Penn Warren, who tell us that if "nothing 'happens,' "then we simply do not have fiction (*Understanding Fiction*, 10).
17. Pratt, *Toward a Speech Act Theory*, 136.

cording to some configuration) limits the range of those possibilities. We can experience a text as meaningful literature only if we assume, even before we pick it up, that it will be patterned in some more or less recognizable way: that it can be seen as an example of or a variation of *some* preexisting genre category or plot type (even if it ultimately undermines it), that some rules of configuration will apply to it (even if the expectations aroused by those rules are ultimately frustrated), that relations among textual elements that *look* like configurations can tentatively be treated as such.[18]

To put it another way: events have a predictive value in fiction that they do not have in life. We can experience the ebb and flow of a text—its resolutions and surprises, its climaxes and anticlimaxes—only if we assume while reading that the author has control over its shape, and that the future is *in some recognizable way* prefigured in the present. For instance, if a seemingly trivial fact is given notice in a text, if that fact does not have any apparent value for signification (for instance, as character revelation), *and* if there is a configuration in which that fact would have predictive value, then we should presume that that configuration holds, feeling the joy of confirmation when it does, the joy of frustration when it does not. If I mention to my wife in real life that our daughter is especially trusting and unsuspicious of strangers, my remark has no particular predictive value, except to the superstitious—indeed, superstition can perhaps be defined as the application of literary rules of configuration to reality. But the expression of the same sentiment sets up a different pattern of expectations in a novel. In Dixon's *Leopard's Spots,* Tom's first daughter has been killed when blacks tried to abduct her; he later expresses his fears about his second:

> "Lord, there's so many triflin' niggers loafin' round the county now stealing and doin' all sorts of devilment, I'm scared to death about that child. She don't seem any more afraid of 'em than she is of a cat."
> "I don't believe anybody would hurt Flora, Tom,—she's such a little angel," said Gaston kissing the tears from the child's face.[19]

18. One of the reasons that it is easier to read texts that have been published than those which have not is that the knowledge that the text has passed through editors helps assure us that this rule has been adhered to. For a good discussion of the importance of publication, see Pratt, *Toward a Speech Act Theory,* 116–25.

19. Dixon, *Leopard's Spots,* 366 (bk. 3, chap. 4).

No experienced reader should be surprised when Flora in turn is abducted, raped, and murdered—especially given the racist premises of the novel. The only surprise is that Dixon dilutes the potential pleasure of the pattern he has set up by fulfilling his reader's expectations within two pages, instead of building up suspense.

These two basic rules underlie many of the more specific rules of configuration, to which I will now turn.

Rules of Undermining

It is scarcely possible for a human being to be happier than was Lord Leaton at this time. In the prime of his manly life, blessed with a fair wife in the maturity of her matronly beauty, and a lovely daughter, just budding into womanhood, endowed with an ancient title, an immense fortune, and a wide popularity, Lord Leaton was the most contented man in England.[20]

The first of the two metarules of configuration means, among other things, that readers can expect situations of inertia to be upset. Thus, for instance, when a work begins with a claim of a permanent and static state of affairs (as *Emma* begins with Emma's security) or a claim of an inevitable future (as the film *War Games* opens with the military's insistence that its computer cannot fail), we can expect the stability to be undermined. The precise application depends, however, on a number of variables. (1) The probability that a state of affairs will change depends, in part, on the reliability of the person claiming it to be permanent. It makes a difference, for instance, whether a character or an omniscient narrator makes the claim, as well as whether the fallibility of that character is itself an issue (as it is in *War Games*). Thus, when the omniscient narrator of *Bleak House* tells us that the case of Jarndyce and Jarndyce is "perennially hopeless,"[21] we are not intended to invoke the rule of undermining.

20. Emma D. E. N. Southworth, *Allworth Abbey; or, Eudora* (New York: Hurst, 1876), 27 (chap. 1).

21. Charles Dickens, *Bleak House* (Boston: Houghton Mifflin/Riverside, 1956), 3 (chap. 1).

(2) The content of a claim affects our judgment about the likelihood of its reversal. Claims of perfect crimes and foolproof get-rich-quick schemes are particularly unreliable. Thus, when Thomas Bass opens *The Eudaemonic Pie* with the confident belief that the computer in his shoe will turn him into a winner at Las Vegas, the authorial audience expects that something will go wrong, especially when his boast is given double notice (it appears at the end of the first chapter, and is printed in italics as well).

> Like a basketball player watching a free throw sail up and into the basket, I lean back on my heels and wait. I turn to the cocktail waitress and order a Tequila Sunrise. I watch the Filipino puff his cigar. I smile at the pit boss. I'm not even looking as the croupier calls out the number 13 and places his pyramid on top of my bet. *Why would anyone play roulette,* I think to myself, *without wearing a computer in his shoe?*[22]

Indeed, almost any assured statement of intention at the beginning of a narrative raises *some* doubt in the authorial audience as to whether it will in fact be carried out.

> Terence Kelly, a rising young professor of Latin at the university, was inaugurating a new way of life for himself on this particular Wednesday in November, 1946 which happened to be his twenty-fifth birthday. It was known to himself as "the new program," and was a program of detachment. "Hands off! Hands off other people! Let them alone!" So it might be expressed, in brief.[23]

This is likely to be a novel about a man who finds himself entangled.

(3) Specific application of the rule depends on whether the initial situation or the predicted future is positive or negative. The way in which this factor influences the reading process, however, depends heavily on the novel's period and intended audience. For instance,

22. Bass, *The Eudaemonic Pie* (Boston: Houghton Mifflin, 1985), 14. Although this book is not a novel, it does rely heavily on novelistic techniques for its effects—so much so that many of the early critics had difficulty believing it was true.
23. Francis Steegmuller, *Blue Harpsichord* (New York: Carroll and Graf, 1984), 9 (pt. 1, chap. 1).

nineteenth- and twentieth-century European and American canonical fiction, especially after the rise in popularity of naturalistic techniques, has a strong streak of pessimism. In these texts, negative situations, such as economic deprivation, can be expected to be more stable than positive ones. Thus, it is reasonable for a reader to assume that the poverty of the Joads in Steinbeck's *Grapes of Wrath* has a good chance of continuing—in contrast to even the moderate middle-class comfort of Charles and Emma Bovary. American popular literature of the era, however, is aimed at different readers, and uses different generic patterns; on the whole, it is not so uniformly pessimistic. Thus, when we pick up Horatio Alger's *Ragged Dick* and find a chipper young street urchin polishing shoes, the authorial audience—which is radically different from Flaubert's—will expect his lot in life to improve.

Under the general rule of undermining lie a number of more specific rules. For instance, the rule of the lure of the unfamiliar governs our expectations by suggesting that novels are more likely to move from the familiar to the unfamiliar (although perhaps back again at the end) than vice versa. Eric Ambler's *State of Siege*, for instance, begins as the hero, Steve Fraser, who has been working as an engineer on a dam project in Sunda, is about to return to London. It would be highly unusual for a novel, particularly an adventure story, to begin with a trip from the exotic back to the well known. And while, as it reads, the authorial audience has to entertain the remote possibility that *State of Siege* will develop into a how-London-has-changed-while-I've-been-away novel, it is more prepared for what actually does happen—Fraser's departure is delayed, and his adventures take place against an Asian background. Even novels that seem to begin with returns rather than departures often actually move into the unfamiliar: although *The Idiot* begins with Myshkin's arrival back in Russia, from Myshkin's point of view it is still a trip from his familiar and protected Swiss habitat to a strange and threatening one.

Similarly, we have the rule of chutzpah: When a character states with assurance that which he or she has no good reason to believe to be the case, we can expect that he or she will turn out to be wrong, especially if the claim is important for the outcome of the plot. When Oedipus claims to possess greater wisdom than the oracle, it is reasonable to expect that he will be shown up. When, in Harriet E. Wilson's *Our Nig*, Mary Bellmont's illness arouses "no serious apprehensions" in her parents, the authorial audience can reasonably expect the illness to grow severe.[24] When Mrs. Norris, in Austen's *Mansfield Park*, says to Sir Thomas, during a discussion of whether to bring Fanny into the house,

> "You are thinking of your sons—but do not you know that of all things upon earth *that* is the least likely to happen; brought up, as they would be, always together like brothers and sisters? It is morally impossible. I never knew an instance of it"[25]

—the authorial audience is being asked to predict that the "morally impossible" marriage will in fact come to pass. Similarly:

> He lay again on the bed, his mind whirling with images born of a multitude of impulses. He could run away; he could remain; he could even go down and confess what he had done. The mere thought that these avenues of action were open to him made him feel free, that his life was his, that he held his future in his hands. But they would never think that he had done it; not a meek black boy like him.[26]

So thinks Bigger Thomas in Richard Wright's *Native Son* as he contemplates the murder of Mary Dalton and his attempt to extort ten thousand dollars from her parents. And his very sense of freedom is intended to make the authorial audience feel all the more surely that he is hopelessly trapped—more hopelessly trapped than his predecessor, Big Boy (in "Big Boy Leaves Home," from *Uncle Tom's Children*), who feels less confident about his possibilities of escape from a similar situation. And even without any knowledge of the actual course of European history, a reader could reasonably expect Macmaster to be proven false when, in *Some Do Not . . .*, he says ("loftily"): " 'You're extraordinarily old-fashioned at times,

24. Wilson, *Our Nig; or, Sketches from the Life of a Free Black* (New York: Random House, 1983), 106 (chap. 10).

25. Austen, *Mansfield Park*, ed. R. W. Chapman, 3d ed. (London: Oxford University Press, 1932), 6 (bk. 1, chap. 1).

26. Wright, *Native Son* (New York: Harper and Row/Perennial, 1966), 179.

Chrissie. You ought to know as well as I do that a war is impossible—at any rate with this country in it.' "[27]

Like most rules, the rule of chutzpah has generic and historical exceptions. Heroes of classical detective novels—especially heroes based on the Holmes/Poirot model—are allowed an unpunished arrogance denied to most other characters. So are heroes of myth and certain Party representatives in strict Socialist Realist texts. Indeed, the particular types of characters that a culture exempts from this rule is probably one of the more revealing markers of its ideology.

Of course, *Some Do Not . . .* was written for readers who *did* know something about the course of European history, which brings us to another rule often invoked by novels set in particular time periods—the rule of imminent cataclysm. If a story begins at a specified moment right before a generally known upheaval (the French Revolution, World War II), we are probably being asked to read with the expectation that that upheaval will influence the course of the novel. Even without the hints that appeared on the paperback cover, the reader of *The White Hotel* could reasonably assume that the Holocaust would influence the working out of the plot. Any post-Holocaust book about European Jewish life in the late 1920s is probably intended to be read in the context of what we know historically took place—and the more stable and secure the political and economic position of those Jews appears to be, the more likely it is that we are expected to apply the rule of imminent cataclysm. Similarly, the authorial audience's expectations as it reads post-1929 American novels dealing with the lives of the well-to-do before the stock market crash should in most cases be guided by knowledge that the market will collapse.

Of course, authors are free to ignore this rule—although they make the reader's task easier if they signal that they are doing so. Stendhal's "Editor's Note" about the date of the composition of *The Red and the Black* ("This work was ready for publication when the crucial events of July occurred")[28] does more than dis-

---

27. Ford Madox Ford, *Some Do Not . . .* , bound with *No More Parades* (New York: NAL/Signet, 1964), 26 (pt. 1, chap. 1).

28. Stendhal, *The Red and the Black*, trans. Lloyd C. Parks (New York: NAL/Signet, 1970), unnumbered page.

sociate him from the events of 1830. It also serves to warn readers that they should *not* apply the rule of imminent cataclysm in their reading of the text that follows. But the very fact that Stendhal felt the need to mark his text in this way is an indication of how strongly this rule pulls on readers.

The rule of imminent cataclysm, of course, applies only to works written after the cataclysm in question. Dirk DeJong's decision to become a bond salesman in *So Big*—published in 1924—is intended to set up entirely different expectations from Junior's decision to follow the same path in Margaret Ayer Barnes' *Edna His Wife* from a decade later. But this is one of those areas where actual readers may find it hard to recapture the experiences of the authorial audience. It is easy to *say* that the rule of imminent cataclysm does not apply in *So Big*—it is another thing for real readers to cleanse their minds of their knowledge of American history as they read, and to avoid predicting the shape of the text based on their knowledge of events about which the author knew nothing. Obviously, the problem is most severe with historically distant texts, but since the world is always changing, even recent texts may pose problems. Margaret Atwood's *Bodily Harm* was published in 1982, but within a year and a half, its references to Grenada took on substantially different connotations for most actual readers.

Even in novels without such historical grounding, there is a parallel rule: If the course of action seems smooth, then anything that *looks* like a potential obstacle has a likelihood of turning into one. Much of our sense of anxiety as we read *Native Son* comes from Bigger Thomas' inability to burn Mary Dalton's bones after he has killed her. We see this as a possible obstacle to his success, and hence we expect it to trip him up. Similarly, the following passage in Zola's *Thérèse Raquin* not only tells us explicitly when the comfortable adultery of Thérèse and Laurent will end, but also warns us implicitly of what will push them into violent action: "This life of alternating excitement and calm went on for eight months. The lovers lived in perfect bliss. Thérèse was no longer bored, and had nothing left to wish for; Laurent, sated, coddled, heavier than ever, had only one fear, that this delectable existence might come to an end."[29] And if even potential obstacles are absent, then readers should probably expect one to emerge. The more central the action in question is to the plot, the more likely the obstacle will be. In *Bodily Harm*, Lora asks Rennie to pick up a box at the airport for her in St. Antoine—a small Caribbean island just made independent of England and on the edge of an explosive election. She assures her that the package does not contain drugs, and to Rennie it looks like a simple job with "no complications."[30] But the authorial audience realizes that it would not be worth mentioning were it not likely to prove more complex than it seems, and it consequently awaits the outcome of the trip to the airport with trepidation—trepidation crucial to the intended reading experience.

Let me stress once again that a rule of configuration can be important in a text both when the expectation it activates is fulfilled and when it is not. The humor of the following passage by James Cain works only if we know the rule and are surprised when it does not apply:

> But pretty soon Captain Madeira, he come to me and says I was to go on duty. And what I was to do was to go with another guy, name of Shepler, to find the PC of the 157th Brigade, what was supposed to be one thousand yards west of where we was, and then report back. . . . So me and Shepler started out. And as the Brigade PC was supposed to be one thousand yards west, and where we was was in a trench, and the trench run east and west, it looked like all we had to do was to follow the trench right into where the sun was setting and it wouldn't be no hard job to find what we was looking for.
> And it weren't.[31]

Rules of Balance: Focus

Just as rules of undermining furnish the openness demanded by the first metarule of configuration, so the second metarule requires

29. Emile Zola, *Thérèse Raquin*, trans. Leonard Tancock (New York: Penguin, 1962), 75 (chap. 8).
30. Margaret Atwood, *Bodily Harm* (New York: Bantam, 1983), 96 (pt. 2).
31. Cain, "The Taking of Montfaucon," in *The Baby in the Icebox and Other Short Fiction* (New York: Penguin, 1984), 105–6.

rules of order to limit the field of possibility. Among these are rules of balance. Whether or not the author is striving for formal elegance as an end in itself, most standard novels in our tradition are balanced in one way or another. Our knowledge of the various ways in which that balance can be manifested helps us predict the work's shape as we read, and thus share in its intended emotional curve.

Balance can occur along several axes. Some of these relate to what might be called the general focus of the work—its content in the broadest sense. The focus of a work is usually announced in some conventional way, and by knowing rules of focus, the reader can determine the probable boundaries of the novelistic universe that he or she will inhabit. Among the more important axes of focus is central consciousness: most traditional novels maintain some consistency with regard to point of view. For instance, if a novel opens from a particular point of view, readers can reasonably expect that it will be dominated by that point of view or will at least close with it, unless there is a signal to the contrary, such as a frame-tale structure (as in Turgenev's *First Love*), a constant flickering of point of view (as in Bram Stoker's *Dracula*, James Hilton's *Ill Wind*, or Faulkner's *As I Lay Dying*), or an explicit warning from the narrator or author that the focus will shift.

Like all rules of configuration, rules of focus are not prescriptions for producing well-made texts, but authors can use the knowledge that readers will apply them in order to shape readers' experience. Thus, if readers expect the initial point of view to return at the end of the text (as in a musical ABA structure), authors can fulfill that expectation to create a sense of closure. Robbe-Grillet's *In the Labyrinth*, for instance, begins with the word "I"; even though overt references to the first-person narrator disappear—the first person emerges only once more before the end, at the beginning of the last chapter—the authorial audience feels a sense of fulfillment when the novel ends with the word "me." But that sense of fulfillment comes about only because the expectations of return is activated in the first place. Granted, Robbe-Grillet, with his geometrical obsessions and his love of formal ingenuity, is an extreme case. But far less precise writers—even fairly sloppy writers like Dostoyevsky—rely on their reader's application of rules of focus to support closure. Anton Lavrent'evich, the narrator of Dostoyevsky's *Possessed*, offers a limited perspective on events at the beginning of the novel.[32] But while he remains the nominal narrator throughout the text, his persona and limitations fade away for long passages in the middle, where we receive a great deal of information to which he could have no possible access. But when it comes time to wrap up the novel, Dostoyevsky not only resolves his major plot strands and sums up his major themes, but he also returns explicitly to Anton Lavrent'evich's perspective in the last chapter, where "sources" are once again cited for the details of his narration. Similarly, John O'Hara heightens the sense of closure in *Appointment in Samarra* by beginning with the thoughts of Luther Fliegler—who turns out to be a minor character—and then returning to him for the closing paragraphs. Once again, authors may well choose to reverse the expectations they set up. Thus, the shift of narrator toward the end of Goethe's *Sorrows of Young Werther* is intended to wrench us emotionally, but it can work only for the reader who *expects* consistency in point of view strongly enough to feel the dislocation.

It is remarkable, in fact, how strongly the assumption of this kind of consistency operates. I remember my sense of irritation while reading E. Phillips Oppenheim's once-classic spy thriller, *The Great Impersonation*. The novel begins from the point of view of Sir Everard Dominey, who is apparently killed in Africa at the end of the second chapter by his German look-alike, Baron von Ragastein. The novel goes on to center on his killer, who returns to England and takes Dominey's place in order to act as a spy. This shift in perspective gives the novel an odd, off kilter flavor, but the reader who follows his or her instincts, expecting some return of Dominey at the end, will paradoxically find that the novel's effect is dissipated when the expectation is fulfilled. For at the end of the book, we find that Dominey had in fact killed von Ragastein, and that he has been impersonating the German impersonating *him* in order to infiltrate the *German* spy network. Oppenheim had (unconsciously, one presumes) followed this rule of balance even

---

32. For a good discussion of the importance of that perspective, see Ralph E. Matlaw, "The Chronicler of *The Possessed*: Character and Function," *Dostoevsky Studies: Journal of the International Dostoevsky Society* 5 (1984): 37–47.

though in so doing he risked destroying his intended effect, for the reader who expects balance loses the intended shock.

What applies to the perspective from which a novel is narrated applies as well to its central character or characters. Susan Suleiman has made a strong claim that "it is only after having read the whole novel that one can fully distinguish major characters from secondary or minor ones."[33] There is some slippage introduced by the word "fully" here—but we need to remember that in fact, most traditional novels rely on the reader's use of conventional rules to recognize the protagonists almost as soon as they enter the text. Such recognition is particularly easy, of course, in those works (especially common in the nineteenth century) that announce their central characters in their titles (*Jane Eyre, David Copperfield, Anna Karenina, Indiana*). But even in our supposedly more sophisticated literary world today, non–avant garde novelists rely on fairly simple shared conventions to cast a spotlight on their protagonists. Showing up in a position privileged by a rule of notice is one way of attracting attention. In fact, merely being the first-mentioned character in a novel is enough to arouse some expectation—weak, perhaps, but significant—of centrality. Bigger Thomas is mentioned by name twice before any other character is named in *Native Son;* he is also the first character we see. Note also the beginning of Marge Piercy's *High Cost of Living:*

> Leslie was balanced on the hard cushion of an antique chair designed for someone with a three-cornered behind. In front of her, too close, Hennessy straddled a chair backwards and loomed over her, telling loud anecdotes intended as far as she could guess as advertisements. "The minute Ted left the room, she walked over to me and stood there, just looking me up and down. Provocative. I could see she wasn't wearing a bra."[34]

One can reasonably infer from her presence in the novel's first word that Leslie is more likely to be the center of the novel than Hennessy, Ted, or the anonymous "she." The presumption that Leslie is the (or a) main character is supported in several ways: the

33. Suleiman, *Authoritarian Fictions*, 173.
34. Piercy, *The High Cost of Living* (New York: Fawcett, 1978), 7 (chap. 1).

narrator assumes our greater familiarity with her (she is called by her first name, the only other present character by his last), the paragraph describes *her* space (which is being invaded by Hennessy) from her point of view (it is her interpretation of Hennessy's motives that we are given), and Hennessy is so unattractive that an author is unlikely to demand that we keep him company for 288 pages. Similarly, when a novel begins

> I first met her, this girl you'll find soon enough, when she fished me out of the Sacramento River on an occasion when I was showing more originality than sense

—we can reasonably assume that "this girl" will be central to the novel and that the narrator will continue to show more originality than sense.[35]

Thus, while novels may have several main characters, they rarely center on one of them for a long period of time at the beginning and then switch, without preparation, to another—unless the change in focus is intended as an aesthetically significant jolt. Of course, sometimes such shifts *are* prepared for. For more than half of *So Big*, Selina DeJong is the primary character. But both the title and the opening two pages (privileged both) have made it clear that Dirk DeJong is a central subject as well. Thus, when his story eventually takes over from his mother's, we do not feel disoriented. Alice Walker uses a title in much the same way to prepare us for Grange Copeland's centrality in the second half of *The Third Life of Grange Copeland*, even though he has been all but absent from the novel until then. Similarly, *Wuthering Heights* begins with the Cathy II/Hareton generation; this leads the authorial audience to expect that the story it is later told will not stop with Heathcliff and Cathy I, but will continue on to the "present."

When such warnings are not given, disruptions of focus more often than not are used to startle us. In the final scene of Turgenev's *Rudin*, for instance, the protagonist is suddenly seen from a distance as a minor actor on the French barricades in 1848—a shift that underscores Turgenev's criticism of Rudin's presumptuous

35. Cain, *Past All Dishonor* (New York: Knopf, 1946), 1 (chap. 1).

self-importance. But Turgenev's critique only works because we assume the rule of balance to be operative. Without the reader's expectation that Rudin will remain central, his final demotion produces no shock—and without the shock, there is nothing for the reader to interpret as a critique.

Dostoyevsky's *Gambler* violates the rule in a radically different way. While it is quite common for a novel to begin in medias res with regard to its story, this one seems to begin right in the middle of its *narration*. The opening paragraph (as would be appropriate in a real journal) gives us few hints about who is who, or who is important:

> At last I have come back from my fortnight's absence. Our friends have already been two days in Roulettenberg. I imagined they were expecting me with the greatest eagerness; I was mistaken, however. The General had an extremely independent air, he talked to me condescendingly and sent me away to his sister. I even fancied that the General was a little ashamed to look at me. Marya Filippovna was tremendously busy and scarcely spoke to me; she took the money, however, counted it and listened to my whole report. They were expecting Mezentsov, the little Frenchman, and some Englishman; as usual, as soon as there was money there was a dinner party; in the Moscow style. Polina Alexandrovna, seeing me, asked why I had been away so long, and without waiting for an answer went off somewhere. Of course, she did that on purpose. We must have an explanation, though. Things have accumulated.[36]

The authorial audience can perhaps conclude that Polina will be important, but the rest of the cast is a jumble. In fact, some of those mentioned are crucial, others very minor. The effect is disorienting, and unmoors us from the comfort of our world so that we can take in the madness of Alexei's. But Dostoyevsky can create his intended effect only because his authorial audience approaches the novel with expectations about how focus is announced—expectations that he can then fail to fulfill.

Balance works with regard to subject matter as well. Just as we

36. Fyodor Dostoevsky, *The Gambler*, trans. Constance Garnett, in *Great Short Works of Dostoevsky*, ed. Ronald Hingley (New York: Harper and Row/Perennial, 1968), 381 (chap. 1).

usually have ways of knowing, fairly soon, who will be the main characters, so we have ways to tell what a novel is likely to be about. Once again, titles are occasionally clear signals (*War and Peace*; Gladkov's Soviet factory novel, *Cement*), but more usually, the text itself counts on shared conventions to inform us about what its primary subject(s) will be. In a sonata-form movement, an experienced listener can usually tell an introduction from the first subject (although occasionally he or she may be fooled—as in the long introduction to the Tchaikovsky First Piano Concerto); similarly, an experienced reader knows how to tell when a significant subject has arrived in a novel—and expects that once it has arrived, it will remain important. To return to *The High Cost of Living*: the opening points to Leslie as a main character, but it also suggests that sex is likely to be a major topic in the subsequent text. It is not simply that sex is given a privileged position. The authorial audience, reading the opening of James' "Daisy Miller" ("At the little town of Vevey, in Switzerland, there is a particularly comfortable hotel; there are indeed many hotels, since the entertainment of tourists is the business of the place"),[37] is not surprised when the novel does not go on to treat the trials and tribulations of the Swiss tourist industry. Nor does the authorial audience of *The Sound and the Fury* prepare itself, after the first page, to settle into a novel about golf. But sex is an interesting, even titillating, subject, as tourism and golf are not—and when a titillating subject is trumpeted at the beginning of a text, it is reasonable to assume that it will be developed. What counts as interesting, of course, is in part socially determined, and therefore varies with historical and cultural context. On this point, as on so many others, actual audiences may therefore not start out where their authors expect them to. Many actual readers of James Cain's *Career in C Major*, approaching it with expectations developed through reading *The Postman Always Rings Twice*, are probably surprised when opera *does* turn out to be the main subject rather than a mere prelude to bloodier matters. One reason why strict Socialist Realist texts seem virtually unreadable to many contemporary American read-

---

37. Henry James, "Daisy Miller," in *The Novels and Tales of Henry James* (New York: Scribner's, 1909), 3 (chap. 1).

ers, in fact, may well be that their central concerns simply do not seem vital.

Rules of Balance: Action

Rules of balance regarding focus restrict the world that a novel will inhabit; rules of balance regarding action inform us about the *events* that will take place in the book to come. One of the most elementary rules is that it is reasonable to assume that repetitions will be continued until they are in some way blocked. Even very young readers get a sense of delight—of anticipation fulfilled— when the wolf phrases his request the same way ("Little pig, little pig, let me come in") for the third time. On a less literal level, the authorial audience expects the narrator's father in Sherwood Anderson's "Egg" to fail as an "entertainer" in part because he has failed at everything else he has tried to do.

Similarly, readers can usually start with the presumption that diverse strands of action will in some way be linked. In *Farewell, My Lovely*, Philip Marlowe has accidentally gotten entangled in the search for ex-convict Moose Malloy, who is wanted for murder. Suddenly, he is phoned by a stranger named Lindsay Marriott and offered some unspecified work. The authorial audience knows immediately that these two plot lines will eventually merge; the surprise of the book is not in the fact of the interconnection, but rather in its specific nature. Similarly, as Carol Billman points out, even the young readers of Nancy Drew books know that "when two suspenseful plot lines are introduced in the first chapter . . . [they] will eventually intersect."[38] This kind of structure, while especially transparent in detective stories, is found more generally as well. Fredric Jameson may be overstating the case, but he is making a shrewd observation when he argues that "the detective story plot merely follows the basic tendency of all literary plots or intrigue in general, which is marked by the resolution of multiplicity back into some primal unity."[39] Once again, of course, the

38. Billman, "The Child Reader as Sleuth," *Children's Literature in Education* 15, no. 1 (1984): 33.
39. Jameson, "On Raymond Chandler," 648.

rule can be as important in texts that do not fulfill expectations as in those that do. Chester Himes disorients us in *Blind Man with a Pistol* because we keep waiting for the parallel plots to merge; but the effect only works on a reader who knows the rule and builds false expectations on it.

Some rules of action, though, are much more complex than the rules of repetition and parallel. As one example, let me turn to the variations on what I call the other-shoe rule: when one shoe drops, you should expect the other. To put it in musical terms: just as an experienced listener, hearing the opening phrase of the Mozart G Minor Symphony (K. 550), immediately develops expectations about how the second phrase is likely to sound, so when we read novels, we learn to predict what sorts of things are likely to follow from what is first presented. Readers have learned to expect literary events to come in patterns of antecedent and consequent. Obviously, the other-shoe rule often involves notions of cause and effect, and in this way, it is related to the causal rules of signification discussed in Chapter 3. But whereas rules of signification allow us to determine the meaning of an event by moving from the effect to the cause, the other-shoe rule allows us to move in the other direction, to predict the consequences of an event by moving from cause to effect.

One version of the other-shoe rule is that it is generally appropriate to assume that events will produce results—that noticeable events that will not have consequences have probably been left out, unless they are included for their signification value, are inherently amusing, or are intentional red herrings. Like all rules of configuration, this one allows readers to develop a sense of anticipation, one that authors can foster and resolve, or frustrate. Pushkin is able to create a sense of anxiety in *Eugene Onegin* because his authorial audience expects that Eugene's decision to flirt with Lensky's fiancée, Olga, will have serious consequences—we are intended, in other words, to experience Lensky's death in the ensuing duel not as a surprise but as the fulfillment of an evil premonition. Alternatively, this rule can be invoked and not fulfilled in order to surprise. Only if Austen's readers apply this rule can her failure to provide the promised complications have the intended comic effect:

Elfrida had an intimate freind [*sic*] to whom, being on a visit to an Aunt, she wrote the following Letter.

TO MISS DRUMMOND

DEAR CHARLOTTE

I should be obliged to you, if you would buy me, during your stay with Mrs Williamson, a new & fashionable Bonnet, to suit the complexion of your

E. FALKNOR

Charlotte, whose character was a willingness to oblige every one, when she returned into the Country, brought her Freind the wished-for Bonnet, & so ended this little adventure, much to the satisfaction of all parties.[40]

Relationships follow antecedent/consequent patterns, too. As a general rule, we expect that strong attractions and dissonances between major characters in novels will have consequences; the more notice that such attractions and dissonances are given, the stronger our expectations will be. We should be especially alert to relational tensions introduced at the very beginning of a book. From the opening pages of *The Idiot*, we can confidently expect that the sharp contrast between Myshkin and Rogozhin—with its paradoxical overtones of attraction and repulsion—will continue to generate action in the novel, and we achieve a sense of completion when they finally join together in their homoerotic vigil over Nastasya's bed toward the end of the novel.[41] Likewise, at the beginning of *The Virginian*, when the hero forces Trampas to back down after Trampas calls him a "son-of-a _____" (the event eliciting the now-classic line, "When you call me that, *smile*"), we expect the antagonism between them to be resolved in the end, for "a public back-down is an unfinished thing."[42] Similarly, the opening paragraph of *The High Cost of Living* discussed above suggests that the conflict between Leslie and Hennessy (or at least between what they represent in this scene) will bear some of the

40. Jane Austen, "Frederic and Elfrida," in *Minor Works*, ed. R. W. Chapman, rev. B. C. Southam (London: Oxford University Press, 1969), 4–5 (chap. 1).

41. It is significant, though, that the novel does not end with this reconciliation, but rather with the epilogue, including Aglaya's marriage. The effect of that jarring post-resolution will be discussed in Chapter 5.

42. Owen Wister, *The Virginian* (New York: Macmillan, 1902), 29–30 (chap. 2).

weight of the novel that follows. And no experienced reader of *Pride and Prejudice* has difficulty seeing, quite early in the text, that the working out of the relation between Elizabeth and Darcy will be central to the action.

It is not only what people do in novels that sets up the anteced-ent/consequent pattern; it is also what they say. As I suggested above, for instance, it is generally appropriate to assume that warn-ings and promises will be followed up. When Leonard, in Cain's *Career in C Major*, is preparing for his career as an opera singer, his teacher/partner/lover Cecil warns him about "the bird." When Leonard asks her what that is, she replies " 'Something you'll nev-er forget, if you ever hear it.' "[43] Under the circumstances, Cain expects us to read the rest of the book haunted by the fear that Leonard will in fact come to hear the bird. The reader who does not apply the proper rule here—who does not recognize the way that the warning is intended to color our experience of the text—will be unable to share the mounting suspense that lies at the heart of the novel's effect.

Obviously, not all promises made in a text carry equal weight. Those made by minor characters, for instance, are less forceful than those made by major characters; those that promise events that will be significant for the plot—as we suspect it will turn out at the time the promise is made—are more forceful than those which promise something tangential. In the Cain example above, the warning is marked in several ways: It is stated by one of the two central characters, and it is repeated—with a clarification of its potential consequences. When Leonard asks, " 'Suppose they give *me* the bird?' " Cecil replies, " 'Then I'll have to get somebody else.' " Since the romantic relationship between Cecil and Leonard is crucial to the plot, the warning is thus doubly underscored by the repetition. In contrast, the promise made by Mary and Liz in *The High Cost of Living*, when Leslie comes over for dinner, has less impact:

Every plate was different, from rummage sales, and "Everything comes from the land, everything!" except the cheap red wine in gal-

43. Cain, *Career in C Major*, in *Three of a Kind* (Philadelphia: Blakiston, 1944), 36 (chap. 5).

lon jugs. "But we don't see why we can't make our own wine eventually. We have grapes started."[44]

Mary and Liz are minor characters, to whom we have just been introduced; the question of the success or failure of their farm seems irrelevant to the concerns of the story, at least as it has developed so far. The authorial audience does not therefore take their remark to be a strong signal about how to approach the rest of the book.

Maxims often function in the same way that warnings and promises do. Those that are given prominence in a novel—especially when they come toward the beginning—create the expectation that they will be followed up. Some maxims, of course, are explicitly predictive in that they pose a specific link between the present and the future by telling what sorts of events follow from situations like the present one. "A man of tact, intelligence, and superior education moving in the midst of a mass of ignorant people, ofttimes has a sway more absolute than that of monarchs."[45] But even maxims that do not explicitly promise consequences of present situations can often be appropriately treated as predictive if they are neither justifications for actions that have just taken place nor guides to signification. Take the following:

"It is a law of nature that we overlook, that intellectual versatility is the compensation for change, danger, and trouble. . . . Nature never appeals to intelligence until habit and instinct are useless. There is no intelligence where there is no change and no need of change. Only those animals partake of intelligence that have to meet a huge variety of needs and dangers."[46]

Or,

"Let me tell you this, as you don't seem to know it. The two go-getting things in this white man's civilization are force and cunning.

44. Piercy, *High Cost,* 120.
45. Sutton E. Griggs, *Imperium in Imperio* (New York: Arno/New York Times, 1969), 7 (chap. 1).
46. Wells, *Time Machine,* 65.

136

When you have force or power you make people do things. When you haven't you use cunning."[47]

On the surface, they appear to be simply expressions of general truths rather than promises. But because of the conventional way in which such maxims are used in novels, it is appropriate to treat them as promises—that is, as promises that the truths they proclaim will be exemplified as the novel progresses.

This is how the authorial audience treats the wisdom passed on to Selina in the first chapter of *So Big*, by her father, right before he dies (what more privileged position?): " 'There are only two kinds of people in the world that really count,' " he tells her. " 'One kind's wheat and the other kind's emeralds.' "[48] Obviously, the reader is intended to experience a sense of resolution when the maxim turns out to sum up the text at its recapitulation near the book's end. But that experience is not built into the text itself; it is available only to the reader who applies previously learned rules of configuration at the maxim's first appearance, and thus activates the expectations that the novel finally fulfills.

Tasks and questions operate in a similar way. It is generally reasonable to expect important questions to be answered and major tasks to be confronted, although (at least in nineteenth- and twentieth-century novels) failure to *fulfill* the task is more common than failure to answer questions. Assumptions that these rules operate is one of the necessary conditions to responding as intended, in particular to detective fiction. In one of the Encyclopedia Brown stories, for instance, we are told that a warning note has been typed on a piece of paper with "The quick brown fox" typed on the other side. In the real world, one can infer virtually nothing from this fact. But since this is a story in which a definite solution is promised, we are entitled to assume that something *can* be inferred. Thus, we look at the clue not to ask, "What does this tell us?" but rather, "Since this is guaranteed to tell us something definite, what could that something definite be?" It is

47. Claude McKay, *Banjo: A Story without a Plot* (New York: Harcourt Brace Jovanovich/Harvest, 1957), 241 (chap. 19).
48. Ferber, *So Big*, 7 (chap. 1).

only in this very limited conventional context that the reader can conclude that the writer of the note had recently bought a new typewriter or repaired an old one.[49]

Antecedents and consequents can work in reverse, as well. If a strange event is narrated, it is normally a signal for the narrative audience to look forward to an explanation of its causes. This is different from rules of signification regarding cause; in those cases, we *assume* the causal connections that are not given. In these configurative cases, in contrast, we do not have the necessary information to determine causes on our own; we thus wait for the text to tell us the causes. A familiar form is the let-me-tell-you-why configurations found, for instance, in Pushkin's "Shot" (from the *Belkin Tales*) and Kuprin's "Idiot." In the latter, the narrator is surprised by Zimina's compassion toward an idiot stranger: "To tell the truth, I shouldn't have expected from him such sincere compassion towards a stranger's misfortune." This leads to a story: " 'If you'll allow me,' " says Zimina, " 'I'll tell you why the sight of an idiot moves me to such compassion.' "[50]

Applying the other-shoe rule and its variants is not without its difficulties, however—for what constitutes a dropped shoe depends on history and culture. In the nineteenth century, colds were not the minor inconvenience that they usually are today; getting soaked in the rain therefore had more serious consequences. The contemporary reader who is not attuned to that historical difference is apt to be more surprised by the lengthy illnesses of Jane Bennet and Mr. Lockwood than Austen and Brontë intended. Similarly, sexual relations between unmarried people implied a set of consequences in the nineteenth century (one thinks of Lydia and Wickham) that they no longer do. It may be poignant when Philip Marlowe and Linda Loring part simply as friends after their night together in Chandler's *Long Goodbye*, but it is neither shocking nor scandalous, and the authorial audience does not expect them to be punished in some way for their actions.[51] Once again, learn-

49. Donald J. Sobol, "The Case of the Litterbugs," in *The Case of the Exploding Plumbing and Other Mysteries* (New York: Scholastic, 1978), 40–45, 70.

50. Alexander Kuprin, "The Idiot," in *A Slav Soul and Other Stories*, trans. Mr. and Mrs. Stephen Graham (London: Constable, 1916), 39–40.

51. They do get married after *Playback*, but I doubt that that outcome was foreseen by Chandler when he wrote *The Long Goodbye*, and it certainly has no impact on the way the authorial audience reads the novel.

ing to read authorially involves learning historical and cultural norms.

Correct application of the other-shoe rule depends on our understanding of genre as well. Virtually any event or statement can imply some consequences; authorial reading involves the ability to sort out those for which the consequences are likely to be vital in the text. To a large extent, this comes about through rules of notice: the important antecedents will usually be marked. But we also need to know what sorts of things are appropriate in what sorts of works: antecedents are often noticed *because* they have the potential to lead to consequences that the genre requires.

Indeed, the whole notion of cause and effect in literature is radically genre bound. What is relevant to our ability to foresee textual turns is less our knowledge of what certain conditions lead to in reality than our knowledge of what they lead to in the kind of novel in which they are appearing. Antagonism is probably not, in fact, the most fertile breeding ground for true love, but it is the only breeding ground in at least one variant of the popular romance. Take, similarly, our ability to foresee the climax of John D. MacDonald's *Girl in the Plain Brown Wrapper*. Maureen Pearson Pike has apparently tried to commit suicide three times in three different ways (pills, slit wrists, hanging). It does not matter whether such a series of attempts is really psychologically possible. What matters is that Travis McGee has informed us, with scientific authority, that suicides rarely try to kill themselves even in two different ways, and in this genre, as I have noted, such absolute statements by the narrator are to be treated as true. This, in turn, leads us to believe that someone is really trying to murder her—not because, in reality, that is the usual cause of fishy suicides, but because in this genre, anything that looks murder related should be treated as such. Furthermore, we suspect her husband, a man who has accumulated considerable wealth through somewhat questionable real estate deals. Again, this is not because of anything in reality, but because of a rule of ethical enchainment that applies to Travis McGee novels: People who engage in shady financial transactions are to be treated as capable of murder. (This is one of those cases where signification and configuration merge: our sense of the character's ethics is really a matter of our expectations of what sorts of actions he or she is likely to perform.) When it is hinted that maybe a jump will be next, we take it seriously; when we find out that there is to be an opening at her husband's new office on the top of " 'that big new building at the corner of Grove Boulevard and Lake Street? Twelve stories? Lots of windows?' "— then the authorial audience treats it as a signal from the author to approach that event with trepidation.[52] In fact, if we know the genre well enough, we can even guess that McGee's race to the opening will not be fast enough to save her—the novel needs a mangled body more than it needs a heroic rescue.

In "Literature in the Reader: Affective Stylistics," Stanley Fish argues that the reader's experience (what *"happens* to, and with the participation of, the reader") is "the *meaning"* of a text.[53] To a large extent he is right, and although he does not use my terminology, his analyses show how this meaning is radically dependent on the reader making predictions about the text using rules of configuration. The reader he posits, to be sure, has such a limited repertoire of rules of configuration that he or she has a fairly limited set of responses. As I noted earlier, the effect of anticipation is for Fish—at least, in this essay—almost always the shock of surprise. With a stronger understanding of configuration, of course, a reader may have a fuller set of textual responses—but in any case, the moment-to-moment curve of the text is "meaningful" as an aesthetic experience only in the context of *some* rules of configuration, and it can only be the curve that the author intended in the context of those rules expected of the authorial audience.

Still, this is not the only kind of meaning that texts have. After we have finished them, we tend to think about them retroactively, reshaping them in the process. This activity opens up a different kind of literary form and calls upon the last set of rules—rules of coherence.

52. MacDonald, *The Girl in the Plain Brown Wrapper* (New York: Fawcett, 1968), 155.
53. Fish, *Is There a Text?* 25.

5

The Austere Simplicity of Fiction: Rules of Coherence

"I've lost my faith in pure coincidence. Everything in life tends to hang together in a pattern."

Ross Macdonald, *Black Money*

The Nature of Coherence

Coherence (or its frequent surrogate, unity) has held a high rank in the critical court—especially during the 1940s and 1950s, when New Criticism dominated American academic practice. As Cleanth Brooks puts it, "The primary concern of criticism is with the problem of unity—the kind of whole which the literary work forms or fails to form, and the relation of the various parts to each other in building up this whole."[1] Or, as he and Robert Penn Warren put it when writing specifically about fiction, "Successful fiction always involves a coherent relating of action, character, and meaning. . . . Most of the failures in fiction could be stated as failures in coherence."[2] Similarly, for Murray Krieger, "The object whose creation the poet supervises wants above all to be one, a unified and complete whole."[3] And despite our current romance with theory (in particular, with deconstruction), the majority of critical work being done today still aims at setting out the basic coherence of literary works, their "unity" or "basic pattern" or "overarching meaning."

1. Brooks, "My Credo," 72.
2. Brooks and Warren, *Understanding Fiction*, 27. See also Brooks' claim that bad poetry is "chaotic and incoherent," whereas a good poem has "coherence of statement" and "unity of style" (*Well Wrought Urn*, 256, 76, 251).
3. Krieger, *Theory of Criticism*, 32.

True, like *form, coherence* has been difficult to define, in part because it occurs along so many literary axes. At times, coherence is defined as a formal relation among elements in the text itself; that is how Culler, for instance, sees it when he lists "the binary opposition, the dialectical resolution of a binary opposition, [and] the displacement of an unresolved opposition by a third term" among the basic types of unity.[4] Alternatively, coherence can be treated as a quality of the vision of the poet or of the world he or she describes. This seems to be what is happening when Eliot claims that if a poem is to interpose "no obstacle to the reader's enjoyment," it needs to present a view of the world that "the mind of the reader can accept as coherent, mature, and founded on the facts of experience."[5] Sometimes, the term is used in more restricted ways, as when Seymour Chatman uses it to refer to consistency of reference: "Another restriction on selection and inference is *coherence*. Narrative existents must remain the same from one event to the next. If they do not, some explanation (covert or overt) must occur. If we have a story like 'Peter fell ill. Peter died. Peter was buried,' we assume that it is the same Peter in each case."[6]

Coherence not only means different things to different critics. To complicate matters, coherence as an aesthetic category is even more strongly colored by ideological overtones than notice, signification, and configuration. Of course, other literary conventions have ideological aspects as well. Rules of ethical enchainment, for instance, make sense in so-called realistic texts only if the reader begins with an assumption about the integrity of the human personality. But the ideological pull on coherence is greater than that on other types of convention. Indeed, to read the discourse of the New Critics, one sometimes wonders whether coherence is an aesthetic attribute at all. Although that discourse is often framed as a defense of ambiguity, in fact the New Critics had a limited tolerance for conflict and uncertainty. They tended to treat ambiguity not as an end in itself (that is, neither as a goal nor as a last

---

4. Jonathan Culler, *Structuralist Poetics*, 174.
5. T. S. Eliot, *Use of Poetry*, 87.
6. Chatman, *Story and Discourse*, 30.

step), but rather as an obstacle eventually to be overcome through resolution. Thus, for all their praise of irony, Brooks and Warren, in *Understanding Fiction*, reject any irony that "preclude[s]" resolution, for such irony leads to "smug and futile skepticism." Instead, they stand for an irony that "force[s] the resolution to take stock of as full a context as possible."[7]

This insistence on resolution has its analogue in Brooks and Warren's views of human experience more generally. For many writers, from Aristotle on, the coherence of art is what separates it from life: "It was a little too pat," notes Philip Marlowe in *The Big Sleep*. "It had the austere simplicity of fiction rather than the tangled woof of fact."[8] But for the New Critics, coherence seems to be what *binds* art and life. Brooks puts it in cosmic terms: "Man's experience is indeed a seamless garment, no part of which can be separated from the rest."[9] But this almost metaphysical claim has social variants, too. The stress on conflict/resolution, for instance, privileges certain kinds of political values through its implicit appreciation of compromise. The New Critics' vision of coherence has psychological implications as well, especially in their discussion of fiction. According to *Understanding Fiction*, the very definition of fiction demands an acceptance of a common sense understanding of "human nature"—common sense, in this case, validating a bourgeois conception of the individual. The New Critics insist that "thoughts and actions must ultimately be coherent."[10] More broadly, "the domain of fiction is . . . the world of credible human beings. . . . What it excludes at either end is the world of pure abstraction: economic man, Mrs. Average Housewife, the typical American, *homo sapiens*; and at the other extreme, the mere freak, the psychological monster, the report from the psychiatrist's casebook."[11] New Critical discourse, furthermore, naturalizes this notion of the individual—that is, presents it

---

7. Brooks and Warren, *Understanding Fiction*, xix. See also Mark Schorer on the ambiguity of *Sons and Lovers* ("Technique as Discovery," in *Essays in Modern Literary Criticism*, ed. Ray B. West [New York: Rinehart, 1952], 197–98).

8. Raymond Chandler, *The Big Sleep* (New York: Pocket, 1950), 157 (chap. 25).

9. Brooks, "My Credo," 74.

10. Brooks and Warren, *Understanding Fiction*, 173.

11. Ibid., 170.

as if it were coextensive with human experience in general. "Our judgment of probability and our notion of credibility in general are based firmly upon the way in which *the human mind* works and upon the experience that we have had as human beings" (emphasis added).[12] It is therefore not accidental that in the New Critical view of fiction, the individual receives more stress than the social.

Thus, as I suggested in my Introduction, when New Critics discuss coherence, they are often judging a work's content as much as its structure. For example, in explaining why an anecdote related by Francis Parkman does not count as fiction, Brooks and Warren end up criticizing not the structure of the episode, but its content—specifically, the view it offers of human character. Parkman's point, they claim, is "to show that the characters of the plainsmen do not fit the 'standard rules of character' which are accepted in more civilized societies. He is merely using the episode as a sociological example." To make the episode fiction, they imply, an author would not only have to "develop . . . the character of Beckworth (which is exactly what Parkman does not do)" but would also have to arrive at a *different conclusion*, such as that "individuals cannot be judged by rule of thumb; every individual character is unique and has mixtures of good and evil in it."[13]

Coherence, then, often serves as a vehicle by which ideological biases are smuggled into literary discussions disguised as objective aesthetic qualities. Beyond that, the very claim that coherence is valued turns out, in practice, to be paradoxical. Recent reader criticism is making increasingly clear that when critics discuss coherence, their true subject is less a quality in the text or the author than an activity on the part of the readers (or, more particularly, their public representatives, literary critics)—what Susan Horton has aptly called "the critic's rage to pattern."[14]

At first, the distinction between coherence as a textual property

12. Ibid., 27.
13. Ibid., 24.
14. Horton, *Interpreting Interpreting*, 40. Culler similarly claims that the unity of texts "is produced not so much by intrinsic features of their parts as by the intent at totality of the interpretive process: the strength of the expectations which lead readers to look for certain forms of organization in a text and to find them" (*Structuralist Poetics*, 91). See also Wolfgang Iser's notion of "consistency-building" in *The Act of Reading*, esp. 118–25.

and making coherent as a critical activity may seem simply another front along which the objectivists and subjectivists (or formalists and reader critics) continue their endless skirmishes. Perhaps it is. Yet it is an especially important area of conflict with serious implications for the process of canonization. For works differ markedly in the degree of activity they require in order to be made coherent.

On the one hand, to return to the text-as-swing-set metaphor of Chapter 1, we have essentially preassembled texts, where all that is left for the reader is grabbing on to the trapeze. These are the most extreme examples of what Roland Barthes calls "readerly texts" (*textes lisibles*)[15]—Harlequin Romances and Horatio Alger novels, for instance. Here, the rules of notice, signification, and (especially) configuration are working well. There seem to be no extraneous details or complicated symbolic patterns; their endings easily and completely satisfy the desires and expectations aroused at their beginnings. They thus require no special rules of coherence—and no special effort—for the reader to make sense of them. For just as rules of notice presuppose that not all things are equally important, so rules of coherence presuppose that a work is not apparently coherent—that there are some surface incoherences that need to be explained in some way, or at least made the subject of our critical discourse. But these preassembled texts lack such surface ruptures; to their authorial audiences, they appear coherent simply on their face. Often, in fact, their coherence is explicitly trumpeted. Alexander Kuprin's story about a servant named Yasha, for instance, tells us point-blank how we should make sense out of Yasha's apparent inconsistencies. The last paragraph reads:

> And now that I am nearly what may be called an old man, I go over my varied recollections now and then, and when I come to the thought of Yasha, every time I say to myself: "What a strange soul—faithful, pure, contradictory, absurd—and great. Was it not a truly Slav soul that dwelt in the body of Yasha?"[16]

15. Barthes, *S/Z*, 4.
16. Alexander Kuprin, "A Slav Soul," in *A Slav Soul and Other Stories*, trans. Mr. and Mrs. Stephen Graham (London: Constable, 1916), 13.

Entitling the story "A Slav Soul" only binds its elements together more tightly. It is significant that such texts are rarely taken seriously in current academic critical discussion.

Other texts, in contrast, are completely incoherent. These are the swing sets that arrive without the proper screws, with mismeasured poles and warped seats. In the end, their inconsistencies are unmanageable, and there seems no sense to their structures or to their systems of signification. Such works are rarely the subject of critical discussion either. For the most part they remain unpublished—a sign that literature maintains higher quality control than many other industries.

But between these lies a third category of works: works that leave us baffled and confused until we apply the proper procedures to them—works that are just pieces of wood and rope until we find the proper assembly techniques and apply the proper effort.

Now if coherence itself were really viewed as a literary virtue, it would be the first type of text that received the greatest critical praise; in practice, however, the academy has by and large come to privilege the third, taking members of the first group seriously only when it is possible to prove that their true coherence is not the coherence that appears at first glance. Thus, while Brooks and Warren insist that a good story should "convey a definite 'point,' a definite idea or meaning," they hasten to add that it need not be (and rarely is) expressed explicitly.[17]

Of course, not all reading communities share this preference for the not-yet-coherent. Contemporary readers of romances probably do not; nor, in all probability, did Homer's original audience. But at least the contemporary academic critical community seems to have adopted Barbara Herrnstein Smith's principle that "art inhabits the country between chaos and cliché."[18] Whatever is said in critical pronouncements, the academy puts high value not on coherence per se, but rather on the activity of applying rules of coherence to works that are not evidently unified, but that can be made so through critical manipulation.

Behind the valorizing of coherence, then, lies a preference for

17. Brooks and Warren, *Understanding Fiction*, 23.
18. Smith, *Poetic Closure*, 14.

works with disjunctures, with at least some surface ruptures and
inconsistencies. This preference is just as strong in New Criticism
as it is in post-structuralism. The two critical camps may be moving in opposite directions, the former trying to smooth over the
gaps, the latter trying to widen them; but their differing critical
activities tend to be nourished in the same literary soil. This is
why post-structuralism, in contrast to feminism, has not led to any
fundamental shift in the canon, even though it may shuffle the
respective rankings of particular writers.[19]

In arguing that coherence is more usefully discussed as an activity by readers rather than a property of texts, I am not arguing
that the coherence that results is unintended by the author. The
conventions by which we make novels coherent can, like other
literary conventions, be shared; and writers can plan their effects
with the understanding that these rules of coherence will be applied. The gaps found in texts, in other words, are not necessarily
either errors or even ambiguities—they may well be intended as
opportunities for us to apply rules of coherence in some guided
fashion. In fact, as we shall see, this is often one of the strongest
ways an author can express his or her meaning.

We can find those intended meanings, though, only if we assume
that they are there. Indeed, the fundamental rule of coherence is
parallel to the second metarule of configuration: We assume, to
begin with, that the work *is* coherent and that apparent flaws in its
construction are intentional and meaning bearing. As Northrop
Frye puts it, "The primary understanding of any work of literature
has to be based on an assumption of its unity. However mistaken
such an assumption may eventually prove to be, nothing can be
done unless we start with it as a heuristic principle."[20]

Rules of coherence are invoked whenever a text appears to resist
such an assumption. I shall examine three sets of them, corre-

19. Culler has a different explanation of deconstruction's tendency to center on
canonical texts; see *On Deconstruction*, 280.

20. Frye, "Literary Criticism," in *The Aims and Methods of Scholarship in Modern Languages and Literatures*, ed. James Thorpe (New York: Modern Language
Association, 1963), 63. See also Gary Saul Morson: "To take a verbal text as a
literary work . . . is to assume in principle (1) that everything in the text is potentially relevant to its design, and (2) that the design is complete in the text that we
have" (*Boundaries of Genre*, 41).

sponding to three ways in which texts can appear to be incoherent.[21] First, texts can be insufficient—that is, they can be apparently incoherent because of gaps in their fabric, holes that need to be filled in. Second, works can be overabundant—they can have a surplus of information that we need somehow to tame, including details that seem to contradict one another and that we need to reconcile. Finally, works can be simply disparate—and we need rules to help us bundle them together into convenient packages. These categories, to be sure, are rough—and it is not always clear whether a particular activity by a reader responds to one kind of apparent incoherence or another. Nonetheless, this classification provides us with a preliminary scaffolding for discussing some of the activities by which readers make works coherent. Let us look at each of these situations in turn.

License to Fill

Miss Binney stood in front of her class and began to read aloud from *Mike Mulligan and His Steam Shovel. . . .* [Ramona] listened quietly with the rest of the kindergarten to the story of Mike Mulligan's old-fashioned steam shovel, which proved its worth by digging the basement for the new town hall of Poppersville in a single day. . . .

"Miss Binney . . . —how did Mike Mulligan go to the bathroom when he was digging the basement of the town hall?"

Miss Binney's smile seemed to last longer than smiles usually last. Ramona glanced uneasily around and saw that others were waiting with interest for the answer. . . .

"Well—" said Miss Binney at last. "I don't really know, Ramona. The book doesn't tell us. . . . The reason the book does not tell us . . . is that it is not an important part of the story. The story is about digging the basement of the town hall, and that is what the book tells us."[22]

---

21. For a different classification of the processes for making texts coherent, see Mary Louise Pratt, *Toward a Speech Act Theory*. Pratt has been especially successful in working out the ways that assumptions of unity govern reading activities.

22. Beverly Cleary, *Ramona the Pest* (New York: Dell, 1982), 22–24.

No work of literature can tell us everything that the characters do or think; instead, selected moments, thoughts, and events are flashed on the page. Chekhov's "Grasshopper," for instance, starts with the wedding of Olga Ivanovna and Dymov, followed by a general description of their life as newlyweds. But chapter 3 jumps to Whitmonday, chapter 4 to an evening in July, chapter 5 to September 2, and chapters 6 and 7 take place the next winter. How do we know what is going on in the interstices?

Perhaps the most common procedure for dealing with such holes is to assume, with Miss Binney, that "the reason the book does not tell us . . . is that it is not an important part of the story." Miss Binney is certainly correct that authors often leave out what is unimportant; one of the reasons actual readers interpret and evaluate texts differently is that their perspectives on what is important differ:

> Miss Binney spoke as if this explanation ended the matter, but the kindergarten was not convinced. Ramona knew and the rest of the class knew that knowing how to go to the bathroom *was* important. They were surprised that Miss Binney did not understand, because she had showed them the bathroom the very first thing. Ramona could see there were some things she was not going to learn in school, and along with the rest of the class she stared reproachfully at Miss Binney.[23]

But the Chekhov example cited above suggests that Miss Binney's claim is not universally true, even for authorial readers. Despite her arguments, and despite the claims of such critics as Robert Champigny ("In the case of a piece of fiction . . . filling gaps would amount to creating another fictional world"),[24] there are many works of fiction where important events *do* occur in textual lacunae. One may think at first of classical detective stories, which ask the reader to use information at his or her disposal to close the crucial gap and figure out who done it. Such stories, though, while

23. Ibid., 24–25.
24. He continues: "One of the differences between fictional individuals and 'real' individuals is that a character cannot be assumed to exist outside what the text says about him" (Champigny, *What Will Have Happened*, 20). Champigny qualifies this position later in his text.

they may allow an opportunity to play with rules of coherence, do not finally depend on them, for they traditionally end with explicit solutions for those readers who have not been able to fill in the gaps on their own. In fact, the pleasure of the text in detective stories resides primarily in the reader's *inability* to figure out what has happened until told. More to the point is the early work of Robbe-Grillet where he takes his cue from this genre, but radicalizes it in a fundamental way. The solution to the mystery is never explicitly given in *The Erasers*, and the plot of *The Voyeur* centers around a blank moment in the middle of the text that the reader has to fill in on his or her own.

But it is not only avant-garde novelists who demand that their readers fill in the blanks.[25] Although the rape of Clarissa occurs between two chapters, Richardson assumes that we will be able to extrapolate from what we are told, logically and readily. Tolstoy leaves unarticulated the crucial part of a conversation between Dolly and Anna, expecting his readers to be able to peer behind his ellipsis:

> "I shall not have any more children."
> "How do you know you won't?"
> "I shan't, because I don't want them."
> And in spite of her agitation Anna smiled on noticing the naive expression of curiosity, surprise and terror on Dolly's face.
> "After my illness the doctor told me . . ."
> . . . . . .
> "Impossible!" said Dolly, with wide-open eyes. To her this was one of those discoveries which leads to consequences and deductions so enormous that at the first moment one only feels that it is impossible to take it all in, but that one will have to think it over again and again. [Ellipsis in original][26]

25. Indeed, Iser would argue that such gap filling is characteristic of *any* real literary text. See, for instance, *The Implied Reader.* See also Stanley Fish's attack on Iser's position, "Why No One's Afraid of Wolfgang Iser," *Diacritics* 11 (Spring 1981): 2–13. Fish's objections might seem to apply to my arguments, too, but they dissolve when the distinction between authorial and actual readers is taken into account.

26. Leo Tolstoy, *Anna Karenina*, trans. Louise Maude and Aylmer Maude (New York: Norton, 1970), 577 (pt. 6, chap. 23).

In such cases, what rules permit us to fill in the blanks as the author intended?

First, there is a general rule of inertia. Although rules of configuration lead us to expect that inertial situations will not last indefinitely, we generally expect their undermining to be noted explicitly in the text. Thus we assume, unless we are given reason to believe otherwise, that events in the blank spots continue along the same path as the events preceding them. Since the affair between Olga Ivanovna and Ryabovsky in "The Grasshopper" is more stormy than sweet, therefore, we assume—in the absence of evidence to the contrary—that the same hostilities and recriminations and ambivalences continue in the gap between chapters 5 and 6. Similarly, in Harriet E. Wilson's *Our Nig,* two years pass between chapter 3 (when Fredo is delivered to the Bellmonts and first discovers the virtual slavery in which she is to be held) and chapter 4. The authorial audience is not intended to think that nothing important has taken place; rather, we are expected to assume that the important events have been repetitions of the beatings and degradation that we have already witnessed.

Even when events change course within textual gaps, the authorial audience can usually make correct inferences by applying the realism rule discussed in Chapter 3. Every literary text, as I've argued, depends on areas of congruence between the narrative and authorial audiences. As Seymour Chatman puts it, "We assume that a character has the requisite numbers of eyes, ears, arms, hands, fingers, and toes unless we are informed to the contrary."[27] And narrative gaps can be filled through reliance on the authorial audience's assumptions about the way things are. Thus, to cite Mary Pratt, "If we are not told how a character got from point A to

---

27. Chatman, "Towards a Theory of Narrative," *New Literary History* 6 (Winter 1975): 304. Chatman's argument shows some of the ways in which problematic assumptions about the world may lie behind interpretive inferences: "If a girl is portrayed as 'blue-eyed,' 'blond,' and 'graceful,' we may assume further that her skin is fair and unblemished, that she speaks in a gentle voice, that her feet are relatively small, and so on. (The facts, of course may be other, but we have to be told so, and our inferential capacity remains undaunted. Indeed, we go on to infer a variety of details to account for the 'discrepancy,' too)" (304–5). This passage was revised when it appeared in *Story and Discourse,* 29.

point B, we assume he did so in some normal and untellable [that is, usual or unproblematic] way."[28] When an author, for instance, finishes one chapter at night, with the sentence, "I needed a drink badly and the bars were closed," and begins the next with the sentence, "I got up at nine, drank three cups of black coffee . . . ," we can reasonably assume (unless we are given reason to believe otherwise) that the narrator has spent most of the intervening time drinking alone in his apartment.[29] Jane Austen plays with this rule for comic effect in *Mansfield Park*. After the novel's complications are resolved, and Edmund is finally on the verge of realizing that he is in love with Fanny, she writes:

> I purposely abstain from dates on this occasion, that every one may be at liberty to fix their own, aware that the cure of unconquerable passions, and the transfer of unchanging attachments, must vary much as to time in different people.—I only intreat every body to believe that exactly at the time when it was quite natural that it should be so, and not a week earlier, Edmund did cease to care about Miss Crawford, and became as anxious to marry Fanny, as Fanny herself could desire.[30]

In particular, the realism rule allows us to fill in gaps through cause and effect; unless signaled otherwise, we assume that gaps contain those events that are most likely to produce the effects that we see in the events that are explicitly narrated. In *The Postman Always Rings Twice*, the idea of the murder is at first posed implicitly—but when Frank says, " 'They hang you for

---

28. Pratt, *Toward a Speech Act Theory*, 158.

29. Raymond Chandler, *Farewell, My Lovely* (New York: Pocket, 1943), 65 (chaps. 12–13).

30. Austen, *Mansfield Park*, ed. R. W. Chapman, 3d ed. (London: Oxford University Press, 1932), 470 (vol. 3, chap. 17). Note a similar gesture in *Tom Jones:* "The reader will be pleased to remember that . . . we gave him a hint of our intention to pass over several large periods of time, in which nothing happened worthy of being recorded in a chronicle of this kind.

"In so doing . . . we give him . . . an opportunity of employing that wonderful sagacity, of which he is master, of filling up these vacant spaces of time with his own conjectures; for which purpose we have taken care to qualify him in the preceding pages" (Henry Fielding, *Tom Jones* [New York: Modern Library, n.d.], 74 [bk. 3, chap. 1]).

that,'" the authorial audience can readily determine the subject of their plans, for only thoughts of murder could elicit that response.[31] We are expected to make a similar interpretive move in Southworth's *Allworth Abbey*. The happy marriage between Hollis Elverton and Athenie de la Compte has been broken asunder by a visit from a mysterious stranger, which for unexplained reasons forces Elverton to abandon his wife and child, Alma. The mother turns against her daughter, who grows up virtually alone. When Athenie discovers that Alma is planning to marry Norham Montrose, she tells her that such a marriage—indeed, that love and marriage, period—is impossible. Yet at first, she will not tell her why. She only tells her "'what the objection is *not*'": that Montrose's birth, position, and character are all exemplary, that there is no feud between the families, that her parents loved each other and lived happily "'up to that fatal evening,'" that neither had had a previous marriage that separated them. Finally, Athenie tells Alma that her "'parents' marriage proved the most awful calamity that could have crushed any two human beings,'" that Alma's birth was "'a curse to Hollis Elverton—a curse to me, and deeper still, a curse to you,'" and that she is "'not flesh and blood as others! but something set apart, accursed, that must not join heart or hand with any other human being.'" None of this makes sense to Alma, so finally Mrs. Elverton "whispered in her ear." We do not hear her explanation of the mystery, but we do see Alma's reaction:

> Alma sprang to her feet, gazed with dilated eyes and blanched cheeks in bewildering despair upon her mother's face, as though unable to receive at once the full horror of her words, and then drew her hands wildly to her head, reeled forward and fell senseless to the floor.

Yet while Southworth refrains from telling us explicitly what the secret is, she certainly expects that her reader will, from the effects that have been produced, be able to infer that we are dealing with a case of incest. Indeed, the surprise twist of the plot is not the discovery that the relation between the Elvertons was incestuous, but the final revelation that it in fact was not—a revelation that

31. James M. Cain, *The Postman Always Rings Twice,* in *Cain × 3* (New York: Knopf, 1969), 13 (chap. 3).

produces the intended effect only if the reader has previously concluded that incest *was* involved.[32]

Rules of Surplus

Novels not only leave gaps that we need to fill in; they also, on occasion, provide a surfeit—give notice to too much information. In the easiest cases, that information is simply unnecessary or extraneous. As a general rule, especially when we are dealing with the canonical texts of the Western tradition, we are not expected to assume that such extraneous information results from authorial oversight (like the unexplained death of the chauffeur, Owen Taylor, in *The Big Sleep*). Instead, unless there is evidence to the contrary, we are intended to assume that the surplus is intentional and that we are supposed to interpret it in one way or another, transforming the text so that it is no longer excessive.

More specifically, when notice is given to apparently irrelevant textual features—features that do not contribute to plot or characterization, for instance, or that do not serve some immediate function, like the provision of verisimilitude or local color—then they are to be treated as figurative. The repeated descriptions of the sign advertising Dr. Eckleburg—like the repeated description of the green light at the end of the Buchanans' dock—are thus legitimately treated as metaphors in *The Great Gatsby*, although there would be less justification for so doing if they did not have as much notice as they do. Similarly, while the description of Vevey at the beginning of "Daisy Miller" makes sense as local color—as a setting—the famous description of the turtle crossing the road in the third chapter of Steinbeck's *Grapes of Wrath* does not, and must therefore be treated symbolically. More specifically, the authorial audience assumes a kind of parallelism—that the journey of the turtle is intended, in some way, to reflect on the journeys of the characters in the book.

Surplus can be more difficult to manage, however, when it in-

---

32. Emma D. E. N. Southworth, *Allworth Abbey; or, Eudora* (New York: Hurst, 1876), 274–78 (chap. 20).

volves *contradictory* information. In *Othello*, the Moor offers two different histories for the crucial handkerchief. When talking to Desdemona (act 3, scene 4), he tells her that it was given to his mother by an Egyptian charmer; in the climactic scene of the play, he tells Iago and Emilia that it was "an antique token/My father gave my mother" (act 5, scene 2). This is extra information with a vengeance; how are we to account for the discrepancy?

The most general rule in such cases is "trust the last." If, for instance, a text proffers a series of variations on the same story (as, say, *Absalom, Absalom!* and Anthony Berkeley's *Poisoned Chocolates Case* do), we are generally to accept the final version, rather than one in the middle, as the "correct" one. In part, this ties in with the rule of notice that endings are privileged—for, given the weight our culture puts on truth, that which gets the greatest attention in a text is most likely to be construed as true. It is for this reason that John Fowles realized the futility of giving *The French Lieutenant's Woman* its double ending: "I cannot give both versions at once, yet whichever is the second will seem, so strong is the tyranny of the last chapter, the final, the 'real' version."[33] The trust-the-last rule also fits neatly with a common configuration, what Culler calls "the *pattern of alethic reversal:* first a false or inadequate vision, then its true or adequate counterpart."[34] To put it otherwise, while nineteenth- and twentieth-century narratives on the whole tend to move from the familiar to the unfamiliar, the unfamiliar tends to be increasingly understood.

To be sure, many narratives—*Heart of Darkness* comes readily to mind—move from clarity to ambiguity; but even here, the ambiguity that Marlow confronts is intended to be taken as a truer vision than the false clarity at the beginning of the text. Intellectually, therefore, such narratives generally move from darkness to light, even if they move temperamentally into gloom; in the Western realistic tradition, characters are more likely to be correct after undergoing experiences worthy of narration than before them. Susan Suleiman points out that in the *roman à thèse*, it is unlikely

33. John Fowles, *The French Lieutenant's Woman* (New York: NAL/Signet, 1970), 318 (chap. 55).
34. Culler, *Pursuit of Signs*, 69 (italics in original).

"that a positive apprenticeship will be followed by its opposite. Once the truth has been found, it is inadmissible, in the 'exemplary' world of the *roman à thèse,* that it will be abandoned in favor of error."[35] But this is also generally true of most other nineteenth- and twentieth-century narrative genres where discovering the truth is an issue. Thus Emma Woodhouse's final perception of herself—her recognition of her snobbish and meddlesome nature, her altered views on marriage and her relation to Mr. Knightley— is to be considered by the reader as wiser and more understanding than those views she holds at the beginning of the book.

As with most other rules of reading, though, the proper application of the trust-the-last rule is radically bound up with genre. Although most genres do incorporate this rule, there are types of novels that move in the opposite direction—novels in which characters lose their grip on the truth, move backward in terms of self-awareness. An extreme case is Orwell's *1984:* surely, we are not expected to take Winston's final vision ("But it was all right, everything was all right, the struggle was finished. He had won the victory over himself")[36] as correct. But while extreme, *1984* merely exemplifies what we see in certain other texts. Indeed, many novels centering on characters who sell out (Balzac's *Père Goriot*), go mad (Dostoyevsky's *Gambler,* Robbe-Grillet's *Jealousy*), or fall prey to vice and degradation (*Madame Bovary*) operate in a different way. Such exceptions, though, are usually signaled, for in most of them, there is a strong disassociation of the voices and values of author and narrator (or main character). And we are generally not expected to accept the last vision in a text if it comes from a frankly unreliable character.

In addition, regardless of genre, application of the trust-the-last rule depends on rhetorical context. That is, when the contradiction comes in the spoken words of a character—as opposed to his or her thoughts, or the statements of a reliable narrator—the circumstances in which the words are spoken also put pressure on whether we are to apply the rule of trust the last. In the example from *Othello,* of course, the rhetorical context seems to support,

35. Suleiman, *Authoritarian Fictions,* 90–91.
36. George Orwell, *1984* (New York: NAL/Signet, 1950), 245 (pt. 3, chap. 6).

rather than undermine, our tendency to believe the final version. The first story comes when Othello is trying to terrorize Desdemona so that she will reveal her true feelings; the handkerchief is but a means to further the end of finding out the truth about her. But in the second account, the real subject of the discussion is the handkerchief itself—and Othello is trying to find out the truth about *it*. But in Lermontov's *Hero of Our Time*, where Pechorin describes himself in different terms virtually every time he searches his soul, there is no reason to give credence to *any* version, for in each case, he has reason to lie either to himself or to his audience (for instance, when he is trying to impress the first narrator with his worldliness or trying to seduce Princess Mary through self-laceration). Lermontov, of course, is aware of the problem raised by Fowles—of the tendency of the reader to apply the rule even where it is inappropriate. He has thus structured his novel so that the reader who tries to trust the last account is blocked. Specifically, he confuses the time scheme so that the chronologies of the narration and of the story do not correspond. We see Pechorin near the end of his life well before we read of his youthful adventures, so it is thus not at all clear what the "last" statement really is. Indeed, this temporal complexity is announced in the novel's paradoxical opening line ("In every book the preface is the first and also the last thing"), which introduces a preface where even the author's voice is ironized.[37] This self-conscious thwarting of the traditional techniques for making determinations about the validity of various versions of self offered by the main character is one of the sources of the novel's psychological richness.

A similar structure is used to confuse political issues in Sutton Griggs' 1899 novel, *Imperium in Imperio*. The core of the novel consists of a debate about the appropriate black responses to white oppression. After a notice from "Sutton E. Griggs" vouching for the "truthfulness" of the narrative, the narrator's voice is the first and last we hear, and he supports the conservative position espoused by Belton Piedmont rather than the more violent alter-

---

37. Mihail Lermontov, *A Hero of Our Time*, trans. Vladimir Nabokov and Dmitri Nabokov (New York: Doubleday/Anchor, 1958), 1 (Author's Introduction).

native posed by Bernard Belgrave. But since his opening words are "I am a traitor," and since he has no active presence in the novel that can counteract the negative impression created by that declaration, it is hard to know where we are expected to stand.[38]

Contradictions can occur not only in the content of a text, but in its formal aspect as well, most specifically in the violation of conventional configurations of closure. I will be able to deal with this more fully at the end of the next section of this chapter, where I talk about endings as conclusions.

Rules of Naming, Bundling, and Thematizing

Once done reading a text, readers usually try to tie it up in some way. If a text is short and simple, especially if it has a clear point, this may not prove difficult, any more than it is difficult to get a quart of milk from the checkout counter to your car. But a major text in our tradition is apt to be more cumbersome—and readers need some kind of packaging that allows them to treat it conveniently as a whole, just as they need paper bags and carts when doing more elaborate shopping. There are a number of ways in which texts can be packed up.

For instance, as linguists and philosophers have long maintained, the process of naming serves to take the complex or unfamiliar and make it manageable by putting it in a category, increasing its apparent coherence by stressing some features and downplaying others. The same process occurs in reading. Academic readers, in particular, name and thus classify works—for instance, by appropriating them to particular generic categories, by elucidating their central theme, or by finding their governing metaphoric or mythic structure. Annette Kolodny suggests, for instance, "the tantalizing possibility that metaphor, or symbolizing in general, . . . helps to give coherence to the otherwise inchoate succession of discrete sense data."[39] These naming activities are

---

38. Griggs, *Imperium in Imperio* (New York: Arno/New York Times, 1969), ii, 1 ("To the Public" and "Berl Trout's Dying Declaration"). For a good analysis of similar devices in Sartre, see Gerald Prince, "*La Nausée* and the Question of Closure," 182–90.

39. Annette Kolodny, *Lay of the Land*, 148.

made easier by the fact that readers usually start with the assumption that such a handle is there to be grasped in the first place.

As a general rule, if a reasonable number of textual features unite it with another known textual pattern, then that pattern can legitimately be treated as an appropriate "name" for the artifact in question. The more features that can be subsumed under this name, the more appropriate it is, and the more coherent the bundle is deemed to be. Sometimes, as we have seen, authors themselves suggest the potential bundles: Joyce calls his novel *Ulysses,* and the parallels to the *Odyssey* that are thus uncovered are seen as proof of its coherence. More often, we have to find the names ourselves. It is important to realize that the very act of naming provides a sense of coherence; this is true even when, paradoxically, the name given is the name of some kind of chaos. Thus, we get a sense of some kind of order even when the narrator of William Kennedy's *Legs* points out the incoherences of his text: "I've often vacillated about whether Jack's life was tragic, comic, a bit of both, or merely a pathetic muddle. I admit the muddle theory moved me most at this point."[40]

Bundling can also be facilitated through the use of parallelisms. It is generally assumed, for instance, that parallels along one axis imply parallels along another. In poetry, for instance, parallel syntax is usually assumed to imply parallel thoughts. Similarly, in fiction, Bruce R. Stark is able to argue that there is a *thematic* parallel between Daisy Faye and Ella Kay—the woman who cheated Jay Gatsby out of his inheritance from Dan Cody—at least partly because of the "phonological equivalence" of their names.[41] Indeed, we are generally invited to assume that any elements— characters, plot lines, settings—that *can* be treated as parallel *should* be treated in that way. Of course, like all spatial metaphors, literary parallelism resists Euclidean exactness. Two elements can be called literary parallels if they are variations of the same theme, for instance, if they provide commentary on each other, or even if they serve as counterexamples of each other. Thus, for instance, since Chekhov wrote "The Man in the Case," "Gooseberries," and

40. Kennedy, *Legs* (New York: Penguin, 1983), 166 ("Playing the Jack").

41. Stark, "The Intricate Pattern in *The Great Gatsby,*" *Fitzgerald/Hemingway Annual 1975,* ed. Matthew J. Bruccoli and C. E. Frazer Clark, Jr. (Washington: Microcards, 1975), 57–58.

"About Love" in the form of a trilogy, it is appropriate to see them as three different exemplifications of the same general theme—to see, for instance, the social forces that keep Alehin from declaring his love for Anna as a variant of the social and physical shells in which Belikov encases himself. The stories of Anna Karenina and Levin, in contrast, serve as exemplifications of the opposite trajectories that lives can follow. Interpretive disagreement can often stem from the application of this rule—not only from dispute over *whether* the general rule ought to be applied, but also, once it is applied, from dispute about *how* to do so, about what *sort* of parallels are in fact intended. Is the parallelism between Tom and Huck in *Huckleberry Finn* intended to make us see them as similar—or radically different?

Because of the parallelism rule, collections of stories differ radically from novels. When formally discrete narratives are a novel—as the seven "stories" of Gloria Naylor's *Women of Brewster Place* are—we are entitled to see them as reflections of one another, as different ways of saying what is, in the end, the same story. When stories are merely collected as stories, however, there is no convention allowing us to treat them in that manner. Thus, it makes a tremendous difference in which way we consider such ambiguously structured books as Jean Toomer's *Cane* or John Barth's *Lost in the Funhouse.*

Perhaps the most important bundling technique, however, involves the rule of conclusive endings. The ending of a text is not only to be noticed; there is also a widely applicable interpretive convention that permits us to read it in a special way, as a *conclusion*, as a summing up of the work's meaning. Marianna Torgovnick puts it especially strongly: "An ending is the single place where an author most pressingly desires to make his points—whether those points are aesthetic, moral, social, political, epistemological, or even the determination not to make any point at all."[42] I would phrase it differently: readers *assume* that authors put their best thoughts last, and thus *assign* a special value to the final pages of a text. It is particularly easy for the reader to do so, of course, when the ending is apparently congruent with the text that

42. Torgovnick, *Closure in the Novel,* 19.

precedes—for instance, the moral of a traditional fable or the marriage of a traditional paperback romance. As E. M. Forster puts it, "If it was not for death and marriage I do not know how the average novelist would conclude."[43] Endings, however, are not always so neat, and when they are not, the reader is often expected to reinterpret the work so that the ending in fact serves as an appropriate conclusion. Take, for instance, Lucas Beauchamp's demand for a receipt at the end of Faulkner's *Intruder in the Dust*. We not only notice it because of its privileged position, we are also expected to interpret the novel in such a way that it serves as a satisfactory summing up. In particular, it serves to undercut Gavin's political pronouncements—for the only way to turn that ending into a summation is to assume that Gavin, in contrast to Chick, has failed to attain the wisdom that would make him worthy of Lucas' trust and friendship. Similarly, Huckleberry Finn's decision to "light out for the Territory" could, taken out of context, be read as an introduction to adventures to come, but its placement in the novel we have requires us to read it as a conclusion—a final response— to what he has already experienced.

This is the general reading strategy that allows readers to deal with the formal contradictions that I mentioned at the end of the previous section of this chapter. To exemplify the process, I would like to look at some of the ways that the expectations aroused by the second metarule of configuration—the metarule that leads us to expect balance in a text, to expect that the ending will somehow be prefigured in the beginning—can be apparently frustrated, and the interpretive operations that readers are likely to use to restore balance. Specifically, I will look at two ways in which balance can be upset: through violation (deceptive cadence) and through exaggeration (excessive cadence).

(1) Kenneth Burke suggests that formal excellence requires that a work's ending fulfill—perhaps after considerable teasing—the promises with which it begins. But novels often have endings that do not simply surprise (to surprise, after all, is not necessarily to contradict) but that seem, when we get to them, flagrantly to defy what has come before—which end, as Ives' Second Symphony

---

43. Forster, *Aspects of the Novel*, 66.

does, with what musicians call a deceptive cadence. Ambrose Bierce's "Dame Fortune and the Traveler" provides a transparent example:

> A weary Traveler who had lain down and fallen asleep on the brink of a deep well was discovered by Dame Fortune.
> "If this fool," she said, "should have an uneasy dream and roll into the well men would say that I did it. It is painful to me to be unjustly accused, and I shall see that I am not."
> So saying she rolled the man into the well.[44]

The fable's detour around the expected tag line—especially since it moves in the name of a kind of cynical realism—jolts the authorial audience into questioning the validity of the moral it expected. This is because, by the general rule of conclusive endings, readers are invited to revise their understanding of the beginning of the text so that the ending, which at first seems a surprise, turns out to be in fact prefigured. One common way of doing this is by "thematizing" the jolt so that it becomes the very subject of the text. Thus, Torgovnick argues about *Sentimental Education:*

> Any shift in time-scale at the end of a novel ordinarily involves a movement forward in time; Flaubert parodically inverts this traditional element by having the novel end with an "incident" that had occurred before the beginning of the novel's action. The inversion has thematic value, for it indicates that our heroes' journey through life is regressive rather than progressive.[45]

More generally, the undermining of a conventional ending tends to stress the conventionality of that closure, and hence makes us

---

44. Bierce, *Fantastic Fables*, in *The Collected Writings of Ambrose Bierce* (New York: Citadel, 1963), 640.

45. Torgovnick, *Closure in the Novel*, 115. I, of course, would prefer to reword that final sentence: the inversion indicates regression because it is *assumed* beforehand to have thematic value. See also Jonathan Culler's claim that *"The Waste Land* can be unified by thematizing its formal discontinuities" ("Prolegomena to a Theory of Reading," in *Reader in the Text*, ed. Suleiman and Crosman, 48; much of this essay ended up, in altered form, in chap. 3 of *Pursuit of Signs*). This interpretive technique is applied to ancient as well as to modern texts. See Alice M. Colby-Hall's analysis of the "double ending" of Renaut's *Bel Inconnu* in the special issue of *Yale French Studies* devoted to closure ("Frustration and Fulfillment: The Double Ending of the Bel Inconnu," *Yale French Studies*, no. 67 [1984]: 120–34).

aware of the gap between the authorial and narrative audiences. In works that present themselves as jests—works, like S. J. Perelman's parodies, that are intended primarily to charm—it is possible to interpret the opening of the gap as an end in itself, as a source of surprise and hence amusement. But in works that have greater pretentions to seriousness, we assume, in the absence of instructions to the contrary, that the undermining of a convention is to be read at least in part as a critique of that convention.

There are, in general, two directions such a critique can take. If the primary subject of the work in question is art itself, then we can assume that the convention is being questioned from an aesthetic point of view. Pushkin's ostentatious refusal to wrap up the plot at the end of *Eugene Onegin*, for instance, seems—given the discussion of poetry throughout the text—to be a commentary on literary convention itself.

If, on the other hand, the work seems to be trying to make a statement about the world, we will start off assuming that the convention is being criticized for its falseness when held up to the outside world—at least, the outside world assumed by the authorial audience. Take, for instance, Mark Twain's *Pudd'nhead Wilson*. At first, the text may seem but a variant of the traditional Cinderella pattern. In this plot, an impoverished but deserving person is cruelly abused, even enslaved, but he or she endures and is eventually discovered (usually through some bizarre coincidence, often involving switched infants) and rewarded with wealth and rank. Twain's novel tells the story of a black woman who, to save her child (who looks white) from being sold down the river, substitutes him for the son of one of the local aristocrats. In a climactic courtroom scene, the deception is uncovered, and the true freeman, the virtuous Valet de Chambers, who has spent the first two decades of his life as a slave, discovers that he is heir to a fortune. But just as we are about to delight in his success, there is an unexpected twist.

The real heir suddenly found himself rich and free, but in a most embarrassing situation. He could neither read nor write, and his speech was the basest dialect of the negro quarter. His gait, his attitudes, his gestures, his bearing, his laugh—all were vulgar and uncouth; his manners were the manners of a slave. Money and fine clothes could not mend these defects or cover them up; they only made them the more glaring and the more pathetic. The poor fellow could not endure the terrors of the white man's parlor, and felt at home and at peace nowhere but in the kitchen. The family pew was misery to him, yet he could nevermore enter into the solacing refuge of the "nigger gallery"—that was closed to him for good and all.[46]

This does more than joke about art; it forces the authorial audience to question the ideological assumptions behind the convention: the belief that if we could somehow make our fortunes, we could easily transcend any limitations in our upbringing.

One of the primary targets for many nineteenth- and twentieth-century novelists has been closure itself. The term *closure*, unfortunately, has been confused by its application to at least two radically different concepts. On the one hand, closure can refer to the way a text calls on readers to apply rules of signification; in this sense, a text is "open" if its symbolic meanings are not restricted. Maeterlinck's play *Pelléas and Mélisande*, with its vague but resonant symbols, is open in this way, and it is presumably in this way that Renée Riese Hubert is using the term when she argues that "the modern work of art is essentially open, proposing a dialectic between the work and its interpreter."[47] But closure can also refer to the way that a text utilizes rules of configuration; in this sense, a work is "open" when, for instance, the plot remains unresolved and incomplete even at the end. In this second meaning, *Pelléas*, where both the mismatch of Mélisande's marriage to Golaud and the oddly innocent passion of her adulterous/incestuous love affair with Pelléas are rounded out by the deaths of the lovers, is a fairly closed text.

In the argument that follows, I will be talking about this second kind of closure. More particularly, I would argue that many realistic writers prefer endings in which the full consequences of the

46. Mark Twain, *Pudd'nhead Wilson*, in *Pudd'nhead Wilson and Those Extraordinary Twins* (New York: Harper, 1899), 224 (Conclusion). It is, though, risky to talk about coherence in a work as textually tangled as this one; for a discussion of the problems, see Hershel Parker, *Flawed Texts and Verbal Icons*, chap. 5.

47. Hubert, "The Tableau-Poème: Open Work," *Yale French Studies*, no. 67 (1984): 43. Hubert's claim, of course, applies only to a fairly restricted text-milieu. See also Gerald Prince's distinction between hermeneutic, proairetic, and tonal closure later in that same issue ("*La Nausée* and the Question of Closure," 183).

events portrayed—even the consequences immediately pertinent to the narrative at hand—are neither worked out nor clearly implied. *Crime and Punishment*, as I've noted, ends with Raskolnikov looking toward the future.

> At the beginning of their happiness at some moments they were both ready to look on those seven years as though they were seven days. He did not know that the new life would not be given him for nothing, that he would have to pay dearly for it, that it would cost him great striving, great suffering.

Now it is true that such unresolved endings are sometimes rounded off with a desultory closing of the door, such as the final paragraph of *Crime and Punishment*, which follows the passage just cited.

> But that is the beginning of a new story—the story of the gradual renewal of a man, the story of his gradual regeneration, of his passing from one world into another, of his initiation into a new unknown life. That might be the subject of a new story, but our present story is ended.[48]

Similarly, Robert O'Brien's book for young readers, *The Secret of NIMH*, ends with important unanswered questions about what has happened to some of the major characters, as well as about what will happen in the future. But it still includes the final gesture that brings down the curtain in so many children's stories: "They went to sleep."[49] These easy assertions of well-roundedness, however, do not make these texts substantially different from texts that are more blatant in their failure to tell the whole story, such as Chekhov's "Lady with the Dog," which ends with the following paragraph:

> And it seemed to them that they were within an inch of arriving at a decision, and that then a new, beautiful life would begin. And they

48. Fyodor Dostoyevsky, *Crime and Punishment*, trans. Constance Garnett (New York: Random House/Vintage, 1950), 492 (Epilogue, chap. 2).
49. O'Brien, *The Secret of NIMH* (New York: Scholastic/Apple, 1982), 249 (Epilogue). The novel was originally entitled *Mrs. Frisby and the Rats of NIMH*, but was later renamed to conform to the title of the film version.

both realized that the end was still far, far away, and that the hardest, the most complicated part was only just beginning.[50]

It is important to realize that such lack of closure does not mean lack of *conclusion*. By the rule of conclusive endings, the authorial audience will take these open endings and assume that open-ness itself is part of the point of the conclusion.[51] It will not, however, treat these texts as it treats *Eugene Onegin*, for in *Crime and Punishment, The Rats of NIMH*, and "The Lady with the Dog," art itself is not the primary subject. Thus, the authorial audience is more likely to thematize the apparent incompleteness as an attempt by the author to cast doubt on the social and philosophical implications of the traditional well-made story—most specifically, the implication that stories really do have endings, that lives ever reach a state of rest. "That is the story," writes Alice Walker in "Advancing Luna—and Ida B. Wells." "It has an 'unresolved' ending. That is because Freddie Pye and Luna are still alive, as am I."[52]

Of course, different conventions have different ideological implications—and even the same convention (or its overturn) may have different meanings in different texts, depending on when, where, by whom, and for whom it was written. Thus, for instance, when W. S. Gilbert mocked the Cinderella story in *H.M.S. Pinafore*, he may have been ridiculing certain class pretensions, but he apparently did not see the power of those class pretensions to warp personality beyond redemption. He may have thought that the lucky break was unlikely, but there is no textual indication that he did not believe that with luck the individual could transcend class. Twain sees the convention in radically different terms, for he sees class as *forming* the individual to begin with. Attacks on well-roundedness, too, bear a different ideological weight in different contexts. "The Lady with the Dog," for instance, reflects

50. Anton Chekhov, "The Lady with the Dog," trans. Ivy Litvinov, in *Anton Chekhov's Short Stories*, ed. Ralph Matlaw (New York: Norton, 1979), 235.

51. Prince, although he uses almost the opposite terms, is describing the same paradox when he says that there can be "a closure of uncertainty (making sense of or exploiting inconclusiveness, hesitation, and contradiction)" (*"La Nausée* and the Question of Closure," 188).

52. Walker, "Advancing Luna—and Ida B. Wells," in *You Can't Keep a Good Woman Down* (New York: Harcourt Brace Jovanovich/Harvest, 1982), 98.

Chekhov's sense that humans always have to deal with concrete particulars rather than generalities, and that the course of an individual's future is therefore always unpredictable. In Chandler's *Big Sleep*, as I will show in more detail at the end of Chapter 6, the attack on well-roundedness reflects a political critique of a certain notion of crime promulgated by the classical detective story. The novel violates the primary conventions of the genre, and the rule of conclusive endings allows the reader to treat these violations as a statement, specifically as an attack on the vision of the world that the traditional conventions imply.[53]

(2) So far, I have considered only deceptive cadences. Thematizing a text's conclusion is more complex still when a convention is undermined not by overthrowing it, but rather by following it in such an ostentatious way that it looks absurd—where the cadence is not deceptive, but excessive. Farce is particularly apt to use this mode. In Ludovic Halévy's libretto for Offenbach's *Ba-Ta-Clan*, which concerns a revolutionary conspiracy in China, tragedy is averted at the last moment when it turns out that all the major characters are secretly French. A more pointed example is the rescue of Macheath in Brecht's *Threepenny Opera*. Even without Peachum's explicit criticism of the falseness of the ending ("In reality, their end [i.e., that of the poor] is generally bad. Mounted messengers from the Queen come far too seldom"),[54] the intended reader would have little trouble concluding that he or she should take the arrival of the mounted messenger as a criticism of the lack of realism inherent in all such last-minute rescues.

But the technique can be subtler as well. Southworth's *Allworth Abbey* provides a telling case. Annella Wilder is one of those dashing Southworth heroines like Capitola in *The Hidden Hand*—courageous, spirited, prepared for action while the men wring their hands in despair unable to think of what to do. She seems destined for a life of independence. Yet when the romantic couples are being

---

53. More generally, as Fredric Jameson puts it, the "contaminat[ion of] the central murder" by the "random violence" of what he calls the "secondary plot" ("the search") in Chandler's novels in general is part of a strategy of "de-mystification of violent death" ("On Raymond Chandler," 648–49).

54. Bertolt Brecht, *The Threepenny Opera*, trans. Desmond Vesey and Eric Bentley (New York: Grove/Evergreen Black Cat, 1964), 96.

united in that culminating series of marriages that ends so many comic novels, we find that Annella, too, has been paired up—with Valerius Brightwell. Annella has had no heterosexual romantic attachments in the course of the novel (in part because the men are so far beneath her in character and fortitude); and Brightwell, neither so bright as a button nor so deep as a well, has been entirely incidental to the plot until this point (he utters hardly a word and performs no actions at all). Their union thus seems flagrantly contrived—the conventional configuration of final marriages is fulfilled to a degree that the plot itself does not demand, and the artificiality of the convention is thus foregrounded almost as much as it would have been if it had been reversed. The effect is that the reader begins to doubt *all* of the marriages—and perhaps the institution itself.

Or is that the intended effect? Like all interpretations, this one requires the application of rules that preexist the text and that may not be appropriate to it. Surely, whether a given actual reader sees the ending of *Allworth Abbey* (or, for that matter, the formally similar ending of *Sense and Sensibility*) as subversive will depend to a large extent on his or her politics and prior opinion of the author's talents and outlook. If one takes the current deprecatory attitude toward Southworth and assumes that she didn't know what she was doing, one can conclude that the book is merely conventional. Similarly, if a given actual reader thinks that Chandler was not a skilled novelist, he or she may not apply the rule of conclusive endings to his texts, and may, as Stephen Knight does, conclude that his novels are simply poorly plotted.[55] Indeed, it is specifically because of his refusal to apply certain kinds of rules— in part because he sees Chandler as a popular novelist—that Luke Parsons can conclude that his novels are *not* a "serious indictment" of American society (if they were, they would have been "a boon to the propagandists of the Kremlin"): "His books, after all, are detective stories. . . . Just because Mr. Chandler writes so well, we must take care not to apply to him inappropriate literary standards."[56]

55. Knight, *Form and Ideology*, esp. 150–51.
56. Luke Parsons, "On the Novels of Raymond Chandler," *Fortnightly Review*, May 1954, 351. For a fuller analysis of this novel, see my "Rats behind the Wainscoting."

Applying *appropriate* standards—there's the difficulty. For disputes about appropriateness are bound to lead to disputes about interpretation and ultimately about evaluation. Let me now turn to this problem and show in more detail both how interpretive disagreements can arise and how, as cultural critics, we might learn from them.

PART II

THE POLITICS OF INTERPRETATION

6

Through *The Glass Key* Darkly:
Presupposition and Misunderstanding

> We must analyze the language of contemporary criticism it-
> self, recognizing especially that hermeneutic systems are not
> universal, colorblind, apolitical, or neutral.
>
> Henry Louis Gates, Jr.,
> "Writing 'Race' and the Difference It Makes"

Presuppositions and the Ambiguity of Interpretation

Even among critics not particularly concerned with detective
fiction, Dashiell Hammett's fourth novel, *The Glass Key* (1931), is
famous for carrying the so-called objective method to nearly ob-
sessive lengths: we are never told what the characters are thinking,
only what they do and look like. Anyone's decisions about anyone
else's intentions (which have life-and-death consequences in this
underworld of ward politics) are *interpretive* decisions, dependent
on correct presuppositions—on having the right interpretive key.

The novel's title, in part, refers to this kind of key. Ned Beaumont, the protagonist, has to determine what kind of relationship
to have—indeed, what kind of relationship he is *already* having—
with Janet Henry. One of his major clues about what is going on in
her mind is a dream that she tells him, a dream that climaxes in an
attempt to lock a door against an onslaught of snakes. Dream interpretation is difficult enough to begin with, and Janet Henry
compounds the difficulty by telling the dream twice. In the first
version, her attempt to lock the door succeeds; in the second, the
key turns out to be made of glass and shatters. Ned Beaumont, in
deciding which dream to use as his key, chooses the second (as do
most readers)—but it is an intuitive choice, not a logical one.

173

If the model of the reading process I have advanced in the first five chapters of this book is correct, then Ned Beaumont's situation can serve as an emblem of the situation faced by any reader. Interpreting a book, too, requires us to make a choice about what key to use to unlock it, and that choice must often rest on the same kind of intuitive leap.[1] Specifically, an actual reader's interpretation of a specific text is at least in part a product of the assumptions with which he or she approaches it, including assumptions about the rules appropriate for transforming it. In this chapter, I will show in more detail how presuppositions interact with interpretation by examining more closely how readers might go about making sense of two specific novels—one a fairly arcane avant-garde text (Witold Gombrowicz' 1965 *Cosmos*) and one a novel aimed at a broader audience (*The Glass Key*). My aim is neither to propose new interpretations nor to guide readers to correct ones. Rather, my aim is to offer concrete examples of an analytical approach that clarifies the sources of certain ambiguities. This in turn allows us to see the misinterpretations produced by actual readers in particular cultural contexts as useful material for cultural analysis. Specifically, using *The Big Sleep* as my case in point, I will show how we can "read" misreadings in order to illuminate the political pressures implicit behind them.

Before getting to actual cases, however, it is necessary both to reiterate how I am using the term *misreading* in this book and to distinguish among several kinds of misreadings. As I suggested in Chapter 1, I am using the word in a specific and restricted way that refers *not* to interpretive practices that ignore authorial intention, but rather to interpretations in which the reader *aims* at joining the authorial audience, but fails. Whether a given interpretive transformation of a text is a misreading or not, in other words, is less a matter of how you transform the text than a matter of what activity you think you are performing at the time. Misreadings in

---

1. Gary Saul Morson makes a similar claim about what he calls "boundary works," where "it is uncertain which of two mutually exclusive sets of conventions governs a work. . . . Doubly decodable, the same text becomes, in effect, two different works" (*Boundaries of Genre*, 48). Morson tends to see this as a quality inhering in special genres—whereas, as I shall argue, it is characteristic of a wider variety of texts.

this sense, therefore, are failed attempts to join in one particular social practice, not successful attempts to engage in some different social practice. To give a concrete example: a Freudian analysis of Nabokov's *Invitation to a Beheading* is not a misreading (and in fact could be an extremely illuminating interpretive performance) if the interpreter is uninterested in reading the text as Nabokov wished; but a reader *is* misreading if he or she assumes that the application of the theories of the "Viennese witch-doctor" (as Nabokov called him)[2] is part of the interpretive arsenal of the authorial audience.

Misreadings in this sense can come about in several ways. I will set aside two of them at the outset: those that stem from actual misperceptions of the physical marks on the page (I had a student who, in reading the descriptions of Paul Madvig in *The Glass Key*, consistently misread the word "blond" as "blind") and those arising from fundamental ignorance of the meanings of words (my son, reading his first Hardy Boys book at the age of six, thought their father's name, Fenton Hardy, was an alias, because the book said that he had "made a name for himself" in the New York Police Department). Beyond that, misreadings fall generally into two categories. First, the reader can misapply the rules. Thus, for instance, a reader may know that a text's opening is noticeable, but may fail to recognize that the first words are introductory, and that the real opening comes later. Or a reader may understand that Dr. Eckleburg's sign in *The Great Gatsby* is intended as a metaphor, but may interpret it incorrectly as an image of hope.

The second category is both more interesting and, as I shall show, more revealing. Certain acts of misreading result not from the misapplication of rules, but from the application of the *wrong* rules. As I have argued, not only are there a vast number of implicit conventions of reading to be learned before we can understand anything as complex as a novel; more significant, there are different rules for processing different books. Indeed, if there is any analogy between literary and linguistic systems, we must view *Life with Father* and *The Sound and the Fury* not only as different

---

2. Vladimir Nabokov, *Invitation to a Beheading*, trans. Dmitri Nabokov (New York: Capricorn, 1959), 8 (Foreword).

utterances, but also as manifestations of the equivalent of different languages.

What makes a reader apply the wrong rules to a text? There are, of course, many reasons. Readers read within limits imposed by their cultural and economic environments; and as beings with subjective concerns, they have the power to apply rules in a personal or eccentric fashion. Furthermore, even readers trying to recover the author's intended meaning may find themselves facing alternatives that are difficult, if not impossible, to decide among. There is always a variety of sets of rules that one can apply to a text; and while some texts are more or less resistant to certain kinds of misreadings, it is the case—more often than those of us committed to the notion of "better" and "worse" readings would like to believe—that a work will leave considerable leeway, and that several different interpretive strategies will work equally well. How this takes place can be seen by looking more closely at one common cause of this last kind of misreading: ambiguity of genre. My purpose is not to suggest that this is the only or even the most important source of misreading, but simply to offer, in some textual detail, an example of the kind of analysis my proposed model permits, one that can be readily applied to other kinds of misreading as well.[3]

We often think of genre designation as one of the last acts a reader performs—and to some extent it is true that a work's *precise* generic placement is often unclear until we have finished reading it. But some preliminary generic judgment is always required even before we begin the process of reading. We can never interpret entirely outside generic structures: "reading"—even the reading of a first paragraph—is always "reading as."

The notion that we always "read as" is fairly widespread in critical discourse. No one is apt to think it eccentric when Fernando Ferrara says "just as one can study *A Midsummer Night's*

---

3. For a discussion of possible misreadings of *Pale Fire* that are generated by the novel's ambiguity about the nature of its narrative audience, see my "Truth in Fiction: A Reexamination of Audiences," *Critical Inquiry* 4 (Autumn 1977): 121–41.

Dream as document, one can also study *Das Kapital* as fiction";[4] everyone who has worked on *The Turn of the Screw* has had to confront the question of whether it should be "read as" a ghost story. And the terms used to describe various modes of reading are often genre terms: a "ghost story." But critics do not always follow through on the implications of this terminology. For if we take this usage seriously, it suggests that genres can be seen not only in the traditional way as patterns or models that writers follow in constructing texts, but also from the other direction, as different packages of rules that readers apply in construing them, as ready-made strategies for reading.[5]

This is not to deny the possibility that any text, examined in detail, calls into operation a specific and unique collection of rules; on a more general level of analysis, however, any work shares a large number of rules with other works of the same genre—there are, as the Chicago neo-Aristotelians insisted, *kinds* of works. Just as details can come in more or less familiar configurations, so rules come in generic packages: we often apply rule D because it is usual to do so in texts where we have already applied rules A, B, and C. And if we use the notion of genre as preformed bundles of operations performed by readers in order to recover the meanings of texts, rather than as sets of features found in the texts themselves, then we can see that correct reading requires, among other things, a correct initial assumption about the genre that a work belongs to—and that misreading follows in the wake of erroneous placement.

Two implications of this definition of genre need to be spelled out here. First, genre categories can overlap. Depending on *what* rules we choose to focus on, a given work may appear to fall into

---

4. Ferrara, "Theory and Model for the Structural Analysis of Fiction," *New Literary History* 5 (Winter 1974): 252. See also Barbara Herrnstein Smith's claim, "One's perception of and/or response to an event not only determine but are determined by how one classifies it: what we 'see,' and how we subsequently behave toward it, will depend on what we see something *as*" (*On the Margins of Discourse*, 48). Likewise Stanley Fish: " 'Social satire,' 'comedy of manners,' and 'piece of realism' are not labels applied mechanically to perspicuous instances; rather, they are names for ways of reading" ("Working on the Chain Gang," 204).

5. Morson argues from a similar perspective; see *Boundaries of Genre*, viii–ix.

several different generic classes. Faulkner's *Intruder in the Dust*, for instance, asks to be read as a classical detective story. It calls on us to apply the genre's basic rule of notice that virtually any detail can turn out to be important; it also calls on us to use the genre's familiar rules of configuration to put together such elements as a murder, a false suspect, a detective, and a detective's sidekick in such a way that we are led to expect a certain kind of closure—one built on climactic surprise revelation—which the novel in fact provides. At the same time, *Intruder* is a personal-discovery novel—a didactic novel that jolts us into accepting a particular view of the world because it carries us toward a climax in which Chick suddenly acquires a key bit of knowledge that fundamentally alters his world view.[6] As such, it calls for application of *that* genre's usual rules, including the rule of signification requiring us to generalize from the protagonist's discoveries to larger political and philosophical statements.

Second, genre categories can be broader or narrower. Depending on *how many* rules we choose to consider in our definitions, the categories that result can vary in their specificity from such broad classes as "epic" through such smaller groupings as Todorov's "fantastic"[7] on to ever more precise categories. As a result, genres can even include one another: the class "escape fiction" includes the smaller grouping "classical detective fiction," which in turn includes the "classical locked-room mystery."

My analyses of ambiguities in *Cosmos*, which involves fairly narrow generic categories, and *The Glass Key*, which involves genre on the broadest possible level, may help clarify the range of problems involved in choosing interpretive strategies.

Getting to the Bottom of Things

As my first case study, let me delineate some of the interpretive processes a reader is likely to call upon while trying to make sense

---

6. For a fuller discussion of the way Faulkner combines these two generic structures, see my "Click of the Spring: The Detective Story as Parallel Structure in Dostoyevsky and Faulkner," *Modern Philology* 76 (May 1979): 355–69.

7. See Tzvetan Todorov, *Fantastic*, esp. chap. 1, with its incisive attack on Northrop Frye's genre categories.

out of Witold Gombrowicz' avant-garde novel from 1965. *Cosmos'* plot revolves around two young men who seek a quiet refuge in the Polish countryside. Their peace, however, is repeatedly shattered by trivial, but slightly off kilter, incidents which they probe in search of deeper significance. A crack in the ceiling, for instance, is interpreted as an arrow, which they feel compelled to follow. This arrow eventually leads them to a hanging twig, which in turn reminds them of a bird they had seen hanging some time before. As a consequence of such "events," they become convinced of the presence of an underlying order, although its precise nature remains obscure. Their adventures grow more and more grotesque, and the novel climaxes when their landlord, a man who gets his erotic pleasures from what he calls "berging" (subtle masturbatory activities, such as rolling up tiny pieces of bread), takes his family on a picnic that secretly celebrates a love affair of nearly twenty-seven years ago—an outing that culminates, for undisclosed reasons, in the hanging (a suicide?) of his son-in-law.

At first, the novel appears to belong to a genre that has flourished especially since the 1950s: the ironic-grasping-at-straws-in-the-meaningless-abyss novel. Here, the protagonist, caught in a metaphysical void, manufactures a meaning for his or her experiences—a meaning that the reader can see is false. The genre has its antecedents at least as far back as *Don Quixote*, and it has developed by way of such texts as Turgenev's haunting *Knock, Knock, Knock*, the story of a nonentity who manages to reconstruct the world around him in such a way that he becomes a "fatal" romantic hero—a reconstruction that ultimately pushes him into suicide. In its most modern form, the genre is best exemplified by Butor's magisterial *Passing Time* (*L'Emploi du temps*). In this novel, Jacques Revel tries to get to the bottom of events in part by weaving them into the Theseus story—a myth that the authorial audience recognizes as inappropriate. This mythologizing leads to the unraveling of Revel's life, as he incorrectly interprets the motives of others and looks forward to consequences that we know are not forthcoming.

Cosmos seems to fit the same pattern: by the end of the book, the reader realizes that the events do not hold any deeper metaphysical meaning. As Patricia Merivale puts it, the narrator "conspicuously fail[s] to make a satisfying pattern. . . . [The title is] an ironic comment on this failure."[8] Despite its humor, then, this novel about a frustrated search for coherence offers a despairing vision of a decentered universe.

Or does it? Is this initial assumption about *Cosmos'* genre really correct? Perhaps Gombrowicz' novel belongs to a countergenre— the there-is-a-bottom-to-the-abyss-after-all genre in which apparent failures to find coherence in the world really do, in the end, succeed. In its simplest versions, the there-is-a-bottom countergenre distinguishes itself readily from the ironic-grasping genre, because the reader is explicitly shown the meaningful pattern beneath the apparent chaos. Thus, for instance, in O. Henry's "Furnished Room," the reader, privy to several points of view, accumulates a total store of information not available to any of the individual characters, and is thus able to see a meaning behind events that seem random to those experiencing them. But not all members of this countergenre are so straightforward. In the variant represented by Nabokov's "Vane Sisters" (and, in some critics' views, by *The Real Life of Sebastian Knight* and *Pale Fire* as well),[9] a further twist is added by *hiding* the pattern from the reader. In "The Vane Sisters," as I have pointed out, the true meaning is announced in an acrostic that inverts the apparent message of the story.

Knowing about the Vane-Sisters variant can easily produce interpretive vertigo. For once readers start reading with the suspicion

8. Merivale, "The Aesthetics of Perversion: Gothic Artifice in Henry James and Witold Gombrowicz," *PMLA* 93 (1978): 993. See also the claim by Edward Czerwiński and Bronisława Kast that "Gombrowicz in his last novel, constructed a 'cosmos of chaos' out of a world in which order, or at least a semblance of one, once existed" (" 'Berging' Gombrowicz: A Reappraisal of 'Form-Fastening,' " *Polish Review* 23, no. 4 [1978]: 52). Czerwiński and Kast see their view as a minority position; it is, however, widely shared. George Gömöri, for instance, claims that the hero "follows up the imaginary threads which lead nowhere" ("The Antinomies of Gombrowicz," *Modern Language Review* 73, no. 1 [1978]: 128); Ewa Thompson points out that the narrator's ideas are "grounded in incomplete evidence" and criticizes him for his naiveté ("The Reductive Method in Witold Gombrowicz's Novels," in *The Structural Analysis of Narrative Texts: Conference Papers*, New York University Slavic Papers, vol. 3, ed. Andrej Kodjak, Michael J. Connolly, and Krystyna Pomorska [Columbus, Ohio: Slavica Publishers, 1980], 201).

9. See, for instance, Susan Fromberg [Schaeffer], "Folding the Patterned Carpet: Form and Theme in the Novels of Vladimir Nabokov," Ph.D. diss., University of Chicago, 1968.

that an author might be hiding coherence not only from the characters, but from the audience as well, it becomes nearly impossible to distinguish the ironic-grasping genre from the there-is-a-bottom countergenre in practice. As I have suggested, any trained academic reader, by the nature of his or her education, is skilled in applying rules of coherence, including rules of naming, and can thus find a pattern in virtually anything. If such a reader begins with the supposition that there might well be a hidden pattern, therefore, the chances are that one will be found, whether intended or not. And once it is found it is nearly impossible to determine whether it is imposed on, rather than invited by, the text.

A reader looking for such a pattern, for instance, might well find, beneath the surface of Gombrowicz' novel, a concealed series of references to the Viennese composer Alban Berg, and especially to his 1926 composition for string quartet, the *Lyric Suite*. This allusive web, when uncovered, is astonishingly powerful as an intertext for rules of naming, for it ties together many apparent surface disjunctures, thus ironically undercutting the naive reader who thinks that the apparent meaninglessness of the novel's events ironically undercuts the ever-hopeful protagonists.

And what more appropriate vehicle for a secret message? For the *Lyric Suite* itself is a work with a coherence hidden from all but the initiated. Indeed, until recently, the piece was generally accepted as absolute music with no programmatic content. It was only in 1977 that George Perle turned up a copy of the score that the composer had annotated, revealing that the music was in fact an elaborate but covert love letter to Hanna Fuchs-Robetten, with whom Berg had had a brief affair and for whom he maintained a lasting passion. Several elements in the score that had seemed mere oddities until then—such as the quotations (from *Tristan* and Zemlinsky) and the pervasive use of the numbers 10, 23, and their multiples (for instance, in metronome markings and measure numbers)—turned out to have precise programmatic meaning (the quoted passages both deal with the burdens of passion; 10 refers to Hanna, 23 to Berg himself). Similar programmatic intentions determined the structure of the basic row and its constituent motifs (based in part on the initials of the lovers); and the last movement was revealed to be an accompaniment to a setting of Baudelaire's

"De Profundis Clamavi," although the vocal part is not in the published score.

As I have suggested, the Berg piece successfully binds together a large number of textual elements that otherwise seem simply random. Of course, the works are thematically related: both concern a brief affair that provides the secret center for a man's life. And the technical concerns of the novel and the quartet are related as well: the issues of permutation and combination that are constantly raised in *Cosmos* mirror, with uncanny accuracy, the problems of tone-row construction that so intrigued Berg. But more powerful still is the series of what appear to be explicit allusions to Berg, the *Lyric Suite*, and his life and works in general. The landlord's coining of the word "Berging" to refer to his secret, forbidden erotic activities is only the most evident of these allusions. Beyond that, many of the characters have names that tie them to Berg's circle of family and friends. These names are, for the most part, far from common, and do not therefore seem a likely result of mere coincidence. One of the protagonists is named Fuks (the match with the name of Berg's beloved is even closer in the English translation, where it is Fuchs),[10] while the landlord's daughter and Berg's wife share the name Helena/Hélène. The landlord's family name is Wojtys (Berg's most famous work is *Wozzeck*, although the Gombrowicz spelling is closer to Büchner's original *Woyzeck*, on which the opera was based). Two characters, Lulus and Lulusia, have names (and, perhaps, sexual mores) that echo Berg's other opera, *Lulu*. And the son-in-law is doubly knotted to Berg's Violin Concerto. Most obviously, he is named Ludwik (Louis in the English)—and Berg wrote the piece for his violinist friend, Louis Krasner. But he is tied to the concerto in another way as well. The concerto was intended as a requiem for Manon Gropius, the young daughter of Alma Mahler (for a while Hanna Fuchs-Robetten's sis-

---

10. Gombrowicz, *Cosmos*, trans. Eric Mosbacher, in *Three Novels* (New York: Grove, 1978). Mosbacher has translated not from the original Polish, but from earlier French and German translations, which may explain some of the name changes—although the change from Lulus and Lulusia to Lolo and Lola makes little sense. Although I have glanced through the Polish version, *Kosmos* (Paris: Instytut Literacki, 1970), I cannot say that my Polish is fluent enough that I could claim to have "read" the original.

ter-in-law) and architect Walter Gropius—and Louis happens to be an architect, too. In addition, the number of chapters (10) is the number that Berg used to represent Hanna in the score. The secret tryst turns out to have taken place just short of 27 years ago—just as the *Lyric Suite* was finished just short of 1927. Indeed, the picnic takes place one month and three days before the actual anniversary—an apparently pointless detail, except if it is seen as a veiled reference to Berg's number 13.

My aim here is not to argue for one or another interpretation of the text. Rather, my point is that the experience of reading the novel depends radically on the reader's starting point. It is not simply a matter of whether the reader has some arcane bit of information that adds a bit of resonance to the text: the *whole meaning* of the novel is reversed according to where the reader is before reading. Virtually any reader before 1977—and almost any non-musical reader thereafter—is apt to see the novel as confused and unsettled. But anyone who knows Berg's history and is prepared, before reading the book, to entertain the possibility of a secret message, will easily be able to apply rules of coherence so that *Cosmos* resolves into a perverse puzzle in which the hidden solution completely inverts the surface meaning. Indeed, once you see this hidden solution, it is almost impossible to ignore it. True, the historical facts strongly suggest (although they can never fully prove) that Gombrowicz could not have intended it, since the affair between Alban and Hanna was a closely guarded secret at the time he wrote the book. Yet so powerful is the pull of patterning as we read that it is difficult to believe that the references are not really there, if you are predisposed to find them in the first place.

Popular Fiction as a Genre

One might argue, of course, that the interpretive problems I have pointed out in *Cosmos* stem from its postmodern sensibility, and from the ambiguous and closely intertwined nature of the two genres competing for the reader's allegiance. And, to be sure, Gombrowicz' chosen techniques serve to magnify the problems of reading. But they magnify them, they do not create them; similar difficulties are likely to occur, to a greater or lesser extent, when reading many other literary texts, and when dealing with *any* genres, even the ones that seem least problematic on the surface. To demonstrate the range of the problem, let me take up a case at the opposite end of the literary spectrum, *The Glass Key*, which involves a genre distinction of the broadest type: the distinction between what are generally thought of as "popular" and "serious" (or "elite") texts.

At first, the popular/serious distinction may not appear to be a genre distinction at all. But if one accepts the description of reading and the definition of *genre* I have presented above, it follows that not all common genres have generic names. That is, by looking at genres in terms of shared reading conventions—rather than in terms of the preformed textual types that the academy has classified—we find ourselves with the possibility of categories that are not traditionally treated as genres, but that have all the attributes of genres and that can illuminate our cultural practices if they are so considered. This is certainly true of the popular/serious distinction. Granted, this distinction is about the broadest possible, so the rules that apply are both extremely general and subject to numerous exceptions. Still, we can say that, as a genre, popular literature—at least, if we restrict our discussion for the moment to American and British novels from the 1920s to the 1980s—seems to differ from so-called serious fiction in two ways. (Parallel differences would no doubt hold for other countries and other periods, but for the sake of my argument here—the problems faced by a reader of a particular American text from the 1920s—such concerns can be bracketed.)

First, popular fiction emphasizes a different category of reading rules. Roland Barthes has made a similar claim, although of course in different terms, when distinguishing popular tales from the psychological novel—one of the epitomes of serious fiction in the period I am discussing. "Some narratives," he writes, "are predominantly functional (such as popular tales), while some others are predominantly indicial (such as 'psychological' novels)."[11] In Barthes' own vocabulary, popular tales tend to be more metony-

11. Barthes, "Introduction," 247.

mic, while psychological novels are more metaphoric; translated into more traditional terms, this means that popular tales are more plot oriented, psychological novels more character oriented. Recast in my terminology, his remarks suggest that when we read popular fiction, we tend to stress operations of configuration, while in reading psychological novels, we tend to emphasize operations of signification.[12] If an element is brought to our attention by a rule of notice in a work of pop fiction, therefore, we tend to consider it in terms of what it may tell us about plot outcome, rather than in terms of what it may reveal about the inner states of the characters and the world of the book. Thus, for instance, in Anthony Olcott's thriller, *Murder at the Red October*, the protagonist, Ivan—a security officer at a Moscow hotel—snatches a doll that he finds under the bed of a mysterious American who has been murdered, in order to give it to his girlfriend's daughter. It is a noticeable event, in part because it comes at the end of a chapter; but since this is a popular novel, we are expected to think of the theft in terms of what complications are likely to result, rather than in terms of what it reveals about Ivan's character. It is for this reason that Fredric Jameson is able to argue that certain chance perceptions of "the inessential" are possible in popular fiction, but not in "great literature," where the reader is "obliged" to treat them as "directly infused with symbolic meaning."[13]

Pop and serious fiction differ not only according to which type of rule their readers put into effect more often, but also with respect to the particular rules that readers are asked to apply within each category. Take rules of notice. Although specific rules of notice vary considerably within subgenres, there are three general ways in which operations of notice differ radically between popular and serious texts. First, attention to textual nuances is greatly influenced by the speed with which we read, and our current cultural

---

12. The same claim, in only slightly different terms, is made by Billie Wahlstrom and Caren Deming, who argue that locations in works of popular fiction (like *Spiderman*) are "a device to amuse us and to provide some obvious plot complications," whereas those in serious art (like *Ulysses*) have "a further metaphoric dimension" ("Chasing the Popular Arts through the Critical Forest," *Journal of Popular Culture* 13 [Spring 1980]: 421).

13. Jameson, "On Raymond Chandler," 626.

context encourages us to zip through popular texts carelessly. In part, we see this in marketing strategies. The sales of certain popular titles in airports, train stations, and supermarkets, for instance, reflects a context in which speedy reading is assumed; so does the rapid turnover of the stock of romances.[14] And these sales practices confirm more widely held assumptions about reading speed. The tendency of college students to divide literature into classroom reading and summer reading is one manifestation of these assumptions. So is George P. Elliott's claim that the pace of the thriller "forbids that contemplation which is essential to reading great fiction."[15]

Second, notice is also affected by the number of times we read a text—indeed, by the number of times we think it capable of being read. For if a reader accepts Wayne Booth's dictum that "we quite properly ask that the books we call great be able to stand up under repeated reading,"[16] it will seriously affect the expectations, and hence the attentiveness, with which he or she approaches a given work, even the first time through. The printing of popular texts in cheap, nondurable editions, the stress on their newness—which, by implying that last month's novelties are no longer worth considering, also implies that this text will not be worth reading next month—all encourage a lack of attentiveness as we read.

Third, as I have argued, what we attend to in a text is also influenced by the other works in our minds against which we read it. Particular details stand out as surprising, significant, climactic, or strange in part because they are seen in the context of a particular intertextual grid—a particular set of other works of art. And we tend to hold popular and elite fiction up against different backgrounds. Thus, for instance, when Leon Howard asserts that "few detective novels invite comparison with specific works of 'serious' fiction,"[17] he is not so much stating a "fact" about the properties

---

14. For an excellent discussion of the marketing strategies of popular romances, see Janice Radway, *Reading the Romance*, esp. chap. 1.

15. Elliott, "Country Full of Blondes," *Nation*, April 23, 1960, 355–56.

16. Booth, *Rhetoric of Fiction*, 256. See also Kenneth Burke's discussion of the kinds of texts that are rereadable in "Psychology and Form."

17. Leon Howard, "Raymond Chandler's Not-So-Great Gatsby," *Mystery and Detection Annual* (1973): 1.

of detective stories as making a claim about the "proper" intertextual grid on which to map them. As a consequence of such differences in background, the same detail will be read differently, depending on the type of text in which it is found. When Turgenev gives the name Tatyana to the mother of his heroine in "Assya," we are expected to pay attention to his choice because the novel continues the literary tradition that includes Pushkin's *Eugene Onegin,* whose heroine Tatyana serves as a major model for women in nineteenth-century Russian fiction. But when Olcott gives the same name to the heroine of *Murder at the Red October,* we are not expected to register that fact as particularly important (even though Olcott himself is a brilliant scholar of Russian literature), because we are supposed to read it against a different background.[18] Similarly, while readers are apt to look out for ciphers and anagrams in serious post-Joycean fiction (without such predisposition, the anagrams in Fuentes' *Death of Artemio Cruz* would be invisible),[19] we are not apt to do so in a popular spy novel—even one that, like Robert Littell's *Amateur,* concerns a code breaker who has discovered, encoded in *The Tempest,* proof that Bacon wrote Shakespeare's plays.

Even when what is noticed is the same in popular and elite art (for instance, a title), there is often a difference in the rules of signification applied to it. As a general rule, titles in serious novels during the period under discussion are to be treated metaphorically or symbolically. More specifically, we are expected to treat them as one guide to the specific directions outward in which the novelist intends us to read; as Wayne Booth points out, "It is interesting to note how much more importance titles and epigraphs take on in modern works, where they are often the only explicit commentary the reader is given."[20] The title *Absalom, Absalom!,* for instance, serves, among other things, to remove the novel from a specifically

---

18. Of all the claims about authorial meanings in this book, this is the only one that comes from personal communication with the actual author involved.

19. See Santiago Tejerina-Canal, *La Muerte de Artemio Cruz: Secreto Generativo* (Lincoln: University of Nebraska Press, forthcoming). Since I do not read Spanish, I have not read this monograph; I have, however, discussed the issue of anagrams with its author.

20. Booth, *Rhetoric of Fiction,* 198, n. 25.

Southern context and place it in a larger frame. It is for this reason that a teacher, at a loss for an exam question about a serious novel, can usually ask, "Why is the book called *For Whom the Bell Tolls?*" Or *Their Eyes Were Watching God?* Or *Gravity's Rainbow?* But in reading popular novels, we are normally expected to treat their titles, on the whole, as broadly descriptive (they give clues about genre and general content) and discriminatory (they help distinguish one book from another so that we will know whether we have read it already). Indeed, mass-market books often depend as much on numbering as on title for identification—as I well remember from my years as a collector of Hardy Boys books. One could not reasonably ask students to write for an hour on the question, "Why is this book called *The Drums of Fu Manchu?*" because Sax Rohmer chose his title with the expectation that its function for the reader would be more circumscribed. He expected his reader to be able to recognize from the jacket that his novel was an adventure story in a particular series and that it was a different book from *The Mask of Fu Manchu;* he did not intend it to provide a springboard for generalization or metaphoric association, or to provide an authorial norm otherwise missing from the text.

Rules of configuration differ for the two types of literature as well. As I have already suggested, popular novels tend on the whole to encourage activities of configuration rather than activities of signification. Furthermore, we read popular literature, in general, expecting less complex and ironic plot patterns. In addition—as I will demonstrate in detail later in this section—the particular configurations you impose on or expect in a book depend, in part, on the books you are reading it against.

Finally, in elite art, we demand—and seek out—greater and more elaborate forms of coherence. We are, for instance, more apt to look at apparent inconsistencies as examples of irony or undercutting, whereas in popular novels, we are apt to ignore them or treat them as flaws. This, too, has something to do with the speed of reading—as well as with the reader's tendency, in fiction presumed to be serious, to reread, to refine interpretations, and to exercise ingenuity.

But as I have argued, correct determination of genre—and of the appropriate interpretive rules—is not automatic. It is not even logical. That is, there is no way to determine *by reason alone* what rules apply in a particular case. When, in *Dr. No*, the villain captures James Bond and assures him that he will die, we should expect that the prediction will turn out false. That is not because there is any logical imperative to do so, but rather because we live in a community where it is conventional to apply the rule of chutzpah at such a moment in the plot in novels that present themselves as Fleming's does. But not all novels are so unambiguous in their self-presentation.

I am not here taking the fashionable position that all books are, by their very nature, inherently undecipherable. Quite often, a text will give fairly precise signals as to how the author intended it to be taken. For instance, Erle Stanley Gardner's title *The Case of the Sleepwalker's Niece* nudges us into a pop strategy of reading by blocking a metaphorical interpretation, just as the title *The Sound and the Fury*, by forcing us both into metaphor and into Shakespeare, steers us into the serious mode. The recurring religious imagery of Nathanael West's *Miss Lonelyhearts*—which begins with Shrike's poem in the very first paragraph—makes it nearly impossible for an experienced reader to infer that the author wanted it treated as a nonsymbolic popular tale; the flat, unresonant prose of most paperback romances discourages the kind of attentiveness that is central to elite-novel reading strategies.[21]

But other works are more confusing—even a work as apparently straightforward as Spillane's *Vengeance Is Mine*. Its title can be treated as a pop title, a marker to distinguish it from, yet relate it to, *I, the Jury*. But it can also be interpreted as a serious title, as a call to read the novel in the context of Tolstoy (whose *Anna Karenina* starts with the same biblical citation)—and hence to notice its ironic religious implications and to adopt a critical attitude toward the arrogant hero who takes God's work on himself.

Now the attempt to read as authorial audience is ideally a process of matching presuppositions against unfolding text, and revising strategies if the text moves in unanticipated directions. And it would be comforting to believe that the reader who assumed at

---

21. For an excellent discussion of this subject, see Radway, *Reading the Romance*, chap. 6.

first that *Vengeance Is Mine* was the title of a serious ironic novel would soon find that reading corrected by other elements in the text. But as we have seen argued theoretically by such critics as Stanley Fish,[22] and as we have seen demonstrated practically in the variety of readings put forward by our academic journals, it is not always easy for a text to win over a reader who is predisposed to finding in it meanings and values that the author did not intend—even (perhaps especially) when the reader is sincerely trying to join the authorial audience. Given the frequent references to hell and damnation, to playing God, to "making" people; given the antagonist's name, Juno, and the frequent references to Olympus; given what can be interpreted as its references to Balzac's "Sarrasine" (references especially noticeable in an intellectual climate greatly influenced by Barthes' *S/Z*)—it would not be hard to read the novel ironically.

I am not claiming that such an ironic reading, if it were presented as the interpretation of the authorial audience, would be a good one. Rather I am saying something quite different: Bad as it is as an authorial reading, it would not necessarily run against stumbling blocks in the text. In other words, the success of any genre placement—that is, the degree to which any particular reading strategy makes sense of a text—is no guarantee that one has successfully joined the authorial audience. *Vengeance Is Mine* is a popular novel, and thus requires us to approach it with the proper presuppositions. And there is a basic rule of coherence in popular literature: While subtle references or allusions to elite culture (for instance, the discussions of opera in Mary Burchell's Harlequin romance, *Masquerade with Music*) may be read as enhancements for the pleasure of elite readers, those allusions cannot be read as a basic undermining of the apparent overall meaning of the text. The ironic reading of Spillane, whatever its textual grounding, would be wrong as an interpretation of the author's intentions, just as Samuel Rosenberg's ingenious reading of Sherlock Holmes, however successful, is probably wrong: Doyle most likely did *not* have Nietzsche in mind when he invented Moriarty.[23] In neither case,

22. See, in particular, the later essays in Fish, *Is There a Text?*
23. Rosenberg, *Naked Is the Best Disguise: The Death and Resurrection of Sherlock Holmes* (Indianapolis: Bobbs-Merrill, 1974).

though, does the text itself dictate conclusively what rules ought to be applied. Whether you hit upon the right reading will often depend on what you think it likely to be before you begin. Thus, as I have suggested before, whether we pay particular attention to the name Marlow that Eric Ambler gives his hero in *Cause for Alarm* (1939) or the name Marlowe that Chandler gave to *his* hero in *The Big Sleep* that same year will depend on whether we read their texts as popular thrillers (and hence against other popular thrillers) or as serious novels (and hence, perhaps, against the tradition that includes the works of Conrad). And to a large extent, the very act of connecting *The Big Sleep* to one or another of these literary traditions *makes* it into a particular kind of text for the reader processing it.

This brings me back, at last, to *The Glass Key*. As I noted at the beginning of this chapter, the novel itself raises the issue of how presuppositions influence interpretation. In analyzing the discussions of Janet Henry's dream as a metaphor for reading, though, I had already made a decision to treat the novel as serious rather than as popular. But the book is nowhere near so transparent as I pretended it was; in fact, it holds itself open for placement in either broad genre.

Take the opening sentence: "Green dice rolled across the green table, struck the rim together, and bounced back." Whether the novel is popular or serious, this is a privileged position, and in either genre it raises questions for the reader. But *what* questions it raises—that is, what expectations it nourishes, how it is experienced—differ radically for each. If we assume that it is a popular detective story, we will tend to emphasize configurational questions: Who is throwing the dice? Will he or she win or lose? How will the outcome trigger future actions? If we approach it as if it were a serious novel, we will stress questions of signification: What is the role of chance in this novel? What are the symbolic implications of the phrase "bouncing back"? Yet the book that follows does not serve as a strong corrective for either of these readings. Whichever path we choose, the novel follows through; the game does generate much of the early action, but the images of chance and resilience are central to the novel's metaphoric structure.

As I noted above, genres can overlap. One might therefore argue that these two reading strategies are not mutually exclusive, and that the good reader can ask all of these questions at once, reading the novel as a member of both classes simultaneously. Perhaps that is true of these initial questions (although I suspect only academics would actually read this novel in that way). But there are other consequences of genre placement that demand an either/or decision about reading strategy. This is clearest with regard to configuration. If we construe the book as a popular novel, subgenre "detective story," we will be on the lookout for a particular configuration—a problem, a false solution (often stemming from a false confession) about three-quarters of the way through,[24] a correct solution about ten pages from the end, and a postclimax wrap-up of secondary importance. And if we look for that pattern, we will find it. Reading with these expectations, we will not for a moment believe Paul's "confession," and we will concentrate more on the solution than on the wrap-up. The book will not, even in this reading, be particularly jolly, but its despair will be muted by the reader's privileging of the positive results of Ned Beaumont's investigation.

But if we read it as a serious novel, subgenre "personal-discovery novel" (under the spell of Proust, Conrad, and Faulkner), we will be alerted to another potential configuration, one in which the correct solution will come earlier than it would in a detective story, but will be followed by something even more important—an examination of its psychological and philosophical ramifications. If we are on the lookout for this configuration, we will find it, too, with a bit of a twist. Using this reading strategy, we are more likely to believe Paul's confession and be surprised by the arrival of a second solution; in any case, we will be more interested in the consequences of the truth than in the facts of the murder itself. In this reading, therefore, we will give less attention to the solution and will stress the novel's final image more strongly: Ned Beaumont staring at an empty doorway, a doorway we will tie metaphorically to the door in the dream and all the other doors and entryways into psycholog-

24. See Barbara Gerber Sanders' extreme claim that "the climax in the action traditionally occurs near the 3/4 point in novels" ("Structural Imagery in *The Great Gatsby:* Metaphor and Matrix," *Linguistics in Literature* 1, no. 1 [1975]: 56).

ical blanks that give this book much of its troubling character when it is construed as a serious novel.

Intellectually, perhaps, we can have it both ways and call the novel some kind of hybrid. But for any actual act of reading, we must choose one genre or the other (or some discrete third): we cannot be both surprised and not surprised, and we cannot both emphasize and de-emphasize the emptiness and lack of resolution of the final paragraph. In precisely the same way that initial genre choice substantially colors our experience of the avant-garde *Cosmos*, so it radically influences our reading of *The Glass Key*.

Scapegoating Carmen: Reading Misreadings

So far, my argument in this chapter has centered on one of the reasons—generic ambiguity—that texts are so often open to misreadings. As I have suggested before, though, my primary concern is not with exploring generic ambiguity itself, but with offering an exemplary kind of analysis that can be turned to other problems as well. Rather than pursue this direction further, therefore, either by hunting down additional specimens of generically ambiguous texts, or even by trying to build up a typology of misreadings (a project that threatens to be both endless and drab), I would like now to see how the examination of the presuppositions behind the reading process can help us answer a parallel, and I think more important, question, one that has hovered throughout. Given the potential ambiguity of texts, what makes a reader aiming at an authorial reading choose to apply one strategy rather than another?

There are, of course, many possible reasons, often depending on the specific individual doing the reading. But sometimes particular misreadings are widespread rather than idiosyncratic—and I would argue that such *persistent* misreading usually has its origins, not in the readers as individuals, but in the culture that has taught them to read. We can therefore often uncover forces at work in a society by reading its misreadings, by studying the ways that readers have misappropriated the texts they live with. Specifically, to the extent that we can determine what rules readers actually do apply when they try unsuccessfully to recover an author's intentions, we can illuminate the categories informing their thoughts, and consequently the ideological pressures working on them.

Why turn to *mis*readings? Can't the works themselves—or the authorial interpretations of them—give us cultural insights? Yes, but of a different kind—or, to be more accurate, of two different kinds. First of all, to the extent that a work provides messages, espouses values, criticizes or supports its culture, we can determine—within limits, of course—the author's vision of things. We can, for instance, determine Dostoyevsky's attitudes toward Roman Catholicism by reading *The Idiot*, just as we can learn Proust's attitudes toward Wagner or (by a vastly more circuitous route) toward homosexuality by reading *Remembrance of Things Past*. A great deal of useful criticism is aimed at precisely such determinations.

Second, and more subtly, determining the nature of the authorial audience—specifying the presuppositions on which a text is built—can inform us about what authors assumed about their readers. The gratuitous violence toward blacks in *I, the Jury*—a violence that the text apparently sees no need to justify—spotlights more than Mickey Spillane's racism; it also betrays the racist attitudes he routinely expected in his readers. And to the extent that authors are shrewd observers of their times, such assumptions can be even more revealing than an author's own more or less explicit moralizing. Unfortunately, it is not always easy to tell when an author has been shrewd in this regard. I used to believe that the popular success of a novel could serve as at least partial evidence, but I have been forced to modify that point of view for two reasons. First, even if readers do read as an author intended, we cannot be sure of their own predilections. For whatever we feel about the status of authorial intention, it appears that until fairly recently, most people read texts at least *as if* they were trying to extract the author's meaning. To the extent that a particular past reading matches the author's intention (regardless of how it matches up with our own responses to the text), we can therefore never be sure how much it actually incorporates the ideology of the actual reader, and how much it merely represents that reader's attempt to join the authorial audience—to follow the instructions of the text, to "accept" (provisionally, perhaps) the ideology it calls for. Thus, for instance, it would be hard to draw any conclusions about an actual reader's views on monarchy as a system of social organization from his or her acceptance of the rightfulness of Richard the Lionhearted's claim to the throne in *Ivanhoe*. Second, as I have argued above, texts can be popular without being understood. Thus, the commercial success of a work has no necessary bearing on the degree to which the author made the right guesses about his or her readers. Chandler's *Big Sleep*, for instance, was intended as a critique of a conservative political position, but his point was consistently missed, even by his admirers. Thus, reading the novel tells us little about what his readers actually thought.

But if we cannot learn about Chandler's readers from reading Chandler, we surely can learn about them by looking at how *they* misread Chandler. For a reader's attempt and *failure* to join the authorial audience implies that something is keeping him or her from applying interpretive strategies that the author, at least, believed to be more or less readily available. The source of that failure may lie in the reader (lack of experience, personal eccentricity) or in the author (poor technique, unrealistic expectations about how readers would respond). But in any case, the mismatch itself provides a starting point for further investigation: it offers a possible instance of ideological interference by indicating a point in the culture where two individuals have different understandings about what presuppositions should underlie a reading of the text.[25]

Let me illustrate this claim in more detail, showing how the strategies employed by critics when they read *The Big Sleep* (and critics are, after all, merely people who get paid to read under public scrutiny) can teach us something about the structure of misogyny, not the misogyny of the novel itself, but the misogyny of the world outside it.

As I suggested in Chapter 5, *The Big Sleep* is a subversive book

---

25. Some of these ideas were originally developed in colloboration with Janice Radway for a paper entitled "The Hidden Mind: Authorial Intention and Literary Texts as Historical Documents," which was delivered at the American Studies Association meeting on November 4, 1983. I am grateful for her permission to use them here. For Radway's own analysis of the problems involved in trying to learn about actual readers by looking at the texts they consume, see *Reading the Romance*.

that seeks to encourage a socially critical attitude by forcefully overturning the basic rules of the detective story genre (at least, its classical variant represented by such writers as Christie), thus forcing its readers to apply rules of coherence that look beyond the conventions to their ideological implications. Those conventions, of course, have been widely discussed by critics from W. H. Auden to S. S. Van Dine, and different critics have listed them in different ways. Nonetheless, there are three rules that show up implicitly or explicitly on nearly every list. First, in S. S. Van Dine's words, "There must be but one culprit." Second, the detective must always win and restore order; as Van Dine puts it, "The detective novel must have a detective in it; and a detective is not a detective unless he detects." And third, the crime must originate in some personal quirk, succeeding temporarily only because it operates behind a veil of deception; the criminal, therefore, can always be unmasked through rational procedures—what Van Dine calls "logical deductions."[26] In other words, the classical detective story centers on a single villain whose transgressions stem from "a little kink in the brain somewhere,"[27] a villain who can be (and is) brought to justice by a single detective through logic rather than force.[28]

Stated in this way, of course, these are rules for the proper construction of texts; but they have analogues in rules for reading, as well. Most obviously, they parallel rules of configuration, governing our expectations about what is likely to occur in a classical detective story (it is appropriate to expect that there will be a single villain, etc.). But they also serve as rules of signification. In a classi-

---

26. S. S. Van Dine, "Twenty Rules for Writing Detective Stories," in *The Art of the Mystery Story: A Collection of Critical Essays*, ed. Howard Haycraft (New York: Grossett and Dunlap/Universal Library, 1947), 190–91.

27. Agatha Christie, *The Mystery of the Blue Train* (New York: Pocket, 1940), 172.

28. There are, of course, exceptions—but they make a point of their unusualness. Thus, Josephine Tey ends *The Man in the Queue* as follows:

"Well," I said to him, "it has been a queer case, but the queerest thing about it is that there isn't a villain in it."
"Isn't there!" Grant said, with that twist to his mouth.
Well, is there? [*The Man in the Queue* (New York: Pocket, 1977), 222 (chap. 18)].

cal detective story, we are normally asked to see the villain—that is, the cause of crime—as an individual; it runs against the grain of the genre to treat him or her as a metaphor for larger social problems. Likewise, the practitioners of the genre expect us to see the detective as a positive representation of the power of an individual to overcome evil, not as a symbol of the weakness of the solitary human being.

This aesthetic formula is not innocent; it serves a political function, supporting what John Cawelti calls "the moral fantasy that human actions have a simple and rational explanation and that guilt is specific and not ambiguous."[29] Addressing the anxieties of a bourgeois audience troubled by the possibility of social revolution, Christie, for instance, puts fear to rest by insisting that evil is individual in nature and can therefore be uprooted without social change by a single competent person. As Stephen Knight puts it, the "meaning implicit in the organic structure" of writers like Doyle and Christie—where "criminal events [are] resolvable by a skilful, persevering agent"—"responds to bourgeois ideas of personal effort through diachronic time towards the improvement of one's moral and physical position."[30]

Chandler's novel is quite different. Here, evil is multiple and social in origin, and the detective is unable to contain it. As E. M. Beekman puts it, "the artificial jungle of the hothouse grows into that of a perverse society of sex, money, murder, immorality and betrayal. . . . A corrupt universe can house no justice."[31] A rough outline of the story may make this break with convention clearer. Philip Marlowe is hired by General Sternwood to take care of Arthur Gwynn Geiger, a bisexual porn merchant who is blackmail-

---

29. Cawelti, *Adventure, Mystery, and Romance*, 132. But see Jameson's claim that the detective story is "a form without ideological content, without any overt political or social function" ("On Raymond Chandler," 625).

30. Knight, *Form and Ideology*, 151. Knight, however, sees the role of the hero as less important in Christie than I do; see esp. his chap. 4. See also Geoffrey H. Hartman: Mystery stories "are exorcisms, stories with happy endings that could be classified with comedy because they settle the unsettling" ("Literature High and Low: The Case of the Mystery Story," in *The Fate of Reading and Other Essays* [Chicago: University of Chicago Press, 1975], 212).

31. Beekman, "Raymond Chandler and an American Genre," *Massachusetts Review* 14 (1973): 164.

ing Carmen, the general's younger daughter. Marlowe intuits, however, that Sternwood really wants him to trace the missing husband of his older daughter Vivian, a former bootlegger named Rusty Regan. Regan has mysteriously vanished, and there are rumors that he has run off with Mona Grant, the wife of racketeer Eddie Mars. After three or four murders (depending on how you count the ambiguous death of the chauffeur) and some strong-arming by the local authorities who want him to lay off the case, Marlowe finds Mona, but is himself caught by Mars' hit man, Lash Canino. Mona—whom he dubs "Silver-Wig"—helps him get away; he kills Canino and then goes back to the Sternwood mansion where it appears that the traditional denouement is to take place.

But *The Big Sleep* has worked up to a traditional resolution only to retreat from it. Yes, we do discover something. Carmen, angry at Marlowe for repelling her attempts at seduction, tries to shoot him. We learn that she had murdered Regan for the same reason, and that Mars and Canino, who had helped get rid of the corpse in a sump, have been using their knowledge to put the screws on Vivian. But by this point in the novel, so much has happened that Philip Marlowe's discovery of what had happened to Regan seems anticlimactic; it surely does not constitute a real answer to the questions that the novel has raised. Nor, for that matter, does Vivian's agreement, at Marlowe's insistence, to put her sister in an institution, really seem an adequate restoration of order. In Chandler, as Beekman notes, "the purported solution does not tidy things up since there is no end to a waking nightmare."[32] But lest we miss the hollowness of the denouement, Chandler purposefully exaggerates the irritation by preparing a configuration that never takes place; throughout the novel, he has built up a growing antagonism between Marlowe and Eddie Mars, only to leave it hanging at the end.

We are made to expect this confrontation in a number of ways. First, as is evident even from the plot summary, the events of the novel are both complex and episodic, and are quite hard to tie together. But there is one link, other than Marlowe, holding it all

32. Ibid.

together: Mars is involved, although often behind the scenes, in all of the action of the book. Indeed, *The Big Sleep* was put together by Chandler out of material scavenged from "Killer in the Rain" and "The Curtain," and Mars is the only character (other than Marlowe, of course) in the novel with an equivalent in both of those early stories. (True, General Sternwood and Carmen are involved in *incidents* that originated in both of the stories; but as characters, they only have analogues in one or the other. Thus, the general takes on some of the plot function of Tony Dravec in "Killer," but they have no character resemblance.) Rules of balance therefore lead us to expect that these primary antagonists will in fact have it out. Second, Chandler uses a verbal trick to reinforce their position as antagonists: Mars' name is an echo of Marlowe's. Chandler was especially fond of this device; in the later novels, Marlowe is mirrored, in different ways, by such characters as Mrs. Murdock, Lindsay Marriott, Moose Malloy, and especially Paul Marston. In this case, the phonetic parallel is a signal for us to apply rules of signification and coherence to read Mars as Marlowe's primary opponent. Third, Marlowe's most bitter and most extended—hence his most noticeable—verbal assault in the novel is directed at Mars.

> "You think he's just a gambler. I think he's a pornographer, a blackmailer, a hot car broker, a killer by remote control, and a suborner of crooked cops. He's whatever looks good to him, whatever has the cabbage pinned to it. . . . [Jones is] a dead little bird now, with his feathers ruffled and his neck limp and a pearl of blood on his beak. Canino killed him. But Eddie Mars wouldn't do that, would he, Silver-Wig? He never killed anybody. He just hires it done."[33]

Marlowe unleashes this diatribe to Silver-Wig, and its vehemence grows partly from his growing involvement with her. This competition for her affections, of course, further arouses our expectation of a showdown: there is a rule of balance that rivals have to meet. Finally, near the end of the novel, Chandler explicitly and

33. Raymond Chandler, *The Big Sleep* (New York: Pocket, 1950), 179–80, 182 (chap. 28). Further references to this edition are made in the text.

ostentatiously drops the first shoe. After telling Vivian to seek professional care for Carmen, he tells her of his plans.

> "Forget Eddie. I'll go see him after I get some rest. I'll handle Eddie."
> "He'll try to kill you."
> "Yeah," I said. "His best boy couldn't. I'll take a chance on the others." [213, chap. 32]

Yet while the Howard Hawks film version ends dramatically as Mars is machine-gunned by his own thugs, the novel promises this confrontation only to fail to fulfill it. In fact, Marlowe never does "handle" Mars; instead, Chandler closes the novel with a despairing meditation, in a privileged position.

> What did it matter where you lay once you were dead? In a dirty sump or in a marble tower on top of a high hill? You were dead, you were sleeping the big sleep, you were not bothered by things like that. Oil and water were the same as wind and air to you. You just sleep the big sleep, not caring about the nastiness of how you died or where you fell. Me, I was part of the nastiness now. Far more a part of it than Rusty Regan was. . . .
> On the way downtown I stopped at a bar and had a couple of double Scotches. They didn't do me any good. All they did was make me think of Silver-Wig, and I never saw her again. [213–14, chap. 32]

Yet from the first reviews that greeted the novel, most critics have missed its irresolution. Thus, instead of interpreting it as a critique of the politics upheld by the traditions of the genre, they have instead read it as a heroic text, seeing not Marlowe's final despair, but rather his knightly—albeit muted—triumph. In other words, the text has been misread in such a way that it appears to provide a resolution. Even John Cawelti touts Marlowe in *The Big Sleep* as an example of a hero who "confronts, exposes, and destroys this web of conspiracy and perversion."[34] Philip Durham similarly decides that he was "the traditional American hero bringing fair play and justice where it could not be or had not been administered."[35] Why have they done so? And how?

34. Cawelti, *Adventure, Mystery, and Romance*, 149.
35. Philip Durham, *Down These Mean Streets a Man Must Go: Raymond Chandler's Knight* (Chapel Hill: University of North Carolina Press, 1963), 33. See

In part, the phenomenon can be explained by a tendency of readers to find what they expect and want in a text. As I. A. Richards puts it, "When any person misreads . . . it is because, *as he is at that moment,* he wants to. . . . Every interpretation is motivated by some interest."[36] Readers are likely to expect and want this kind of resolution for a number of reasons. On one level, of course, experiences with previous detective stories have had their toll. In addition, as I have argued (and post-structuralist critiques of traditional reading practices would support this claim), there is a general tendency in most reading to apply rules of coherence in such a way that disjunctures are smoothed over so that texts are turned into unified wholes—that is, in a way that allows us to read so that we get the satisfaction of closure. This interpretative technique is taught explicitly in school; and it may be connected to an innate psychological drive for closure.

But there are political reasons as well. Even if the desire for closure is cross-cultural, its *particular* manifestations are always social. We cannot explain why children's stories so often end with characters going to sleep simply by trotting out a generalized desire for closure. This particular closure is common under these circumstances—but less so in adult fiction—because in our culture children's stories often serve the social function of preparing children to go to sleep. Similarly, Janice Radway has eloquently demonstrated how the particular forms of closure found in popular romances respond to tensions within the structure of contemporary patriarchy.[37]

I suspect that readers in our culture tend to seek out (or impose) this particular kind of resolution—explanation with punishment—in *The Big Sleep* for much the same reason that they read detective stories in the first place: they want to be soothed, not irritated, and they do not want to confront Chandler's abyss and its demand for radical social change. As George P. Elliott puts it, we all have a malaise about the order of the world, and we like "to read a story which produces in the reader a safe version of the same

---

also his claim, about Chandler's novels in general, that "the action and violence more or less covered up the fact that everything came out all right in the end" (97).

36. Richards, *Practical Criticism: A Study of Literary Judgment* (New York: Harcourt, Brace, and World/Harvest, 1964), 229.

37. Radway, *Reading the Romance,* esp. chap. 4.

thing and which purges this induced tension";[38] and while this may be less true with so-called elite art, it is widely felt to be true of popular texts.[39] It is thus not coincidental that the earliest reviews not only passed over the novel's irresolution, but also ignored Chandler's *social* analysis of evil. Almost uniformly, they stressed the theme of personal degeneracy rather than social corruption. The *New Yorker*, for instance, called it a "pretty terrifying story of degeneracy"; Ralph Partridge referred to the "full strength blend . . . of sadism, eroticism, and alcoholism"; the *Times Literary Supplement* described the novel's plot as Marlowe's trying "to conceal from an aged general the misadventures of his two degenerate daughters."[40] Even the more astute critics tended to see *The Big Sleep* as a collection of characters—mostly vicious, but at least individuals—rather than as a portrayal of a social situation.

Most readers, in other words, seem to misread Chandler for the same reasons they misread most disturbing books—they want to defend themselves against unwelcome points of view. But the question of the readers' *motives* for reading the novel as they do is only half the question. Even if I am right about *why* they do so, we still have to confront the even more vexing question of *how* they do so. For while readers tend to find what they want to find in books, there are, for most readers, limits to the process. Behind any persistent interpretation must lie not only some persistent desire to read in that fashion; at the same time, there must also be some coherent interpretive strategy, some approach to the text that makes *that* reading seem a plausible, even inevitable, consequence of the words on the page. For any interpretation, in other words, it

38. Elliott, "Country Full of Blondes," 356. For a different perspective on this problem, see Stephen Knight's claim that Chandler holds a "conservative and elitist position" (*Form and Ideology*, 136–38).

39. See Russel Nye's claim that "popular art confirms the experience of the majority, in contrast to elite art, which tends to explore the new" (*The Unembarrassed Muse: The Popular Arts in America* [New York: Dial, 1970], 4). See also Donald Dunlop, "Popular Culture and Methodology," *Journal of Popular Culture* 9 (Fall 1975): 375/23–383/31; Dwight Macdonald, "A Theory of Mass Culture," in *Mass Culture: The Popular Arts in America*, ed. Bernard Rosenberg and David Manning White (Glencoe, Ill.: Free Press/Falcon's Wing, 1957), 59–73.

40. "Mysteries," *New Yorker*, February 11, 1939, 84; Ralph Partridge, "Death with a Difference," *New Statesman and Nation*, June 10, 1939, 910; "Detective Stories," *Times Literary Supplement*, March 11, 1939, 152.

ought ideally to be possible to trace the steps that allow readers to transform the text in that particular way.

In this case, the process of interpretation involves treating the novel primarily as a popular novel (stressing the solution) rather than as a serious one (stressing the indecisive conclusion). In addition, it has to involve an act of scapegoating: in order to create a sense of resolution in a morally chaotic situation, someone must be seen as the wrongdoer and appropriately punished. And even for those critics who did not explicitly name anyone as *the* guilty party, it is clear who they must have had in mind. For given the novel's structure, there is only one possibility: if anyone's punishment redeems the world, serves as an emblem of the triumph of justice, it has to be Carmen Sternwood's, since the discovery that she killed Rusty Regan is the closest thing to a standard, formulaic detective story conclusion that we find in this novel. Thus, for instance, John Cawelti, claiming that there is a single criminal (although one usually tied to a larger organization) in the hard-boiled formula, goes on to name Carmen as the criminal in *The Big Sleep*.[41] Stephen Knight obviously believes the same when he claims that "Chandler's ultimate villains are always women."[42] Dennis Porter, more explicitly, calls Carmen the "archcriminal" of the novel: "That the archcriminal turns out in the end to be the perverted baby doll who falls into Marlowe's arms on the fourth page of the novel has about it the swift and unanswerable finality of the best punch lines and, in the context, warrants the sustained darkness of mood with which the novel ends."[43] At first, that may

41. Cawelti, *Adventure, Mystery, and Romance*, 147–48.

42. Knight, *Form and Ideology*, 157. See also Gavin Lambert's claim that *Farewell, My Lovely, The Lady in the Lake*, and *The High Window* are "dominated by portraits of a deadly female of the American species, combing [*sic:* combining?] the power-drive of one Sternwood sister and the psychosis of the other. . . . His novels are a notable addition to the popular mythology that represents death as a woman" (*The Dangerous Edge* [New York: Grossman, 1976], 220, 233).

43. Dennis Porter, *Pursuit of Crime*, 143. Elsewhere, he claims that Marlowe's journey is "unnecessary as part of the effort to catch *the* criminal—Carmen even pretends to faint into Marlowe's arms in that first scene—but it is made indispensible for the moral education of the investigator and, even more importantly, for the appropriate aesthetic experience of the reader" (39, emphasis added). Porter does mention, however, that Chandler "points to the psychological and even socioeconomic causes of crime" (41). One of the few critics to see Carmen as a victim is Hartman; see "Literature High and Low," 220–21.

seem a fairly reasonable interpretive move, but the more I think about it, the odder it seems. It is not simply that the text itself does not make this move inevitable; it does not even make it easy. Not only, as I have pointed out, does Chandler go out of his way to underscore Mars' villainy; in addition, he tries to block this potential reading by minimizing Carmen's role in the evil around her.

Carmen is a fairly complicated character. On the one hand, to be sure, she has the characteristics that allowed the anonymous blurb writer for my printing to give her top billing: on the front cover as "a luscious mantrap," on the back as a "female . . . as crooked as a snake—and twice as deadly."[44] Through the novel, she is described in terms that recall serpents and rodents. We are told that "her breath hissed" (79, chap. 15), that "her small sharp teeth glinted" (142, chap. 24), and that her laughter reminds Marlowe twice of "rats behind the wainscoting" (60, chap. 12; 143, chap. 24). And her name, taken from Merimée's novel (a Chandler favorite), hardly conjures up notions of purity and fidelity.

If that were all there were to her, of course, her transformation into a scapegoat would be unproblematic. But surely that is an incomplete description. After all, Merimée's Carmen, whatever her faults, is not a villain. As a smuggler, her crime is simply an attack on an irrational economic structure; as a woman, her crime is simply an attack on bourgeois, patriarchal respectability. In the end, she is a victim whose sacrifice solves nothing, although it salves male pride. This inherited role of victim, rather than villain, is emphasized by Chandler's imagery, too. His description of Carmen as an animal is clouded by his constant references to her as an incapable child: Marlowe's first crack to the butler Norris is "you ought to wean her" (4, chap. 1), a remark that fits well with a recurring strand of babylike imagery: she sucks her thumb, "turning it around in her mouth like a baby with a comforter" (3, chap. 1); her handwriting is "sprawling" and "moronic" (10, chap. 2); she is described at one point as looking "like a bad girl in the principal's office" (59, chap. 12). She can, in fact, barely take care of herself: she is easy prey for blackmailers; she is incompetent with a pistol; after the climactic scene where she tries to shoot Mar-

44. Pocket Books, September 1967 printing.

lowe, she wets her pants (204, chap. 31). No wonder Marlowe never finds her sexually alluring.

Indeed, although she is the person who actually shoots Regan, Chandler consistently suggests that she is just a pawn in the hands of people far more powerful than she is. And he further suggests, at least metaphorically, that her act (the result of a kind of psychotic epilepsy) is but the blossoming of a rottenness that comes to her from her family heritage, a sickness inherited from the oil fields that represent the source of "legitimate" wealth. Carmen, if anything, is but the end of the line for her class, and her institutionalization—far from threatening that class—only serves to bolster it. Carmen, in sum, is neither as intelligent as Spillane's Charlotte Manning (*I, the Jury*) nor as alluring as Pandora, neither as calculating as Temple Drake (Faulkner's *Sanctuary*) nor as self-controlled as Brigid O'Shaughnessy (Hammett's *Maltese Falcon*). She is as pitiable as she is repulsive.

I am not suggesting that Chandler's depiction of her is not misogynistic. It clearly is. But the nature of his misogyny is dismissal and ridicule. His Carmen is infantile; she is too weak to serve as a worthy foil if Marlowe is to be seen as a heroic figure. Yet as we have seen, readers have read her quite differently. Luke Parsons, for instance, suggests a total lack of sympathy on Chandler's part: "In Mr. Chandler's books this association of nymphomania with homicidal tendencies is especially marked. . . . And it is remarkable that Marlowe witholds from them [the nymphomaniacs, including Carmen] the compassion he would allow even a gangster or a millionaire. No doubt this is partly a convention. The plot must have its villainess."[45]

It seems, then, that something happens to Carmen in the act of reading; many readers of the book apparently have, in their interpretive arsenal, some strategy that allows them to increase her monstrosity so that they can put enough blame on her to make her punishment cathartic. The principle clearly has something to do with our culture's denigration of women, but it cannot be quite so simple as a rule of snap moral judgment that, wherever possible,

---

45. Parsons, "On the Novels of Raymond Chandler," *Fortnightly Review*, May 1954, 350.

we should consider a woman the guilty party. Indeed, there seems to be a rule precisely to the contrary, one sufficiently strong to enable Agatha Christie to base an entire novel (I will not spoil it by telling you which one) on the assumption that, unless specifically directed otherwise, readers will assume that all references to a "murderer" are references to a male. Yet there is obviously *some* convention that allows readers to turn against Carmen with special vehemence.

Let me propose here, rather briefly, a candidate for this convention: a rule of enchainment that I call the rule of the dominant negative. When a female character is described as a complex combination of contradictory traits, the reader should give priority to the most negative qualities and should in fact interpret her very complexity as a negative factor on its own. Like all interpretive rules, of course, this one has its exceptions. Not all writers depend on it, not all readers apply it (particularly with rising consciousness about women's positions in our society), and not even the standard, male-centered readings of male texts depend on it regularly. There are certainly cases where women of ambiguous character are viewed in a positive light even in traditional academic readings of canonical texts. But there is no doubt that complexity in a woman is viewed with more suspicion than complexity in a man is. We still live in a literary culture whose norms encourage us to admire King Lear for his involved character, but to demand that our women be as pure as Cordelia. Hamlet, avenging his father's murder, is a sympathetic hero, even though he waffles and even though his sword runs through a couple or more or less innocent victims along the way; Clytemnestra, avenging her daughter's murder, is a snake, even though her resolve is stronger and her aim truer. Thus, as Leland S. Person, Jr., points out, critics have tended to malign Daisy Buchanan for failing Gatsby, even though "no woman, no human being, could ever approximate the platonic ideal he has invented."[46]

The rule of the dominant negative is an indirect consequence of

46. Person, "'Herstory' and Daisy Buchanan," *American Literature* 50 (May 1978): 251.

our polarized view of woman. In our culture, we have a number of categories in which to place women, but they tend to fall into pairs of binary oppositions: madonna/whore, good girl/bad girl, victim/villain. This tendency to dichotomize leads to a particular horror of those who refuse to stay put, for such border straddlers seem to threaten the very order of the universe. Thus, innocent traits in a "guilty" woman serve not to redeem her but to confirm her guilt, doubling the charge against her.[47] Males do not face the same difficulty, however. Since they are viewed as free subjects rather than as objects, they are not fundamentally ordered in clear dichotomies; thus, a combination of attributes is not automatically seen as a crossing of boundaries and a threatening of order. Men, in other words, can be rich as characters; women, on the whole, have the choice of being pure or being monstrous.

The rule of the dominant negative helps explain many things about our culture. In particular, it explains our tendency to blame the victim when she is a woman. We are used to sympathizing with male murderers (Raskolnikov, Pozdnyshev in *The Kreutzer Sonata*) who have redeeming character traits; but when a woman (say, Emma Bovary) is victimized, we often find ourselves looking at her character to find out why she brought it on herself. Only the purest female victims (Drusilla in Southworth's *Changed Brides* and *The Bride's Fate*) can have the sympathy they deserve; this tendency in our society helps prevent us from, among other things, effectively coping with rape.

I do not want to put too much weight on the particulars of this explanation of the misreadings of *The Big Sleep*. For in setting out this hypothesis, my interest is less in *The Big Sleep* and its specific readers than in a general methodological procedure. My primary point is that whatever the specific interpretive strategy that permits it to happen, the scapegoating of Carmen does not take place in the novel; rather, it is an act that readers perform, not idiosyncratically or individualistically, but according to reading strategies

47. For a good discussion of Clytemnestra in these terms, see Nancy S. Rabinowitz, "From Force to Persuasion: Aeschylus' *Oresteia* as Cosmogonic Myth," *Ramus* 10, no. 2 (1981): 159–91.

that their society has taught them and reaffirmed in them before they begin the book. Reading readers, then—whether they be professional critics or friends—is not simply a way of getting a better understanding of a text; it can also help reveal the structures of thought that control us.

7

Some Have Greatness
Thrust upon Them: The
Politics of Canon Formation

> To answer that the *best* novels survive is to beg the question.
> Excellence is a constantly changing, socially chosen value.
>   Richard Ohmann, "The Shaping of a Canon"

As I have been arguing, then, texts are often ambiguous; even readers committed in principle to reading as authorial audience may find that in practice novels often provide insufficient guidance for their own proper decoding and may apparently offer themselves up to contradictory interpretive keys. But it does not follow that they are infinitely open. If a text does not impose itself on readers, it *is* resistant to certain interpretations. Let me return to the swing-set metaphor of the first chapter. As I noted there, if you make a mistake in the process of constructing the swing set, you *may* erroneously produce something internally consistent—and hence never notice your error. But in the process of putting it together, you may also find yourself in a self-contradictory position that forces you to rethink what you have done so far.

There are two circumstances under which this can happen. First, the swing set itself may be defective—the author may have made a mistake, providing signals that encourage readers to apply inappropriate strategies. This can happen with respect to any of the four categories of rules. Thus, for instance, in *The Idiot*, Dostoyevsky seems to invoke the rule of notice that a character whose moral choice generates the primary action is to be read as an important character. Nastasya Filippovna throws a hundred thousand rubles into the fire, in order to see if Ganya is venal enough to

209

pull it from the flames. At this point, the concentration on Ganya's moral choice—and particularly on his moral victory—confirms our initial impression that he is to be a major force in the novel. But he virtually drops out for most of the rest of the book, and his disappearance has no apparent rhetorical function—that is, the violation of the rule does not appear to be aiming at any particular effect. (Dostoyevsky compounds this flaw by a violation of a rule of configuration: he fails to follow through on the conflict set up in the first volume between Myshkin and Ganya.) Knowing the genesis of the novel, one can well understand why Dostoyevsky shifted direction at this point, and why he could not rewrite part 1 (the novel was being published serially while it was being composed); as *The Idiot* stands, though, Ganya's flickering presence remains a weakness in its construction.

Rules of signification can be badly handled, too. Leon Howard, for instance, criticizes Chandler's *Long Goodbye* for failing to conform properly to what I have called the rule of realism.

> The reader of course is given the same information that enables Marlowe to infer that Terry's farewell letter is a fake—i.e., the reference to a mailbox which would not be found in a Mexican village. The validity of this clue for the reader, however, depends upon his faith in Chandler's conformity to a reality that exists outside the novel itself; and this faith cannot be claimed by an author who asks the reader to believe that Terry could be presumed dead and still maintain control over a substantial fortune which he could not have taken with him in his sudden flight.[1]

Similarly, with configuration, it generally mars a novel when an author sets up expectations that are neither fulfilled nor effectively undermined, but simply unutilized. In Southworth's double-volumed novel, *The Changed Brides/The Bride's Fate*, the victimized heroine, Drusilla, learns midway through the narrative that she is an heiress. There are, though, a number of potential obstacles standing between her and her considerable fortune; and the way

---

1. Howard, "Raymond Chandler's Not-So-Great Gatsby," *Mystery and Detective Annual* (1973): 15, n. 1.

that they are mentioned in the text, combined with the abuse Drusilla has received so far, encourages the reader to expect her to confront them. In fact, she gets her rightful money with no difficulty at all, denying us the anticipated pleasure of watching her rise to the challenges.

Authorial failures respecting rules of coherence are most likely in those genres where the pleasure of the conclusion depends on shared notions of fair play. For instance, readers of classical detective fiction expect not only that a coherent solution will be offered, but also that it will be of a specific type—that is, rational. Without this assumed agreement between author and reader, the reader has no grounds for his or her guesswork. Under the circumstances, how is a reader likely to approach Reginald Hill's *Killing Kindness?* It opens with a medium talking to the spirit of a recent murder victim; later, much of what she says turns out to be true. Given the genre, we are entitled to assume that the supernatural cannot intrude, and we are therefore entitled to draw conclusions based on the assumption that the medium must have gotten her knowledge in some other way. The actual solution is therefore likely to frustrate any experienced detective story reader. Although nothing in the text signals the suspension of the convention of rationalism, it turns out that she really is a medium.

If that were all there were to it, evaluating texts—at least, with regard to their technical competence—would be fairly easy. Unfortunately, it is not always easy to distinguish between a defective swing set and a bumbling do-it-yourselfer—and when a text fails to respond to the rules applied to it, it is not always clear whether the text or the reader is at fault. To put it in other terms, there are two ways of rethinking your reading experiences when a text fails to respond to the strategies with which it is approached: You can keep the text and change the strategy, or you can keep the strategy and toss out the text on the assumption that it is thin or incoherent. And when particular reading strategies—such as the New Critical strategies that dominated the 1940s and 1950s—are *normalized*, the latter course is the more likely, regardless of where the problems lie. Indeed, David Daiches goes so far as to validate this procedure explicitly. For the New Critics (including himself), he argues, value is a matter of the "degree to which the work lends itself to" the "kind of treatment" New Critical theory demands.[2]

This, I would argue, is one of the major ways in which the academy makes its evaluations.[3] Canonization is, at least in part, a process by which certain texts are privileged because they work with a normalized strategy or set of strategies. As Annette Kolodny argues, "Frequently our reading habits become fixed, so that each successive reading experience functions, in effect, normatively, with one particular kind of novel stylizing our expectations of those to follow."[4] Thus, for instance, Leon Howard is able to denigrate Chandler's *Long Goodbye*, not only for the problem with signification cited above (which he relegates to a footnote) but even more because it fails to conform to the configuration he expects of a work of the genre he assumes it to be. More specifically, he starts out with the presupposition that the novel fits what I have shown to be popular patterns; when he finds an unexpectedly long epilogue, he blames the text rather than the bias with which he approaches it.[5] Such an evaluative procedure is far from atypical; as a result, canons are always ideological at base, not only in terms of their treatment of content, but even more in their treatment of form, since the reading

2. Daiches, *Critical Approaches to Literature*, 303.

3. Of course, the belief that, as Paul Lauter puts it, "Standards of literary merit are not absolute but contingent" ("Introduction," xx) has become increasingly common in the American academy. See, for instance, Richard Ohmann, "The Shaping of a Canon": "Who attributed [excellence] to only some novels, and how?" Ohmann's concern in his essay is somewhat different from mine: he is looking at the social processes by which the choices of particular readers get institutionalized in the form of a canon. In contrast, I am interested in the ways that the process of reading itself helps lead to those initial choices. I view these approaches as complementary, not contradictory. For some other recent views, see Judith Fetterley, *The Resisting Reader* and "Reading about Reading"; Annette Kolodny, "Dancing through the Minefield" and "A Map for Rereading"; Jane Tompkins, *Sensational Designs*; and the special issue of *Critical Inquiry* (10, no. 1) in which Ohmann's essay appears, and which includes the essay by Barbara Herrnstein Smith, "Contingencies of Value" (1–35).

4. Kolodny, "Dancing through the Minefield," 11. See also Terry Eagleton: "Literary theorists, critics, and teachers, then, are not so much purveyors of doctrine as custodians of a discourse. . . . Certain pieces of writing are selected as being more amenable to this discourse than others, and these are what is known as literature or the 'literary canon'" (*Literary Theory*, 201).

5. Howard, "Chandler's No-So-Great Gatsby," 1–15, esp. 6.

strategies to which they owe their existence always have ideological implications.

The best way to see how politics puts pressure on readers as they evaluate texts is to look closely at a particular pair of texts: one that has succeeded and one that has not. For my first, I have chosen *The Great Gatsby*, almost universally—if sometimes grudgingly—recognized as a classic of American literature. For the second, I have picked Margaret Ayer Barnes' 1935 novel, *Edna His Wife*, since it deals similarly with the difficulties of the long climb up through the American class structure—and, coincidentally, with misplaced Midwesterners in New York. *Edna* is clearly a novel with something to offer, at least to some readers, since it was quite popular at the time it was written; even among scholars of American literature, however, it has been all but forgotten by now. The difference in their status, I would argue, can never be explained by what John Guillory aptly calls "the massively resistant tautology of literary history: that works *ought* to be canonized because they *are* good."[6] Rather, *Gatsby* has been canonized and *Edna* tossed in the can at least partly because of a political bias in the way we have been taught to read. But in order to see how this is so, it is necessary to know something about Barnes' novel.[7]

The story begins in 1900. Edna Losser, whose father is the station master of the Blue Island depot of the Rock Island Line, seems about to marry her shy and clumsy railroad beau, Al. But while at a picnic with her almost-fiancé, she meets the handsome and upwardly mobile young lawyer, Paul Jones. When her bicycle breaks down, he gallantly but forcefully takes her home on a tandem he manages to borrow and—to her shock—kisses her with the somewhat cynical claim, "I always do what I want."[8] Whether by nature or by upbringing, Edna is a "romantic" at heart and is attracted by his appearance, by his energy, and by his self-confi-

---

6. Guillory, "Ideology of Canon-Formation," 174.

7. In my discussion of Barnes' novel, I am especially indebted to Nancy S. Rabinowitz, with whom many of these ideas have been jointly worked out. For a fuller discussion of the structure, meaning, and critical reception—such as it is—of *Edna His Wife*, see our "Legends of Toothpaste and Love."

8. Margaret Ayer Barnes, *Edna His Wife: An American Idyll* (Boston: Houghton Mifflin, 1935), 45 (pt. 1, chap. 1.3). Further references to this edition will be made in the text.

dence—as well as by the fact that he is a foundling. At first, Paul doesn't consider the possibility of a lasting attachment, since marriage does not fit into this stage of the life he projects for himself. But he is swayed by "her small mouth, quivering like a child's mouth . . . her blue eyes, shining with the silver iridescence of a woman's tears" (63; pt. 1, chap. 2.1). Since her parents raise questions about his background, they elope. The remainder of the novel chronicles their worldly rise in the wake of Paul's professional success. Starting in a small Chicago flat, they move to suburban Oakwood Terrace, then to a more fashionable residence on Chicago's North Side, and finally to a chic, modernistic Park Avenue penthouse. But the more Paul succeeds, the less he has in common with Edna, and the more pointless Edna's life becomes. With abundant financial resources and servants to do all her domestic chores, she has less and less intimacy with her family. Remaining very much the same working-class woman whose aesthetic values were derived from Gibson drawings, she finds herself increasingly cut off from the society in which she is supposed to move; the final jolt to her self-esteem comes when Edna learns that, for the last fifteen years, Paul has been having an affair with Katharine Boyne, a famous sculptress of whom she has never heard.

Behind the straightforward story is a strong demystification of democratic capitalist ideology, specifically of the myth of upward mobility—the belief that social advancement is both desirable and possible through shrewdness and hard work. Barnes undermines this myth—not by suggesting, as did many of her contemporaries, that such success is unattainable, but rather by showing that it comes at high personal cost and that the structure of society forces women to pay more than their share. This critique, in turn, forces Barnes into particular rhetorical maneuvers.

For instance, *Edna His Wife* stands in sharp contrast to many apparently similar novels (particularly modern novels) that show how some extraordinary woman (usually artistically talented) is held back by social oppression: Erica Jong's *Fear of Flying*, Margaret Drabble's *Waterfall*, Susan Fromberg Schaeffer's *Falling*. Powerful as those novels can be, they tend to sidestep one crucial aspect of Barnes' analysis. Democratic society, after all, is theoretically structured to protect the interests of the ordinary, not the extraordinary; artists, male and female alike, have traditionally found it hard to adapt. Thus, in *Fear of Flying*, it is hard to tell to what extent Isadora Wing's problems result from her being a woman and to what extent they stem from her being an artist. In order to make sure that her novel has no such ambiguity, Barnes focuses on a woman who is bland to her very core, and thus shows that the *ungifted* woman is crushed by social inequities, too, simply because she is a woman.

For this reason, she has had to create a heroine whose limitations are frankly crippling. Next to Edna, to paraphrase Vladimir Nabokov, Emma Bovary is a Hegel. Emma, at least, reads; since her world view comes from books, there is always the remote possibility that she might stumble upon one that could serve as a corrective. Edna, in contrast, prefers pictures, especially those that tell stories (e.g., 230; pt. 2, chap. 5.2); hence her love of movies. Early on, Paul lends her "a book called 'The Origin of Species', but she could make neither head nor tail out of even the first three pages" (58; pt. 1, chap. 2.1). She doesn't read newspapers, and her ignorance about serious art, music, and literature is almost total. Not surprisingly, Edna's limitations are reflected in a difficulty with words. She thinks in clichés, and stress renders her inarticulate. The best she can manage by way of conversation is a "complicated pretence of interests utterly foreign to her nature, assumed in a passionate desire to please" (58; pt. 1, chap. 2.1). Even when trying to describe something as simple as Mount Vernon, she can only stumble out with, " 'It's somehow—American' " (318; pt. 3, chap. 1.3).

Now on the surface, neither Barnes' plot nor her aims nor her consequent rhetorical choices would necessarily seem to predetermine the quality of her book—it *ought* to be possible to write a good novel within these parameters, just as it is possible to write a bad one. In fact, I think Barnes has succeeded in writing a good book. I am not going to try to prove that here; rather, I am going to try to show that adequate assessment of the novel is rendered unlikely—not impossible, but unlikely—by a masculinist bias in the normalized techniques of reading most academics have been trained to use.

We can see the mismatch between *Edna* and traditional reading strategies if we look at how actual readers are likely to apply the various rules of reading to Barnes' and Fitzgerald's texts. Let me start with rules of notice. As I have pointed out, one way in which a given element becomes noticeable is through the placement of the text on an intertextual grid—that is, *one* of the effects of a literary tradition is that it provides a stock of familiar details, the echoes of which, in subsequent texts, become charged. As a consequence, texts that partake of the academic tradition (which is primarily male) will seem, to academic readers, richer in their details. And given our tendency to associate richness of detail with literary quality (as Brooks argues, "A poem . . . is to be judged . . . by its coherence, sensitivity, depth, richness, and tough-mindedness"),[9] such texts will, other things being equal, appear to be better. Thus, Letha Audhuy is able to justify focusing attention on a few apparently invisible lines in *Gatsby* because they echo *The Waste Land*;[10] T. Jeff Evans is able to center on the word "raw" by holding the text up to "Daisy Miller";[11] John Shroeder can privilege certain details in *Gatsby* because they parallel (perhaps unintentionally) certain details in *Mardi*;[12] other critics can "notice" elements in *Gatsby* by holding it up to the tradition of Chaucer,[13]

9. Cleanth Brooks, *Well Wrought Urn*, 256.

10. Audhuy, "*The Waste Land*: Myth and Symbols in *The Great Gatsby*," *Etudes anglaises* 33, no. 1 (1980): 41–54, esp. 47, 51; Michael Pottorf, "*The Great Gatsby*: Myrtle's Dog and Its Relation to the Dog-God of Pound and Eliot," *American Notes and Queries* 14 (January 1976): 88–90.

11. Evans, "F. Scott Fitzgerald and Henry James: The Raw Material of American Innocence," *Notes on Modern American Literature* 4, item 8 (1980). James E. Miller, Jr., also stresses the importance of "Daisy Miller" in "Fitzgerald's *Gatsby*: The World as Ash Heap," in *The Twenties: Fiction, Poetry, Drama*, ed. Warren French (Deland, Fla.: Everett/Edwards, 1975), 183. Michael A. Peterman, however, following Henry Dan Piper, claims that "there is no evidence that he had read *Daisy Miller* prior to 1925" ("A Neglected Source for *The Great Gatsby*: The Influence of Edith Wharton's *The Spark*," *Canadian Review of American Studies* 8 [1977]: 27).

12. Shroeder, "'Some Unfortunate Idyllic Love Affair': The Legends of Taji and Jay Gatsby," *Books at Brown* 22 (1968): 143–53.

13. Nancy Y. Hoffman, "*The Great Gatsby: Troilus and Criseyde* Revisited?" *Fitzgerald/Hemingway Annual 1971*, ed. Matthew J. Bruccoli and C. E. Frazer Clark, Jr. (Washington: Microcards, 1971), 148–58.

Coleridge,[14] Conrad,[15] and *Citizen Kane*[16]—to limit ourselves arbitrarily to male texts centering around the letter *C*. . . . And because of such interpretive strategies, *Gatsby* is made to seem rich indeed. To be sure, there are occasional references to female texts in the studies of *Gatsby*. Michael A. Peterman, for instance, sees the influence of Wharton.[17] But for the most part, to read the criticism, the novel appears to spring from fathers alone.

A woman writer might very well not wish to partake of that tradition (although her novel may well be tied to a different and forgotten tradition of women's writing), especially if she is writing about a woman who has not been to college and does not read. Sly references, in a book like *Edna*, to Conrad and Eliot could only come from the narrator—and they could only serve the end of increasing the authorial audience's sense of distance from the heroine, which would seriously compromise the intended effect. Nor is Barnes able to use cataclysmic events as a way of attracting notice. This is a novel about a life "dulled by habit" and by "the monotonous recurrence of . . . domestic cares" (128; pt. 2, chap. 2.1). One of the points of the novel is that Paul's financial generosity provides physical comfort only by cutting Edna off from any real engagement with life—and that includes engagement with the historical events that surround her. Being the wife of a successful and brilliant man, she is protected from the war and the Depression—she is "too busy hemming window curtains to hear the shot at Sarajevo" (243; pt. 2, chap. 5.3)—which therefore hardly appear in the novel except in terms of their effect on Edna's domestic life:

14. Leslie F. Chard II, "Outward Forms and the Inner Life: Coleridge and Gatsby," *Fitzgerald/Hemingway Annual 1973*, ed. Matthew J. Bruccoli and C. E. Frazer Clark, Jr. (Washington: Microcards, 1973), 189–94.

15. Harold Hurwitz, "*The Great Gatsby* and *Heart of Darkness*: The Confrontation Scenes," *Fitzgerald/Hemingway Annual 1969*, ed. Matthew J. Bruccoli (Washington: Microcards, 1969), 27–34.

16. Robert L. Carringer, "*Citizen Kane, The Great Gatsby*, and Some Conventions of American Narrative," *Critical Inquiry* 2 (Winter 1975): 307–25.

17. Peterman, "A Neglected Source." Oddly, given Peterman's claims about "Daisy Miller," he provides no solid evidence that Fitzgerald had ever read *The Spark*.

the war, to a large extent, is a matter of using Crisco instead of butter.

Of course, this failure to employ certain traditional rules of notice does not mean that other kinds of notice have not taken their place. In a novel based on different rules, however, crucial details may well be invisible to the reader without the proper key. Writing of a particular textual feature she finds in women's texts, Nancy K. Miller points out, "When these modalities of difference are perceived, they are generally called implausibilities. They are not perceived, or are misperceived, because the scripting of this fantasy does not bring the aesthetic 'forepleasure' Freud says fantasy scenarios inevitably bring."[18] And Naomi Schor defines a whole school of feminist criticism in terms of rules of notice: "The clitoral school of feminist theory might then be identified by its practice of a hermeneutics focused on the detail, which is to say on those details of the female anatomy which have been generally ignored by male critics and which significantly influence our reading of the texts in which they appear."[19] And indeed, there is a great deal to notice in Barnes' book as well, but only if you are prepared to pay attention to the ways that Edna dresses or—even more important—to the fate of particular pieces of furniture amid the shifting interior decors as Edna moves socially. But men, at least—and canons are still formed primarily by men—are trained to prick up their ears at an echo of T. S. Eliot in a way that they are not trained to notice dining room tables. If no details stand out, of course, then all details are equally important. Readers who fail to apply proper rules of notice may well, therefore, think that Barnes' novel is written "in too great detail,"[20] that in comparison to Fitzgerald's, it is undifferentiated and (what amounts to the same thing) boring.

Let me give a particular example. I noted earlier that Edna had difficulty with language. At first, this might seem reminiscent of such characters as Akaky Akakievich in Gogol's "Overcoat" and Golyadkin in Dostoyevsky's *Double*—and for good reasons, since

18. Miller, "Emphasis Added," 42.
19. Schor, "Female Paranoia," 216.
20. Rebecca Lowrie, "A Gibson Girl from the Middle West," *Saturday Review*, November 9, 1935, 7.

in our literary culture, a rule of signification almost inevitably makes linguistic failure stand for broader social incapacity. But if we simply compare Barnes to the male Russians, we are bound to be disappointed. Gogol and Dostoyevsky's own command of language was so great that they were able to portray the stutterings of Akaky Akakievich and Golyadkin in a way that is colorful and amusing.

> "Well, you see, Petrovich, I—er—have come—er—about that, you know . . ." said Akaky.
>
> It might be as well to explain at once that Akaky mostly talked in prepositions, adverbs, and lastly, such parts of speech as have no meaning whatsoever. If the matter was rather difficult, he was in the habit of not finishing the sentences, so that often having begun his speech with, "This is—er—you know . . . a bit of that, you know . . ." he left it at that, forgetting to finish the sentence in the belief that he had said all that was necessary. [Ellipses in original][21]

Next to this, Edna's "It's somehow—American" seems simply drab. (So, for that matter, does Daisy's response to Gatsby's shirts: " 'They're such beautiful shirts. . . . It makes me sad because I've never seen such—such beautiful shirts before.' "[22] But Daisy is not the center of her novel.)

There is, however, another perspective from which to look at this phenomenon. If we take our rules of notice not from traditional male texts, but rather from the female tradition, other elements are foregrounded. As feminist critics have pointed out, there is a special kind of denial of access to language that is peculiarly imposed on women. Lawrence Lipking puts it well: "A woman's poetics must begin . . . with a fact that few male theorists have ever had to confront: the possibility of never having been empowered to speak. The right to *mythos* is the first law of literary creation; not even God could have created light without a word. And women have not been able to forget that law."[23] It is not

21. Nicolai V. Gogol, "The Overcoat," in *The Overcoat and Other Tales of Good and Evil*, trans. David Magarshack (New York: Norton, 1965), 243.

22. F. Scott Fitzgerald, *The Great Gatsby* (New York: Scribner's, 1925), 93–94 (chap. 5).

23. Lipking, "Aristotle's Sister," 67.

accidental, for instance, that in Alice Walker's *Third Life of Grange Copeland*, when Brownfield wants to destroy his "tender" wife, "the first thing he started on was her speech."[24]

Awareness of this female tradition provides a different kind of notice, and makes certain aspects of Edna's inarticulateness stand out. We are more apt, for instance, to notice the small gestures that Paul makes just after their elopement, when it is necessary to send a telegram to Edna's parents telling them about their marriage. Edna finds it hard to write; Paul, in his efficiency, takes over the task, literally taking "the yellow blank from her flaccid fingers" and writing "firmly."

> She had read the message over his elbow as he was writing it and she did not dare to criticize. But the word "cordiality" dismayed her. It was an icy word. Broken phrases of excuse and love and explanation were stumbling through her head—simple phrases, more eloquent than Edna knew in their simplicity—"I'm sorry—I loved him so—forgive me—I love you"—but they were not phrases that she could conceive of confiding to a telegraph operator, or even to William Losser for that matter, a shy and inarticulate man. [88; pt. 1, chap. 2.3]

Paul has, in essence, taken over her right to the word—as he does again and again in the book. When Edna turns down an invitation to the fashionable Wintringhams' in order to watch Jessie perform in the school play, Paul insists that they go to the party after all, and Edna is forced to substitute for her own note of regret an acceptance note written "on Paul's curt dictation" (201; pt. 2, chap. 4.2).

Rules of signification work in a parallel way. First of all, in a move clearly linked to our dismissal of the so-called popular, academic critical practice teaches us to value works that stress signification (especially symbolism) over works that depend largely on, say, configuration. Cleanth Brooks, for instance, takes it as an "article of faith" that "literature is ultimately metaphorical and symbolic."[25] And while New Criticism may no longer be in vogue,

---

24. Walker, *The Third Life of Grange Copeland* (New York: Harcourt Brace Jovanovich/Harvest, 1977), 56 (chap. 14).
25. Brooks, "My Credo," 72.

the critical revolution of the past two decades, whatever else it has done, has done little to counteract the stress on the figurative. As a consequence, there is a tendency to denigrate the real world; good works, we are told, should reveal another plane beyond our mundane lives. Allen Tate, for instance, felt that literature was demeaned by the doctrine of relevance, which claims that subject matter should be "tested . . . by observation of the world that it 'represents.'"[26] And Tate's position is still widely held. Highly wrought and abstract works are thus deemed better than works that deal more directly with the concrete aspects of our experience. Edna herself, though, casts some doubt on this mode of interpretation. At the fateful picnic, before she meets Paul, she listens to a sentimental song "written on a tragic plane." But she immediately rejects the gesture of abstraction, her thoughts "busy with Al. A brakeman had to be away a lot" (29; pt. 1, chap. 1.3). And much women's fiction, including *Edna* itself, because it rejects that automatic preference for the abstract, seems too immediate to be taken seriously. It is for this reason that Lloyd C. Taylor, Jr., is able to claim that "Barnes's reputation will rest upon her accomplishment as a social historian rather than as a literary artist. . . . Her writing has none of the presently popular symbolic or poetic quality."[27]

But in addition, even the signification that women's novels do possess is apt to be missed by academic critics. We have been taught, as Nina Baym puts it, that whaling ships are a better "symbol of the human community" than the sewing circle,[28] just as we have been taught simply not to notice the symbolic richness of women's worlds. As Annette Kolodny puts it,

There was nothing fortuitous, for example, in Charlotte Perkins

26. Tate, "The Present Function of Criticism," in *Essays in Modern Literary Criticism*, ed. Ray B. West, Jr. (New York: Rinehart, 1952), 151.
27. Taylor, *Margaret Ayer Barnes* (New York: Twayne, 1974), unnumbered page (Preface).
28. Nine Baym, *Woman's Fiction*, 14. See also Paul Lauter's claim: "Some of the most popular texts in United States literature present hunting—a whale or a bear—as paradigms for 'human' exploration and coming of age, whereas menstruation, pregnancy, and birthing somehow do not serve as such prototypes" ("Introduction," xvi).

Gilman's decision to situate the progressive mental breakdown and increasing incapacity of the protagonist of *The Yellow Wallpaper* in an upstairs room that had once served as a nursery (with barred windows, no less). But the reader unacquainted with the ways in which women traditionally inhabited a household might not have taken the initial description of the setting as semantically relevant; and the progressive infantilization of the adult protagonist would thereby lose some of its symbolic implications.[29]

In part, that is because we have grown up in a culture in which the phallus is the privileged signifier. In Ernest Jones' phrase, "there are probably more symbols of the male organ itself than all other symbols put together."[30] Less literally, our culture still supports Thomas Dixon, Jr.'s claim that "war is always the crisis that flashes the search light into the souls of men and nations."[31] In other words, we already have a well-developed arsenal of techniques for drawing out symbolism latent in male experiences and the objects of male interest. No college student has trouble writing a paper that takes off from the implications of guns,[32] bootleggers, or a gambler who fixes the World Series. *Gatsby* has thus been a gold mine for critics predisposed to privilege its equation of woman as bitch[33]—or prepared to follow up the implications of its symbolic use of the automobile, a symbol that almost inevitably carries with it a certain attitude toward women (indeed, the Jordan automobile company, one of the apparent sources for Jordan Baker's name, ran ad campaigns that, even more than those of other manufacturers, "associate[d] automobiles with girls and young women").[34] Writ-

29. Kolodny, "Dancing through the Minefield," 13–14. See also her "A Map for Reading," esp. 455–60.

30. Jones, *Papers on Psycho-Analysis*, rev. ed. (London: Bailliere, Tindall, and Cox, 1920), 145.

31. Thomas Dixon, Jr., *The Leopard's Spots: A Romance of the White Man's Burden, 1865–1900* (New York: Doubleday, Page, 1902), 405 (bk. 3, chap. 9).

32. See, for instance, Alexander R. Tamke, "The 'Gat' in Gatsby: Neglected Aspect of a Novel," *Modern Fiction Studies* 14 (Winter 1968–69): 443–45.

33. See, for instance, Bruce R. Stark, "The Intricate Pattern in *The Great Gatsby*," *Fitzgerald/Hemingway Annual 1974*, ed. Matthew J. Bruccoli and C. E. Frazer Clark, Jr. (Washington: Microcards, 1974), 51–61.

34. Laurence E. MacPhee, "*The Great Gatsby*'s 'Romance of Motoring': Nick Carraway and Jordan Baker," *Modern Fiction Studies* 18 (Summer 1972): 208–9; F. H. Longman, "Style and Shape in *The Great Gatsby*," *Southern Review* (University

ing an essay on the implications of such female experiences as child raising and homemaking, or such activities as "reversing a puffed sleeve, or turning a full skirt, or freshening a faded bodice with a new velvet bolero or a satin revere" (16; pt. 1, chap. 1.1)—experiences and activities that form a crucial part of *Edna*—is more difficult for a reader trained in normalized techniques.

Indeed, male texts—at least, American male texts from this period—are apt to parody such concerns. In Raymond Chandler's "Red Wind," Marlowe is having a beer in a bar when a man enters looking for a woman: " 'tall, pretty, brown hair, in a print bolero jacket over a blue crepe silk dress. Wearing a wide-brimmed straw hat with a velvet band.' " Before the man finds her, he is shot down; shortly thereafter, Marlowe meets a woman in his apartment building.

> She had brown wavy hair under a wide-brimmed straw hat with a velvet band and loose bow. She had wide blue eyes and eyelashes that didn't quite reach her chin. She wore a blue dress that might have been crepe silk, simple in lines but not missing any curves. Over it she wore what might have been a print bolero jacket.
> I said: "Is that a bolero jacket?"
> She gave me a distant glance and made a motion as if to brush a cobweb out of the way.[35]

It is not simply the academy's stress of male objects themselves that skews the issue; the process of symbolization itself, as taught, tends to be male. As Judith Fetterley has cogently argued, in canonical American literature universality is defined "in specifically male terms"[36]—a definition that automatically makes *Gatsby* a more "American" book than *Edna*, and hence more appropriate for teaching and research. But masculinization is not found simply in such broad critical maneuvers; the tendency to masculinize as we symbolize is found in our smallest interpretive gestures as well.

---

of Adelaide) 6 (1973): 48–67; John J. McNally, "Boats and Automobiles in *The Great Gatsby:* Symbols of Drift and Death," *Husson Review* 5 (1971): 11–17.

35. Chandler, "Red Wind," in *Trouble Is My Business* (New York: Pocket, 1951), 158, 163–64 (chaps. 1, 2).

36. Fetterley, *Resisting Reader,* xiii.

Glass objects in *Gatsby*, we're told by Robert Carringer, represent not only "the ideal West versus the corrupt East" and "childhood innocence versus adult experience," but also "the loss of a woman."[37]

Third, let us turn to configuration. The canonical, we are often told, transcends the temporary and eccentric, revealing instead what is universal to "mankind." Once we accept this view, the patterns articulated by our traditional genres—tragedy, detective story, *Bildungsroman*—turn out to be more than merely formal. Since those canonical forms encapsulate the essence of being human, they imply what kind of life is worth telling about, and hence what kind of life is most worth living.

Thus, for instance, the aesthetic value of well-roundedness, of consistently returning characters, privileges a certain kind of life and makes other kinds of social reality all but impossible to portray without departing from "good" structure. Well-roundedness might therefore well be incompatible with a realistic slave narrative, since the very point of that narrative might be precisely that you lose your friends and family—indeed, your whole past and any possibility of order, much less progress, in your life—as you are shuffled around.

From a traditional aesthetic perspective, therefore, not only is a novel like Harriet Wilson's *Our Nig* episodic; in making that apparently formal judgment, the very life portrayed in that novel—especially its final chapter—is implicitly devalued in favor of a bourgeois story where relationships grow and develop. From a different perspective, though, one that sees the value of art partly through its ability to articulate social injustices, *Our Nig* would seem far more cannily composed. As Barbara Foley argues in her discussion of "the unremittingly episodic structure of most abolitionist documentary novels," "the hero's destiny was intended to illustrate social trends and conflicts, but it was not conceived as a synecdochic reconciliation of those trends and conflicts. Rather, in the frequent arbitrariness of its conclusion, the abolitionist novel proposed that the conditions for formal completeness and closure were dictated by extratextual as well as textual considerations."[38]

37. Carringer, "*Citizen Kane*," 311.
38. Foley, *Telling the Truth*, 249.

Indeed, from this second perspective, a novel like *Uncle Tom's Cabin* might be downgraded, not because of its episodic nature (often held against it in the academy), but rather for the opposite reason, because Stowe tries too hard to round it off at the end, thus submitting to precisely those social values she is trying to critique.

This coincidence between plot structure and implied social value means, among other things, that the actions of those with access to power (with its corollary, violence) lend themselves to sharply outlined patterns of the sort we have been taught to seek in literary texts. It is easier, that is, to write a traditionally well-formed story about a businessman or a cop than it is to write one about a housewife who doesn't seem to *do* anything. Such a domestic story, because it will not fit the norms of the adventure story or the tragedy, is apt to appear shapeless and diffuse, or—as Hershell Brickell said about Barnes' *Within This Present*—"unnecessarily long."[39] It is not exactly that women's lives are inappropriate to narrative fiction. We have canonical plot structures that deal with women who ruin themselves in adultery (*Madame Bovary, Anna Karenina*) or who remain self-sacrificially steadfast even under extreme adversity (Southworth's *Changed Brides/The Bride's Fate*). But the potential roles for women in such plots are restricted. As Alice Jardine puts it, "If the author is male, one finds that the female destiny (at least in the novel) rarely deviates from one or two seemingly irreversible, dualistic teleologies: monster and/or angel, she is condemned to death (or sexual mutilation or disappearance) and/or to happy-ever-after marriage. Her plot is not her own."[40] In other words, traditional patternings, even though they may vary by genre and nationality,[41] make it difficult to write about particular *kinds* of women.

39. Brickell, "The Literary Landscape," *North American Review* (January 1934): 93.

40. Jardine, "Gynesis," 56.

41. Nancy K. Miller puts it well: "Now, if the plots of male fiction chart the daydreams of an ego that would be invulnerable, what do the plots of female fiction reveal? Among French women writers, it would seem at first blush to be the obverse negative of 'nothing can happen to me.' The phrase that characterizes the heroine's posture might well be a variant of Murphy's law: If anything can go wrong, it will. And the reader's sense of security, itself dependent on the heroine's, comes from feeling not that the heroine will triumph in some *conventionally* positive way but that she will transcend the perils of plot with a self-exalting dignity. Here, national constraints on the imagination . . . do seem to matter: the second-chance rerouting

Because she is not one of those stereotyped female characters, Edna does not lead a life that fits the conventional patterns. The point of the book, as I have argued, is not only to describe the experiences of women and others with limited opportunities for action, but also to cry out against those limitations. Such sharply focused actions as Gatsby's violent death are thus ruled out, and one traditional means of producing what the reader will see as a well-structured story is unavailable. The plot of accepted self-denial is equally ruled out. Barnes' problem is made more difficult by Edna's dullness—and especially by the combination of her dullness and the novel's feminist perspective. There are surprisingly few novels about stupid people—and it is not accidental that most of those in that small pool succeed in achieving traditionally acceptable configurations in part because they have a masculinist perspective. For instance, Marquand's *Melville Goodwin, USA* (1951), about an unsophisticated general who, like Edna, is out of place in the chic social set in which he finds himself, might seem roughly analogous in certain ways to Barnes' novel. But that novel shows us what makes Barnes' task so difficult. Goodwin is a male, and since men (especially military men) have adventures in our society, even the most dull-witted among them have more novelistically shapely things to offer us. *Edna* is, to my mind, a well-shaped book. But to see that shape, we have to be prepared to accept the possibility that the trajectory of a woman's socially determined decline from a useful and pretty young housewife to a fat, elderly cast-off might provide just as good a shape for a novel as the rise and fall of a self-made man chasing the American dream.

Coherence, in many ways, is the most interesting of our categories, partly because it has until recently probably been the most highly regarded aesthetic virtue, but also because coherence is especially subject to prejudgment. As I said earlier, texts do resist some readings: not every critic can turn *Hamlet* into a comedy. But texts rarely resist imputations of coherence: any well-wrought academic who begins with a serious belief that a text is coherent will ultimately be able to make it so. This tends to perpetuate canons; we are more likely to assume (and hence to find) high

---

of disaster typical of Jane Austen's fiction, for example, is exceedingly rare in France" ("Emphasis Added," 40).

levels of coherence in famous books, like Fitzgerald's, than in forgotten novels, like Barnes'.

But the finding of coherence is not entirely a subjective process. Even a reader prepared, from the start, to find coherence in a text would have less trouble with *Gatsby* than with *Edna*, for two reasons. First, coherence, like notice, is often a function of the intertextual grid on which a text is placed; books that are like other canonized texts are deemed coherent by similarity, almost as if they shared a club membership. Indeed, it may not be accidental that critics often fall into figurative language that supports just this notion. David Daiches, for instance, notes that a work "is either admitted into the canon, as it were, or is not. Those admitted have all an equal status."[42] And as I have tried to show, we are more familiar with the male literary tradition. Second, and even more important, one way of finding coherence in a text is to apply rules of naming, specifically to find a universal theme—a central metaphor—that holds it together. Even today, in our supposedly post-structural world, this may still generate more critical writing than any other interpretive gesture. And if your stock of themes consists primarily of such goods as "The American Dream,"[43] "The Earth Mother,"[44] "The Grail,"[45] or "The Homecom-

42. Daiches, *Critical Approaches to Literature*, 302. See also George P. Elliott's discussion—tongue-in-cheek, to be sure, but nonetheless revealing—of "whether Chandler will ever be elected into literary history," whether his "nomination for membership" will be "seconded" by those with "the power to vote him in" ("Country Full of Blondes," *Nation*, April 23, 1960, 354).

43. This is one of the most popular bits of glue used to hold *The Great Gatsby* together. See, for instance, Taylor Alderman, "*The Great Gatsby* and *Hopalong Cassidy*," *Fitzgerald/Hemingway Annual 1975*, ed. Matthew J. Bruccoli and C. E. Frazer Clark, Jr. (Washington: Microcards, 1975), 83–87; V. N. Arora, "*The Great Gatsby*: The Predicament of the Dual Vision," *Indian Journal of American Studies* 8, no. 1 (1978): 1–9; Brian M. Barbour, "*The Great Gatsby* and the American Past," *Southern Review* 9 (Spring 1973): 288–99; Thomas E. Boyle, "Unreliable Narration in *The Great Gatsby*," *Bulletin of the Rocky Mountain Modern Language Association* 23 (1969): 21–26; Peter L. Hays, "*Gatsby*, Myth, Fairy Tale, and Legend," *Southern Folklore Quarterly* 40 (1977): 213–23. See Kolodny's critique of some of the implications of the landscape imagery connected to this theme in *Lay of the Land*, esp. 138–39. See also Peter Slater's discussion of some of its ethnocentrism, "Ethnicity in *The Great Gatsby*," *Twentieth Century Literature* 19 (1973): 53–62.

44. H. Keith Monroe, "Gatsby and the Gods," *Renascence* 31 (1978): 51–63.

45. See, for instance, Robert J. Emmitt, "Love, Death, and Resurrection in *The Great Gatsby*," in *Aeolian Harps: Essays in Literature in Honor of Maurice Browning Cramer*, ed. Donna G. Fricke and Douglas C. Fricke (Bowling Green, Ohio:

ing"[46]—whether or not those themes are seen ironically, as many of them are in analyses of *Gatsby*—male-centered texts will almost automatically seem more coherent, since these themes are more appropriate to male experiences. The same is true if your cohering lens comes from Freudian psychology—for that, too, at least until recent feminist revisions, has presupposed certain limited roles for women.[47]

Edna is held together in a radically different way. Yes, the book, like *Gatsby*, reflects back and forth on itself, repeating themes with subtle variations. But these themes are not "The Grail" or "The Homecoming"—the novel gravitates, rather, around changing attitudes toward birthing, methods of raising children, and the ways that middle age and domesticity can reduce a woman to invisibility. In our current critical climate, few nonfeminist critics are likely to take these as serious themes. It is thus not surprising that Barnes' felicities have gone unrecognized—or, even worse, have been viewed as flaws by critics who refuse to start with the assumption that she knew what she was doing.

Of course, I do not pretend to have given a full account of the reasons behind the relative rankings of authors; canonization is a complex process, and our culture's preferences have multiple causes, many of which I have not even touched on. As I pointed out earlier in the chapter, some texts are, even from the standpoint of their authorial audience, less well put together than others, in the sense that they simply don't do what they're supposed to do when they are transformed by the interpretive procedures they themselves call for. Furthermore, the technology and the economic structure of the publishing industry have their roles in canon formation, as does, in the words of Jane Tompkins, "an author's rela-

---

Bowling Green State University Press, 1976), 273–89. Emmitt puts his argument specifically in terms of the cohering power of thematic analysis. See also Arora, "*The Great Gatsby*"; and Audhuy, "*The Waste Land.*"

46. See, for instance, Ronald J. Gervais, "The Trains of Their Youth: The Aesthetics of Homecoming in *The Great Gatsby, The Sun Also Rises* and *The Sound and the Fury,*" *Americana-Austriaca* 6 (1980): 51–63.

47. See, for instance, A. B. Paulson, "*The Great Gatsby*: Oral Aggression and Splitting," *American Imago* 35 (Fall 1978): 311–30.

tions to the mechanisms by which his or her work is brought before the public."[48] And it is probably the case that texts that disturb in certain ways are less likely to be canonized than others that are safer. Of course, we make a great show of our belief that the point of literature is to get us out of ourselves and to learn new experiences. And there is no doubt that many canonized novels do confront difficult issues in ways that can hardly be considered comforting. But there is a certain kind of repetition in the canon as well, at least in its focus. As Judith Fetterley provocatively puts it, "If a white male middle-class literary establishment consistently chooses to identify as great and thus worth reading those texts that present as central the lives of white male middle-class characters, then obviously recognition and reiteration, not difference and expansion, provide the motivation for reading."[49] To put it in other terms, we may readily canonize books that raise problems—but we seem to prefer it if those problems are the problems of a certain dominant group, for then at least the centrality of that group remains an implicit assumption.

Nonetheless, there can be little doubt that the canon grows as well from the interpretive principles we take for granted. Specifically, part of the preference for Fitzgerald stems from the ways we've been taught to approach literature; many of the criticisms leveled against Barnes—to the extent that she is mentioned at all—are likewise built into our prefabricated ways of reading. To say that the "range of her fiction appears extremely narrow" when compared to Fitzgerald's,[50] much less to criticize her writing for appealing primarily to women,[51] is to say less about the quality of her work itself than about the antifeminism implicit in our most familiar reading strategies.

In arguing this way about Barnes' novel, however, I am not merely making a plug for a favorite text. Nor am I simply attempting to provide an explanation—however incomplete—for a particular canonical choice. Rather, I hope that my arguments will raise

48. Tompkins, *Sensational Designs*, 32.
49. Fetterley, "Reading about Reading," 150.
50. Taylor, *Margaret Ayer Barnes*, 129.
51. Basil Davenport, "Safety First," *Saturday Review of Literature*, December 5, 1931, 345.

questions about how we should act in the face of our culture's evaluations. If canonization resulted merely from inherent qualities in the text, of course, standard academic practice would be justified; we could continue, without worry, to read, study, and teach those texts that are inherently better. If such subjectivists as Robert Crosman and David Bleich were right that readers "make" the texts they read, then there would be no particular reason to change our practices either, since no choices would be demonstrably better (or more harmful) than those that the academy has already made. But if, as I have tried to argue, reading strategies can be more or less appropriate to particular texts, and if there are valuable experiences to be gained from an authorial reading of Barnes' novel, experiences that have been blocked by the imposition of inappropriate interpretive moves, then another course of action suggests itself: to teach ourselves to read in new ways (not simply in *a* new way), ways that are self-conscious about how interpretation itself can be ideological, and ways that can thus help us to make the most of the rich literary heritage that has been passed down to us.

In order to do this, we will have to break away from some strongly entrenched notions—for instance, from the traditional reliance on close reading, which is valorized by New Criticism and poststructuralism alike. Whatever its values—and close reading is certainly a useful skill—it can, if overemphasized, distort our literary experiences. To be sure, close reading is necessary for authorial readings of certain texts, especially a particular kind of lyric poetry. But to the extent that canons celebrate texts that work with approved strategies, treating close reading as a synonym for good reading—as it is generally treated in this country—elevates that kind of poetry into the ideal literary type. As Terry Eagleton puts it, "To call for close reading . . . is to do more than insist on due attentiveness to the text. It inescapably suggests an attention to *this* rather than to something else: to the 'words on the page' rather than to the contexts which produced and surround them."[52] In so doing, it fosters the false belief that highly wrought works are necessarily the best, and that texts—even narratives—that do not share the virtues of Donne and Yeats are inferior, rather than just

52. Eagleton, *Literary Theory*, 44.

different. As long as we privilege close reading as it is currently conceived, without questioning it, we will end up accepting, with but minor modifications, the canon erected on it, with all its ideological biases.

Furthermore, the stress on close reading—which means, among other things, slow reading—tends to restrict the number of texts a reader is likely to be familiar with, and there is no reason to believe that this is inevitably a good thing. Receptiveness to new texts and new literary experiences, after all, does not depend solely on the care with which you approach them. If my arguments here have any validity, receptiveness depends as well on the *range* of your reading, on the *variety* of interpretive strategies that you have at your disposal. The best readers—at least among college students—tend to be those who were the most voracious readers as children; I am not sure that training them, as we do in high school AP classes and in college, to read not widely, but too well—that is, encouraging them to substitute intensive for extensive reading—is an unmitigated blessing. New Critical dogma may insist that, in the words of Brooks and Warren, "before extensive reading can be profitable, the student must have some practice in intensive reading";[53] but the opposite may well be the case: intensive reading may well be a worthless skill for someone who has not already devoured a large and heterogeneous collection of texts. Deep reading, in other words, can complement wide reading, but it cannot replace it, for by itself it is not the magic key to literature; it will open some texts, but will shatter when turned in others.

It is not simply that learning these new, more flexible, and more self-conscious modes of reading will increase the *number* of texts that we can enjoy and learn from. Indeed, were quantity the issue, we could rest content with the current canon, which has more than enough texts to fill up a lifetime. Rather, these new kinds of reading will allow us to enjoy a broader *range* of texts, texts that may give us a perspective on unquestioned cultural assumptions that canonical texts do not. Only in this way, I believe, can reading really serve the process of self-liberation, for only this kind of reading can make us aware of—and hence able to escape from—the limitations imposed by traditional interpretive practices.

53. Cleanth Brooks and Robert Penn Warren, *Understanding Fiction*, xi.

Selected Bibliography

This is not a complete list of works discussed, but rather a selection of those critical works cited in the text which will be of greatest interest to readers who want to explore further the theoretical issues raised in this book. For additional titles, see in particular the excellent bibliographies in the following works listed below: Booth, *Rhetoric of Fiction;* Culler, *On Deconstruction;* Flynn and Schweickart, *Gender and Reading;* Suleiman and Crosman, *Reader in the Text;* and Tompkins, *Reader-Response Criticism.*

Althusser, Louis. "Ideology and Ideological State Apparatuses (Notes toward an Investigation)." In *Lenin and Philosophy and Other Essays,* 127–86. London: New Left Books, 1971.

Barthes, Roland. "An Introduction to the Structural Analysis of Narrative." Trans. Lionel Duisit. *New Literary History* 6 (Winter 1975): 237–72.

———. *The Pleasure of the Text.* Trans. Richard Miller. New York: Hill and Wang, 1975.

———. *S/Z.* Trans. Richard Miller. New York: Hill and Wang, 1974.

Baym, Nina. *Woman's Fiction: A Guide to Novels by and about Women in America, 1820–1870.* Ithaca: Cornell University Press, 1978.

Beardsley, Monroe C. "Textual Meaning and Authorial Meaning." *Genre* 1 (1968): 169–81.

Bleich, David. *Readings and Feelings: An Introduction to Subjective Criticism.* Urbana, Ill.: National Council of Teachers of English, 1975.

———. *Subjective Criticism.* Baltimore: Johns Hopkins University Press, 1978.

Booth, Wayne C. *Critical Understanding: The Powers and Limits of Pluralism.* Chicago: University of Chicago Press, 1979.

——. "M. H. Abrams: Historian as Critic, Critic as Pluralist." *Critical Inquiry* 2 (Spring 1976): 411–45.

——. *The Rhetoric of Fiction.* 2d ed. Chicago: University of Chicago Press, 1983.

——. *A Rhetoric of Irony.* Chicago: University of Chicago Press, 1974.

Brooks, Cleanth. "My Credo: The Formalist Critics." *Kenyon Review* 13 (Winter 1951): 72–81.

——. *The Well Wrought Urn: Studies in the Structure of Poetry.* New York: Harcourt, Brace, and World/Harvest, 1947.

Brooks, Cleanth, and Robert Penn Warren. *Understanding Fiction.* 2d ed. New York: Appleton-Century-Crofts, 1959.

Burke, Kenneth. "Psychology and Form." In *Counter-Statement,* 29–44. Berkeley and Los Angeles: University of California Press, 1968.

Cawelti, John G. *Adventure, Mystery, and Romance.* Chicago: University of Chicago Press, 1976.

Champigny, Robert. *What Will Have Happened: A Philosophical and Technical Essay on Mystery Stories.* Bloomington: Indiana University Press, 1977.

Chatman, Seymour. *Story and Discourse: Narrative Structure in Fiction and Film.* Ithaca: Cornell University Press, 1978.

Crawford, Mary, and Roger Chaffin. "The Reader's Construction of Meaning: Cognitive Research on Gender and Comprehension." In *Gender and Reading,* ed. Flynn and Schweickart, 3–30.

Crosman, Robert. "Do Readers Make Meaning?" In *Reader in the Text,* ed. Suleiman and Crosman, 149–64.

——. "How Readers Make Meaning." *College Literature* 9 (1982): 207–15.

Culler, Jonathan. *On Deconstruction: Theory and Criticism after Structuralism.* Ithaca: Cornell University Press, 1982.

——. *The Pursuit of Signs.* Ithaca: Cornell University Press, 1981.

——. *Structuralist Poetics: Structuralism, Linguistics, and the Study of Literature.* Ithaca: Cornell University Press, 1975.

Daiches, David. *Critical Approaches to Literature.* Englewood Cliffs, N.J.: Prentice-Hall, 1956.

Doubrovsky, Serge. *The New Criticism in France.* Trans. Derek Coltman. Chicago: University of Chicago Press, 1973.

Dworkin, Ronald. "Law as Interpretation." *Critical Inquiry* 9 (September 1982): 179–200.

Eagleton, Terry. *Criticism and Ideology: A Study in Marxist Literary Theory.* London: New Left Books, 1976.

——. *Literary Theory: An Introduction.* Minneapolis: University of Minnesota Press, 1983.

Eco, Umberto. *The Role of the Reader: Explorations in the Semiotics of Texts.* Bloomington: Indiana University Press, 1979.

Eliot, T. S. *The Use of Poetry and the Use of Criticism: Studies in the Relation of Criticism to Poetry in England.* Cambridge: Harvard University Press, 1933.

Fetterley, Judith. "Reading about Reading: 'A Jury of Her Peers,' 'The Murders in the Rue Morgue,' and 'The Yellow Wallpaper.'" In *Gender and Reading,* ed. Flynn and Schweickart, 147–64.

——. *The Resisting Reader: A Feminist Approach to American Fiction.* Bloomington: Indiana University Press, 1978.

Fish, Stanley. *Is There a Text in This Class?: The Authority of Interpretive Communities.* Cambridge: Harvard University Press, 1980.

——. *Self-Consuming Artifacts: The Experience of Seventeenth-Century Literature.* Berkeley and Los Angeles: University of California Press, 1972.

——. "Why No One's Afraid of Wolfgang Iser." *Diacritics* 11 (Spring 1981): 2–13.

——. "Working on the Chain Gang: Interpretation in the Law and in Literary Criticism." *Critical Inquiry* 9 (September 1982): 201–16.

Fisher, John. "Entitling." *Critical Inquiry* 11 (December 1984): 286–98.

Flynn, Elizabeth A., and Patrocinio P. Schweickart, eds. *Gender and Reading: Essays on Readers, Texts, and Contexts.* Baltimore: Johns Hopkins University Press, 1986.

Foley, Barbara. *Telling the Truth: The Theory and Practice of Documentary Fiction.* Ithaca: Cornell University Press, 1986.

Forster, E. M. *Aspects of the Novel.* In *Aspects of the Novel and Related Writings.* The Abinger Edition of E. M. Forster, vol. 12, ed. Oliver Stallybrass. London: Edward Arnold, 1974.

Frye, Northrop. "Literary Criticism." In *The Aims and Methods of Scholarship in Modern Languages and Literatures,* ed. James Thorpe, 57–69. New York: Modern Language Association, 1963.

——. *The Well-Tempered Critic.* Bloomington: Indiana University Press, 1963.

Gates, Henry Louis, Jr. "Editor's Introduction: Writing 'Race' and the Difference It Makes." *Critical Inquiry* 12 (Autumn 1985): 1–20.

Gibson, Walker. "Authors, Speakers, Readers, and Mock Readers." *College English* 11 (February 1950): 265–69.

——. *Tough, Sweet, Stuffy: An Essay on American Prose Styles.* Bloomington: Indiana University Press, 1966.

Graff, Gerald. "The Joys of Not Reading." Paper presented at the Conference on Narrative Poetics, Ohio State University, April 1986.

——. *Literature against Itself: Literary Ideas in Modern Society*. Chicago: University of Chicago Press, 1979.

——. "Literature as Assertions." In *American Critics at Work: Examinations of Contemporary Literary Theories*, ed. Victor A. Kramer, 81–110. Troy, N.Y.: Whitson, 1984.

Guillory, John. "The Ideology of Canon-Formation: T. S. Eliot and Cleanth Brooks." *Critical Inquiry* 10 (September 1983): 173–98.

Hartman, Geoffrey H. *Criticism in the Wilderness: The Study of Literature Today*. New Haven: Yale University Press, 1980.

Hawkes, Terence. *Structuralism and Semiotics*. Berkeley and Los Angeles: University of California Press, 1977.

Hirsch, E. D., Jr. *The Aims of Interpretation*. Chicago: University of Chicago Press, 1976.

——. "The Politics of Theories of Interpretation." *Critical Inquiry* 9 (September 1982): 235–47.

——. *Validity in Interpretation*. New Haven: Yale University Press, 1967.

Holland, Norman. *The Dynamics of Literary Response*. New York: Norton, 1975.

Horton, Susan. *Interpreting Interpreting: Interpreting Dickens' Dombey*. Baltimore: Johns Hopkins University Press, 1979.

Iser, Wolfgang. *The Act of Reading: A Theory of Aesthetic Response*. Baltimore: Johns Hopkins University Press, 1978.

——. *The Implied Reader: Patterns of Communication in Prose Fiction from Bunyan to Beckett*. Baltimore: Johns Hopkins University Press, 1974.

Jakobson, Roman, and Claude Lévi-Strauss. "Charles Baudelaire's 'Les Chats.'" Rev. ed., trans. Fernande M. de George. In *The Structuralists: From Marx to Lévi-Strauss*, ed. Richard T. de George and Fernande M. de George, 121–46. Garden City, N.Y.: Doubleday/Anchor, 1972.

Jameson, Fredric. "On Raymond Chandler." *Southern Review*, n.s. 6 (July 1970): 624–50.

Jardine, Alice. "Gynesis." *Diacritics* 12 (Summer 1982): 54–65.

Jauss, Hans Robert. *Toward an Aesthetic of Reception*. Trans. Timothy Bahti. Minneapolis: University of Minnesota Press, 1982.

Kermode, Frank. *The Sense of an Ending*. London: Oxford University Press, 1967.

Knapp, Steven, and Walter Benn Michaels. "Against Theory." *Critical Inquiry* 8 (Summer 1982): 723–42.

———. "A Reply to Our Critics." *Critical Inquiry* 9 (Summer 1983): 790–800.

Knight, Stephen. *Form and Ideology in Crime Fiction*. Bloomington: Indiana University Press, 1980.

Kolodny, Annette. "Dancing through the Minefield: Some Observations on the Theory, Practice, and Politics of a Feminist Literary Criticism." *Feminist Studies* 6 (Spring 1980): 1–25.

———. *The Lay of the Land: Metaphor as Experience and History in American Life and Letters*. Chapel Hill: University of North Carolina Press, 1975.

———. "A Map for Rereading; or, Gender and the Interpretation of Literary Texts." *New Literary History* 11 (Spring 1980): 451–67.

Krieger, Murray. *Theory of Criticism: A Tradition and Its System*. Baltimore: Johns Hopkins University Press, 1976.

LaCapra, Dominick. *Madame Bovary on Trial*. Ithaca: Cornell University Press, 1982.

Lauter, Paul. "Introduction." In *Reconstructing American Literature: Courses, Syllabi, Issues*. Old Westbury, N.Y.: Feminist Press, 1983.

Lentricchia, Frank. *After the New Criticism*. Chicago: University of Chicago Press, 1980.

Lipking, Lawrence. "Aristotle's Sister: A Poetics of Abandonment." *Critical Inquiry* 10 (September 1983): 61–81.

Lodge, David. *The Language of Fiction: Essays in Criticism and Verbal Analysis of the English Novel*. New York: Columbia University Press, 1966.

Loofbourow, John W. "Literary Realism Redefined." *Thought* 45 (1970): 433–44.

———. "Realism in the Anglo-American Novel: The Pastoral Myth." In *The Theory of the Novel: New Essays*, ed. John Halperin, 257–70. New York: Oxford University Press, 1974.

Lukács, Georg. *Studies in European Realism*. New York: Grossett and Dunlap, 1964.

Mailloux, Steven. *Interpretive Conventions: The Reader in the Study of American Fiction*. Ithaca: Cornell University Press, 1982.

———. "Rhetorical Hermeneutics." *Critical Inquiry* 11 (June 1985): 620–41.

Michaels, Walter Benn. "Is There a Politics of Interpretation?" *Critical Inquiry* 9 (September 1982): 248–58.

Miller, J. Hillis. "The Critic as Host." *Critical Inquiry* 3 (Spring 1977): 439–47.

——. "The Function of Rhetorical Study at the Present Time." In *The State of the Discipline, 1970s–1980s. ADE Bulletin*, 62 (September/November 1979): 10–18.

Miller, Nancy K. "Emphasis Added: Plots and Plausibilities in Women's Fiction." *PMLA* 96 (January 1981): 36–48.

Miller, Robin Feuer. *Dostoevsky and* The Idiot*: Author, Narrator, and Reader*. Cambridge: Harvard University Press, 1981.

Morson, Gary Saul. *The Boundaries of Genre: Dostoevsky's* Diary of a Writer *and the Traditions of Literary Utopia*. Austin: University of Texas Press, 1981.

Ohmann, Richard. *English in America: A Radical View of the Profession*. With a chapter by Wallace Douglas. New York: Oxford University Press, 1976.

——. "The Shaping of a Canon: U.S. Fiction, 1960–1975." *Critical Inquiry* 10 (September 1983): 199–223.

Ong, Walter J. "The Writer's Audience Is Always a Fiction." *PMLA* 90 (January 1975): 9–21.

Parker, Hershel. *Flawed Texts and Verbal Icons: Literary Authority in American Fiction*. Evanston, Ill.: Northwestern University Press, 1984.

Phelan, James. *Worlds from Words: A Theory of Language in Fiction*. Chicago: University of Chicago Press, 1981.

Porter, Dennis. *The Pursuit of Crime: Art and Ideology in Detective Fiction*. New Haven: Yale University Press, 1981.

Pratt, Mary Louise. "The Ideology of Speech-Act Theory." *Centrum*, n.s. 1 (Spring 1981): 5–18.

——. "Interpretive Strategies/Strategic Interpretations: On Anglo-American Reader Response Criticism." *Boundary 2* 11 (Fall–Winter 1981/82): 201–31.

——. *Toward a Speech Act Theory of Literary Discourse*. Bloomington: Indiana University Press, 1977.

Prince, Gerald. "Introduction to the Study of the Narratee." Trans. Francis Mariner. In *Reader-Response Criticism*, ed. Tompkins, 7–25.

——. *Narratology: The Form and Functioning of Narrative*. Berlin: Mouton, 1982.

——. "*La Nausée* and the Question of Closure." *Yale French Studies*, no. 67 (1984): 182–90.

Propp, V[ladimir]. *Morphology of the Folktale*. Trans. Laurence Scott; 2d ed., rev. Louis A. Wagner. Austin: University of Texas Press, 1968.

Rabinowitz, Nancy S., and Peter J. Rabinowitz. "Legends of Toothpaste and Love: Margaret Ayer Barnes and the Poetics of Stupidity." *Papers in Language and Literature* 18 (Spring 1982): 132–50.

Rabinowitz, Peter J. "Rats behind the Wainscoting: Politics, Convention, and Chandler's *The Big Sleep.*" *Texas Studies in Literature and Language* 22 (Summer 1980): 224–45.

Radway, Janice. *Reading the Romance: Women, Patriarchy, and Popular Literature.* Chapel Hill: University of North Carolina Press, 1984.

Riffaterre, Michael. "Describing Poetic Structures: Two Approaches to Baudelaire's 'Les Chats.'" In *Structuralism,* ed. Jacques Ehrmann, 188–230. Garden City, N.Y.: Doubleday/Anchor, 1970.

Rosenblatt, Louise M. *Literature as Exploration.* New York: Appleton-Century, 1938.

Said, Edward W. "Opponents, Audiences, Constituencies, and Communities." *Critical Inquiry* 9 (September 1982): 1–26.

Schauber, Ellen, and Ellen Spolsky. "Reader, Language, and Character." In *Theories of Reading, Looking, and Listening,* ed. Harry Garvin, 33–51. *Bucknell Review* 26, no. 1. Lewisburg, Pa.: Bucknell University Press, 1981.

Scholes, Robert. *Structuralism in Literature: An Introduction.* New Haven: Yale University Press, 1974.

——. "Towards a Semiotics of Literature." *Critical Inquiry* 4 (1977): 105–20.

Schor, Naomi. "Female Paranoia: The Case for Psychoanalytic Criticism." *Yale French Studies,* no. 62 (1981): 204–19.

Schweickart, Patrocinio P. "Reading Ourselves: Toward a Feminist Theory of Reading." In *Gender and Reading,* ed. Flynn and Schweickart, 1–62.

Smith, Barbara Herrnstein. "Contingencies of Value." *Critical Inquiry* 10 (September 1983): 1–35.

——. *On the Margins of Discourse: The Relation of Literature to Language.* Chicago: University of Chicago Press, 1978.

——. *Poetic Closure: A Study of How Poems End.* Chicago: University of Chicago Press, 1968.

Spivak, Gayatri Chakravorty. "The Politics of Interpretations." *Critical Inquiry* 9 (September 1982): 259–78.

Suleiman, Susan Rubin. *Authoritarian Fictions: The Ideological Novel as a Literary Genre.* New York: Columbia University Press, 1983.

——. "Introduction: Varieties of Audience-Oriented Criticism." In *Reader in the Text,* ed. Suleiman and Crosman, 3–45.

Suleiman, Susan R., and Inge Crosman, eds. *The Reader in the Text: Essays on Audience and Interpretation.* Princeton: Princeton University Press, 1980.

Todorov, Tzvetan. *The Fantastic: A Structural Approach to a Literary*

Genre. Trans. Richard Howard. Ithaca: Cornell University Press, 1975.

——. *The Poetics of Prose.* Trans. Richard Howard. Ithaca: Cornell University Press, 1977.

Tompkins, Jane, ed. *Reader-Response Criticism: From Formalism to Post-Structuralism.* Baltimore: Johns Hopkins University Press, 1980.

——. *Sensational Designs: The Cultural Work of American Fiction, 1790–1860.* New York: Oxford University Press, 1985.

Torgovnick, Marianna. *Closure in the Novel.* Princeton: Princeton University Press, 1981.

White, Hayden. "The Politics of Historical Interpretation: Discipline and De-Sublimation." *Critical Inquiry* 9 (September 1982): 113–37.

Wimsatt, W. K., Jr., and Monroe C. Beardsley. "The Intentional Fallacy." In W. K. Wimsatt, Jr., *The Verbal Icon,* 2–18. New York: Noonday, 1958.

Index

Note: For the convenience of the reader, references to the various rules of reading in this index reflect the organization set out in the book. Thus, where appropriate, the name of each rule or class of rules is followed, in brackets, by the more general categories to which it belongs, and the entry ends with a cross reference to the more specific rules or classes of rules that are included within it.

Index

Index

Index

Library of Congress Cataloging-in-Publication Data

Rabinowitz, Peter J., 1944–
  Before reading.

  Bibliography: p.
  Includes index.
  1. Narration (Rhetoric)   2. Reading.   3. Hermeneutics.   I. Title.
PN212.R33   1987   808   87-47602
ISBN 0-8014-2010-5 (alk. paper)
ISBN 0-8014-9472-9 (pbk. : alk. paper)